ESCAPE FROM THE JAPANESE

The Amazing Story of a PoW's Journey from
Hong Kong to Freedom

ESCAPE FROM THE JAPANESE

The Amazing Story of a PoW's Journey from
Hong Kong to Freedom

Lieutenant-Commander
Ralph Burton Goodwin OBE, RNZNVR

Frontline Books

ESCAPE FROM THE JAPANESE
The Amazing Story of a PoW's Journey from Hong Kong to Freedom

First published as *Hongkong Escape* in 1953 by Arthur Barker Ltd., London.

This edition published in 2015 by Frontline Books,
an imprint of Pen & Sword Books Ltd,
47 Church Street, Barnsley, S. Yorkshire, S70 2AS

ISBN: 978-1-84832-929-4

CIP data records for this title are available from the British Library

Printed and bound by CPI Group (UK) Ltd, Croydon, CR0 4YY [TBC]
Typeset in 11.24 / 14 point Palatino

For more information on our books, please email: info@frontline-
books.com,
write to us at the above address, or visit:
www.frontline-books.com

TO PHILIPPA

Publisher's Note

In order to maintain the flavour of Lieutenant-Commander R.B. Goodwin's escape through war-time Asia, we have retained his spelling of the numerous places referred to in the original edition of his book. There is, however, one particular exception to this, Hong Kong. Traditionally the name of this former British colony was Hongkong, but as it is more widely known as Hong Kong we have changed this throughout the text.

Contents

List of Maps

Introduction

On the 25th day of December 1941 the rich prize of Hong Kong fell to Japanese invaders. The furious sounds of battle grumbled to a grudging silence, and all was still. There could be no "Dunkirk" for the beleaguered troops, the enemy was all around, and the survivors of the garrison became prisoners of war (PoW).

Before the event it was my belief that every prisoner would automatically begin to plan his escape, and that a bid for freedom would be the best contribution he could make towards the enemy's defeat. Yet circumstances cloud the issues. When an escape by one or two individuals may bring severe reprisals against those left behind, the course of duty becomes confused; and when men have been weakened by systematic starvation for months, and years, thoughts of further suffering are apt to loom in distorted menace.

The merits of attempting an escape were debated long and heatedly in the prison camps in Hong Kong. From the point of view of the escaper the problem was clear-cut and simple. Success meant freedom and a return to battle; failure meant torture and execution. For those left behind the problem was confused, unpredictable, and therefore the more terrifying. Anything could happen, from a spate of tortures and executions of individuals, to a mass starvation of the whole camp. On the other hand, the Japanese might not take any of the threatened reprisals, though there were few who believed that anything but sadistic cruelty would follow an attempted escape.

When the mutterings and subdued thunders of the Second World War finally burst on an expectant world, a party of ten temporary sub-lieutenants of the New Zealand Division of the Royal Naval Volunteer Reserve sailed from Auckland to begin their war service with the Royal Navy, based at Singapore. It was my fate to be included in that party, and it was my ambition to be detailed to a motor torpedo boat. The Navy had other ideas, and I was told that my thirty-eight years made me too old for such an assignment. Almost two years of routine sea service followed, first in a minesweeper, then in an "asdic" patrol ship, and finally as first lieutenant in the naval tug *St. Aubyn*, which was delivered from Hong Kong to Aden.

From that trip I reached Singapore again late in September 1941, and after a week in HMS *Kedah*, a small armed merchantman, I was sent to Hong Kong to join the 2nd Motor Torpedo Boat Flotilla. Two months later Japan entered the war, and when Hong Kong surrendered it was my misfortune to be in hospital, suffering from a leg wound.

Five MTBs were still afloat, and on Christmas night, with a party of officials and all the fit personnel of the flotilla, they made a dash up the coast to Mirs Bay. There the boats were destroyed, and, guided by the Chinese Admiral Chan Chak, the party made a successful journey across China, to Chungking and freedom.

It was not until the end of February 1942 that I was fit enough to go to the overcrowded North Point Camp. That horrible place was vacated in April, when most of the men went to Shamsuipo (also referred to as Sham Shui Po) Camp in Kowloon, and most of the officers went to the Argyle Street Camp, also in Kowloon. That was to be our home for two years, and then we too were sent to Shamsuipo.

After two months in Shamsuipo I escaped on the night of the 16th-17th July 1944, and after crossing South China to Kunming, I was sent home to Auckland on leave.

Three months were spent in complete relaxation, and then I reported for duty with the MI9 Branch at British Pacific Fleet

Headquarters in Sydney. That appointment gave me an opportunity to follow the fortunes of the prisoners of war in the Far East, and when Japan surrendered I went to Hong Kong with the relieving force as MI9 representative with the Prisoners of War Recovery Party.

The ships of the relieving force, under command of Admiral Sir Bruce Fraser whose flag was flying in HMS *Indomitable,* steamed out from Subic Bay for Hong Kong. A light breeze put dark blue colour on a smiling sea, from which the enemy had gone. But had he? We knew the fanaticism with which he fought towards the end, and there could be no carelessness yet. Aircraft flew from the carrier's deck each day, and at the end of one of those exercises we saw how easily a man could lose his life.

A fighter came in, landed heavily, and broke the arrester wire. Other incoming planes were waved off until repairs were made, and then another came in to land. The day was perfect, and the pilot made a perfect landing. His tail-hook picked up the wire, but then something went wrong. Instead of running out evenly from both sides the wire ran from one side only, with the result that the fighter slewed across the deck as it slowed down. One landing-wheel ran along the scupper for some distance, and when almost stopped the plane toppled over the gunwale. Quite slowly it settled on a twin anti-aircraft gun, almost stopped there and then slipped down, nose first, into the sea. It did not sink, it floated there with its tail in the air, but for some inexplicable reason the pilot did not appear. Under a blue sky and a calm friendly sea he drowned there, one of the last casualties of a war that was already over.

We came to anchor in Hong Kong Harbour on the 30th of August 1945, and the next day I visited the Shamsuipo Camp. There all my old PoW friends were gathered, and there also was Colonel Esao Tokunaga, who had been commanding officer of all prisoner of war camps in Hong Kong. That individual, who had early been christened the "White Pig", revealed the site of the graves of five prisoners who had been murdered, and he began a long justification of his own harsh treatment of the prisoners. He was most insistent that he was merely putting into practice the orders of his senior officers, and that he personally was not to blame. However, when he discovered my identity, Tokunaga's inventions dried suddenly at their source, and I took the opportunity to express some of my own views of that arrogant creature's actions.

The Japanese interpreter present was the same lad who had been on duty at the time of my escape, and when he realised to whom he was speaking, the shock which registered was ludicrous to behold. All Japanese personnel attached to the camp had suffered severe punishment, and some time afterwards this interpreter had said, "Neffer; as long as I live; vill I forget that name of Gootvin." Apparently he had come in for his added share of trouble, and one could almost feel sorry for that unfortunate youth. He was a poor, weak creature, partly crippled, and invariably he was bullied by all and sundry. To the inmates of the camp, for some unknown and obscure reason, he was known as "Deadly Nightshade".

My friends took great pleasure in recounting the happenings at the camp on the day following my escape. At the nine o'clock muster the roll was checked over and over again, and when the Japanese at last found who was missing they searched the camp from end to end. That went on for several hours, until every possible hiding-place, and every impossible one for that matter, had been examined several times over. When finally convinced that neither I nor my body was still inside the wire, the camp commandant had the unpleasant duty of reporting the loss of a prisoner.

The two officers who slept on either side of me, Lieutenant (E.) Chown, RNVR, and Lieutenant Trapman, 12 CRRA, were arrested for interrogation, as also were my two closest friends, Lieutenant Glover, HKRNVR, and Lieutenant Thomson, RNR. Others were also called for brief interrogation.

Lieutenant Thomson recalled a scene when the four who had been arrested were sitting on the ground outside the guardhouse. Dr. Saito, senior medico and most hated of the Japanese, stopped when he reached the prisoners. Looking at Chown, he asked, "How old are you?" Chown replied, "Twenty-five". Saito hissed "S-s-so; you have a long time to live".

Saito then asked Thomson the same question, and on being told "Fifty-one", he merely grunted. Thomson, in his own inimitable way, said he had fully expected Saito to hiss, "S-s-so; you have *not* very long to live".

However, no one suffered any very severe beatings, and reprisals against the camp were very much lighter than they might have been. Any further escapes were made much more difficult, because the Japanese enforced an order that every hut should maintain a sentry at the door from dark to dawn. No one could leave a hut without being identified, and any prolonged absence would be the signal for a search. The result was that after my departure no other escape was attempted.

Now, since many of my fellow prisoners did have hopes of escaping, they can measure their preparations and theories against the realities which confronted me, and they can assess their chances had they been able to take the initial step.

It so happened that Opportunity knocked on my door first, and following the only course that seemed possible in the circumstances encountered, it was my prerogative to put a plan to practical test. I can claim no personal credit for its success, for you will see, as you follow the story, that Luck played all the winning hands.

Lieutenant-Commander R.B. Goodwin OBE, RNZVR

Chapter 1

War Comes to Hong Kong

The dawn was glorious. Soft pearly mists enveloped the harbour of Hong Kong on the morning of the 8th of December 1941, and as the sun rose a warm glow tinted the brown sails of junks as they drifted with a strong tide. Smoke from ferries and steamboats hung in long rich brown streamers in the still air. Passing launches left fleeting pencil lines of wake.

Nature, the supreme artist, ever conscious of intensity of drama in violent contrast, prepared the stage with consummate skill. Even as pale mists melted imperceptibly to the touch of morning sunlight, a storm broke; a storm of hate and passion that was to sweep the East with a searing flame of terror and of agony that was to plunge the lives of millions into misery and despair.

On that particular morning I was enjoying breakfast in the dining-room of "Kingsclere" in Carnarvon Road, Kowloon, when a Chinese "boy" opened the door to announce, "Telephone call for you, Mr. Goodwin".

For days past war with Japan had been momentarily expected, and the reason for that early morning call was a foregone conclusion.

"That you, Goodwin?"

"Yes."

"Kennedy here, there are some important signals in; you had better come down as soon as you can."

"Right; I'll be there in ten minutes."

Lieutenant Kennedy, RNVR, was duty officer at the Motor Torpedo Boat Base at Kowloon, and it was he who had received the fateful signals. Britain and Japan were at war, and at the Base preparations were already under way to evacuate the flotilla to its war station at Aberdeen, a sheltered fishing village on the southern shore of Hong Kong Island. While the latest signals were being discussed in the MTB office there came a distant c-r-ump, c-r-ump of bursting bombs, and the first attack on Kaitak Airfield was in progress.

For the next seventeen days the air about Hong Kong was vibrant with the ceaseless thunder of war. Nights were illumined with the lurid glow of fires, and with the vivid flashes of gunfire and of bursting shells.

The 2nd MTB flotilla was called upon for a multiplicity of duties. Attacking enemy warships, attacking landing-craft, carrying despatches, collecting wounded, evacuating troops from the mainland. In addition the flotilla maintained dark to dawn patrols to seaward of Hong Kong to forestall any surprise attack from that direction.

During the battle three boats were totally destroyed, many casualties were suffered, and the remaining five boats were all more or less damaged by bombs or shellfire. I had been assigned to MTB 10, under command of Lieutenant-Commander Gandy, RN, the commanding officer of the flotilla, and my own active participation in the war came to an untimely end on an exceptionally noisy morning three days before the surrender of the colony.

The gunboat *Cicala*, Lieutenant-Commander Boldero in command, was shelling Japanese positions in Deep Water Bay when heavy mortar fire forced her to withdraw. There was little room to manoeuvre between the wrecks of sunken vessels, and as she went out stern first a flight of bombers unleashed their loads upon her. Stick after stick fell about the little ship, but after each salvo, when the columns of spray had slowly fallen, there she was, still afloat and steaming. Fresh waves of planes came over, and finally three bombs scored direct hits. *Cicala* was mortally hurt, and, with her boats holed, with her steam-pipes broken and her hull shattered, the gunboat was abandoned to the sea. As she slowly sank MTB 10 went alongside to take off survivors.

The hand of Fate was then moving swiftly in my direction. When *Cicala*'s crew had been landed at Aberdeen we prepared to load torpedoes to replace two that had been fired on the previous night, and when that operation was in full swing a field gun opened fire on us from a hill above Deep Water Bay.

The gunners' aim was high at first, but they were rapidly reducing their range and, in imminent danger of following *Cicala* to the bottom of the sea, we cast off from the jetty to zig-zag out through Aberdeen Channel.

Those gunners were very good indeed, and a shell burst close alongside. As I stood against the wheelhouse there came a violent blow on my right thigh, and at the same time the flesh was hauled forward until the skin burst and the strain was suddenly released. A jagged steel splinter had passed through my thigh, and while its entry was marked by only a small puncture, its exit made a hole that could easily accommodate a closed fist. The splinter dropped on deck after hitting the side of the wheelhouse, and it was so hot that it burnt my fingers when I dropped it into my pocket to keep as a souvenir.

MTB 10 was soon out of range, and after field-dressings had been applied to my damaged leg I was landed and carried to a casualty clearing-station at the Aberdeen Industrial School. My recollections of that journey are somewhat hazy, because I was unconscious for varying periods. Shells from the mainland were bursting along the road to the Queen Mary Hospital, so it was almost dark before an ambulance could set out to take a full load of wounded there. Apparently it was not quite dark enough, for shells suddenly began to burst close ahead of the vehicle, and it pulled in violently under a high bank. Then the firing ceased and we went on again, the vehicle crashing and bouncing into the broken road surface. One could forgive the driver his haste to pass the danger zone, but the ambulance was suffering from the strain. After one particularly fierce bump the doors flew open and my stretcher, one of the top tier, began to slide out the back. By grabbing a rail I staved off the immediate danger of being dropped in the road, but the remainder of the journey was completed with almost half of me swaying about in the twilight outside.

The entrance to Queen Mary Hospital was littered with wounded, for all the staffed wards were full and new arrivals had to wait until a new ward was opened up. It was cold there in that draughty foyer, and time passed slowly. Morphia had deadened my senses to such an extent that I was only half conscious, but after what seemed to be two or three hours I was lodged in a spotless bed on the fifth floor, there to pass a restless, feverish night.

Next morning my wound was treated at the operating theatre, and afterwards, back in the ward, I received a great surprise. When serving aboard HMS *Harrow* at Singapore I had had a vivid dream. I was lying in bed in a hospital ward, and coming towards me was a young probationer nurse. She was very plain, with a pimply face, and my thought at the time was: "When there are so many pretty nurses in the world, why should it be my luck to strike this one?" Then, twelve months later, when the effects of the anaesthetic were wearing off and my eyes opened, there was the identical scene before me. It had been my privilege in Singapore to have a preview of one little incident in my life, and it made me wonder if we would ever find the key to the master plan, so that all the future could be seen.

Queen Mary Hospital was reserved for more serious patients, and on the following morning my name was called in a draft to go to the University. All day long, shells and bombs were bursting near the hospital, their thunderous explosions combining with the crash of guns to make the building shake continuously. Night brought relief from most of the uproar, for no more planes came over, and the bark of the anti-aircraft guns was stilled.

Sleep had almost won the day when someone rolled me out of my nice warm bed and carried me down to lie on the floor of a motor-truck. It was a glorious night of black velvet sky and brilliant stars, but it was cold lying there under only one blanket, after the warm comfort of a bed. When fully loaded, the truck drove over dark deserted streets to the University. The road wound along steep hillsides which afforded perfect sites from which hand grenades could be dropped on moving targets, and when buildings were approached the danger from fifth columnists increased. There had been shooting from upper windows, and our escorts talked in hushed whispers when we halted under a high bank overhung with trees. Figures moved silently in the darkness, hurried conversations took place, conversations pregnant with nervous tension, then silence settled down. It was cold waiting there in the dark, and it seemed that we were deserted.

At last the voices came back and we were lifted out, to be carried up hundreds of steps. The wards were all full in that emergency hospital, and I found myself in a corridor on a stretcher made of sacking. That was to be my bed for a week of intense discomfort. Because of the sagging fabric the only position in which I could lie was on my back, and again because of the sagging it was inevitable that I should slide into the same place. The result was that the pain in my leg was completely nullified by a much greater pain that developed at the base of my spine.

All night long cries and groans of pain rose from the floor of the main hall where Chinese casualties were placed. One man who went out of his mind made the nights hideous with his terrible screaming.

On Christmas Day brilliant sunshine streamed from a cloudless sky, but the beauty of the day was rudely shattered by the uproar and pulsing tumult of battle. Shells from Kowloon whined continuously over the University to burst among buildings at a higher level, and with my bed against the front wall I fervently hoped that none of the shells fell short.

The noise died down during the afternoon, and towards evening a strange quietness prevailed. One of the VADs, a vivacious little French girl, came over with eyes streaming tears to announce, "They've surrendered".

That was how I heard the news of the fall of Britain's first bastion in the East. For the past two days surrender had been hourly expected, yet when that simple announcement was made my stomach contracted violently and it required all my strength to resist being physically ill.

From Fort Stanley the 9.2-inch guns continued to thunder distant defiance until eight o'clock p.m., when the commanding officer was finally convinced that the surrender had really been signed. There remained a profound silence, broken only by the occasional crack of a rifle as some looter was discovered at his work.

Into the silence came a muffled throbbing roar, full of significance for me, for I knew that that came from the motors of the five surviving MTBs, tuning up for their last run. The sound faded and was gone. With it went my last link with the free world; I was a prisoner of the Japanese.

What that might mean was quickly taught, the subject of our first lesson being the little lady who had told us, with her tearful voice, the sad news of surrender. She set out one day to find the grave of her husband who had been killed in the fighting, and night was closing down by the time she approached the University again. We heard shots ring out along a nearby road, and later we were to learn that the girl had been raped and brutally murdered by Japanese soldiers. All the tragedy of war had been heaped upon her bright spirit within a few short days, and her passing was the first of a series of incidents that fanned a smouldering resentment into a burning hatred of our captors.

Doctors were far too few, and serious cases fully occupied the time of those available, so for a week my leg was dressed daily by a VAD. One morning she became interested in some gauze adhering to the wound, and after tugging away at it for some time without results, she began to ask a few questions. I suddenly remembered that there was a hole in the back of my leg also, and her attention was drawn to that. There also was a piece of gauze that would not respond to tugging, so the nurse went off to find a doctor.

It had not occurred to me that they did not know the nature of the wound, and after it had been explained the doctor said "Oh! that must be a gauze plug". She thereupon seized the said plug with a pair of forceps, and gave me a rather painful surprise by dragging it right through my leg. My condition was not improving at all, so after a week I was sent back to the Queen Mary Hospital. They kept me there only three or four days, and then sent me on to the Royal Naval Hospital. That was the turning-point for me, for from the day when Surgeon-Commander Cleave, RN, took me in hand the wound healed rapidly, and I was soon walking with the aid of crutches.

The Japanese rarely visited the hospital, so we were surprised and somewhat apprehensive one morning when a large staff car and two truck loads of marines arrived in the compound. With great formality an officer unfolded a paper and, in Japanese, read out a long statement. While that was in progress the marines took station in the wards and corridors, and within a few minutes an order was issued that everyone was to pack at once. The victors had spoken to the vanquished. That day the hospital was to be evacuated entirely.

Patients on the road to recovery, which included me, were sent to St. Albert's Convent at Rosary Hill, while the more seriously hurt went to Bowen Road Hospital. By that time it was possible for me to walk with the aid of one crutch, and we soon settled down to life in our new surroundings. The

Japanese gave orders that no one was to leave the hospital compound, but they put no guards round the area and we had a great deal of freedom. Clouds frequently settled down almost as low as the hospital, and under cover of their thick folds those patients who were fit enough went foraging on the battlefields along the top ridge. Large quantities of clothing and equipment were gathered, and a certain amount of canned goods to augment the rations of the lucky finders.

There were other more gruesome relics of the fighting too, such as a party who had been roped together and then bayonetted to death, and frequently a burial party would set off to perform its sorry task. One day I had crossed the main ridge and was rummaging about some distance down the far side, when suddenly the clouds rolled aside and the whole landscape lay revealed in stereoscopic clarity. Feeling that my own figure was revealed in the same way I lost no time in climbing back into the sheltering mists.

Though sufficient to keep us going, the meals had been very meagre, one result of the low diet being that wounds took much longer to heal than they normally would have done. We were perpetually hungry, and whenever anything could be bought each did what he could to cook little extra dishes. Our chief supplier was an itinerant Chinese who risked the wrath of the Japanese to bring his basket of provisions. Those he sold at rapidly soaring prices. From somewhere several sacks of wheat arrived, and our stomachs were really filled for the first time since the surrender. Some refused to eat that "fowls' food", as they called it, but that only made more for those who would. We found many ways of making it into what were described as biscuits, cakes, or puddings.

A day came when I could really walk without a stick, and then began that pacing up and down, up and down, a pacing that was to continue for two and a half years until the night when its ultimate purpose was achieved. China is a vast country, and my legs would need to be in good shape when the time came to trek across it. At least, that was the insistent thought that spurred me always to keep as fit as possible. The day must come.

Chapter 2

Prisoners of War

On the 25th of February we were ordered to vacate St. Albert's and the sick were sent to Bowen Road Hospital, while those who were almost well were taken by truck to the North Point Camp. On the way there we saw some of the damage caused during the fighting, and we had a fine view of the racecourse where hundreds of motor-cars and buses were parked, spoils of war but, owing to the shortage of petrol, of very little value to the enemy.

Driven by a cold north-east wind drizzling rain was falling when we pulled up outside the camp gates, and there we found that no one had authority for our entry. We waited for two hours, huddling together to gain warmth from one another, and then, with a broad grin upon his face, the camp commandant came waddling across the road, patting his stomach to let us know how well he had been fed. Soaked and frozen after the long wait in the rain we looked at him with eyes of hate, and every one of us would have relished battering his smug yellow face.

Nothing was taken from us during a brief search, and then we were "free" to enter camp.

What had happened? Who were these broken, spiritless, dirty, slovenly, unshaven, gaunt-looking spectres who stared at us with unfriendly, unwelcoming eyes? Could these be those same officers who had so recently looked so immaculate on the dance floor of the Hong Kong hotel? Two months had passed since the last guns boomed, and that scene of demoralisation made us wonder with trepidation what conditions in the camp could be. What forces had been at work to bring men so low in so short a time?

Shown to our respective huts we immediately saw one reason why new arrivals were not welcome. Conditions were terribly cramped. Bunks were arranged in double tiers at right angles to the walls, with a passageway down the middle of each hut. Huts were one hundred and twenty feet long by eighteen feet wide. Often groups of four tiers of bunks were jammed hard together, so that the men in the inside had to crawl over those on the outside to get in or out of bunk. One enterprising soul had escaped the general congestion by rigging a hammock up in the rafters.

Although the appearance of the men made such a deep impression at the time, we were to learn later that it was in the first few months of captivity, when systems were becoming adjusted to a totally altered and hopelessly inadequate diet, which morale in the prison camps was at its lowest ebb.

The dysentery hospital at North Point was a shocking reflection on our captors. That noisome place of healing was situated in a stone stable near the waterfront. The floor was of cobble stones, ventilation and light were provided by two very small windows and a small door, and the interior was always in deep gloom. Two four-gallon cans were the only conveniences provided. Four or five patients were always clustered about each of those inadequate receptacles, needing to use them at the same time, and the place reeked with the stench of ordure which ran among the cobbles and fouled the blankets of those men lying on the ground. It was a horrible place, and repeated requests were made for better hospital quarters. There were several large empty buildings just outside the camp which would have been suitable, but the Japanese cared nothing for our condition and every request was refused.

Lice and bugs began to breed rapidly, and the huts were so congested that it was impossible to keep them clean. At the same time a few of the troops were so careless of their own hygiene that compulsory bathing-parades had to be enforced. Cigarettes were almost unobtainable at times, and men sold all their belongings, including most of their clothing, in order to buy from the guards. One character, known as "Dirty Dick", was finally reduced to a blanket in which he stalked about the camp. This individual's most spectacular feat was to fall through a latrine floor into the outfall from the dysentery hospital, the only result being that he suffered a mild attack of typhoid fever. Anyone else would have died.

A damaged radio had been hidden in the North Point Camp, and that was later repaired and operated by Lieutenant Dixon, RNZNVR. When the camp commandant called for a volunteer to repair his radio, that was Dixon's opportunity. Saying that he would have to have spare parts, he obtained permission to visit a factory. Dixon was a radio technician in civil life, and having reached the factory he went over the stock with the eyes of an expert, and secreted about his person everything that he thought might come in useful. The result of that expedition was that Dixon supplied us for more than a year with news bulletins direct from the BBC.

My own part in dealings with the radio at North Point was a very minor one, though one incident caused me some amusement. The set was to be hidden in a hole cut through the concrete floor of a hut occupied by Lieutenant-Commander Vernall, HKRNVR, and I was detailed to dispose of rubble from the excavation. It gave me rather a surprise one day to walk round the end of a hut into an assembly of Japanese officers and a cinematographer taking scenes within the camp. Of course they could have no suspicions of the contents of my bucket, but just imagine their reactions had they known the origin of that rubble.

Many parties and individuals were perfecting plans for escape, and mine were well advanced, for North Point Camp was on the waterfront and the fence along the seaward side presented no great obstacle. The main difficulty was the harbour crossing to Kowloon, for that would involve a swim of three miles or more, and a careful study of the tides. Flotation was essential for such an undertaking, and, using an electric soldering iron stolen from the factory, Dixon sealed for me a number of empty evaporated milk cans. These were inserted in a long bandolier made from gunny bags, and they fitted well in a harness round my chest and shoulders. A food pack was always kept in readiness, but the weather was still too cold for such a long swim, and my leg was not yet strong enough for the difficult walk that lay beyond. Then, before conditions were suitable, the Japanese stepped in and decided to empty the camp.

On the 18th of April 1942 most of the prisoners in the North Point Camp were transferred to Kowloon, the officers going to the Argyle Street Camp while most of the men remained at Shamsuipo. Any move from one camp to another was always the occasion for a thorough search, so transport of the radio presented a problem. Permission was obtained to take a large basket of vegetables, and the set was hidden inside. Unfortunately, in spite of the commandant's permission the guard at the gate refused to let the vegetables pass, and the precious basket was returned to store without its contents being suspected. Nothing more could be done, so the radio was left in charge of Dutch naval personnel who were left behind at North Point. Later on they were successful in transferring it to Shamsuipo, where it gave good service until finally discovered by the Japanese.

The 18th of April proved to be a lucky day for me, for a trivial incident was important at a later date. My bulky bandolier of empty tins had been replaced by two "Mae West" life-jackets that had been bought for four packets of cigarettes, and those deflated jackets were concealed inside a pillow-case. A particularly poisonous runt of a corporal, when searching my belongings, took great delight in scattering everything on the ground. Even the smallest tins of oddments were emptied and the contents strewn about. When he couldn't find anything suspicious he took away my combined groundsheet and cape, a loss that caused me many a wetting on subsequent parades. The last thing to be examined was my precious pillow, and as he stooped to pick it up I bent quickly, lifted it to the side of my head, closed my eyes and said "pillow". Probably astonished at that performance the corporal grunted and passed on to his next victim, leaving me with a feeling of elation, for all my plans so far had envisaged long swims for which flotation was essential.

A small steamer took the party to Shamsuipo, and when we were all assembled at the camp, Colonel Esao Tokunaga, Commandant of all the PoW camps in Hong Kong, gave an exhibition of his swaggering arrogance which we were to come to know only too well. Combined with his natural obesity his manner earned for him the sobriquet of "The White Pig". Spray flew from his mouth as he stamped and shouted, and he took particular pleasure in venting his foul temper on Commodore Collinson, RN, who was repeatedly pushed on the chest during the harangue. When it was all over the officers were sent to Argyle Street, and as we went we could see the Japanese stealing anything they fancied from the men's kit.

It was almost dark when we reached camp, so we were subjected to only a cursory search before being sent into huts that were the barest one could imagine. There was absolutely nothing in them, there were just bare wooden walls from which every nail or peg had been removed, and bare concrete floors. We settled down to rest on the concrete after a most exhausting day. Our belongings consisted of what we had been able to carry, so although my load was modest because of my damaged leg, it was amazing to see the luggage with which some officers arrived. The previous occupants of the camp had departed with most of the rice "kongs", cooking-pots shaped like deep saucers, so until new ones could be installed meals were even smaller than usual, and the hours at which they were served were erratic.

We had great difficulty at first in cutting enough wood to keep the fires going, for the only tools the Japanese would supply were one small frame-saw, one small hand-saw, and two meat choppers which certainly were never designed to be used on tough wood. That was the equipment with which we were supposed to cut firewood for a kitchen feeding five hundred and eighty men.

At a later date a two-handed saw was provided, and a number of heavy wedges mounted on handles took the place of axes. The angle of those wedges was so blunt that they would continually bounce off a piece of tough wood, and they caused a tremendous amount of aggravating toil that would have been avoided had one or two ordinary axes been supplied. That was one method of applying the mental torture which gave the Japanese such delight, just one of the petty annoyances to which we were subjected throughout our captivity.

Plans of escape were constantly under review. Sometimes alliances were half-formed, but those were always finally discarded because of my belief that a solo effort was the only one that had a reasonable chance of success. Only once was a partnership almost completed, when Brigadier Cedric Wallis of the headquarters staff suggested that we join forces. Our place and method of departure had been agreed, and our attempt was waiting upon suitable weather conditions when the Japanese again interfered. It was decreed that all officers of the rank of colonel and above should be sent to Formosa, and my partner was included in the draft. Before he left the Brigadier bequeathed me a tin of "Bemax", a heart of wheat meal, and that formed a valuable item of food during my subsequent escape.

Many factors had to combine to make an attempt possible, not the least important being the physical and mental condition of the escaper. There were times when, even had outside factors been favourable, my own state was such that the requisite peak of tension could not have been reached. That could be attributed largely to poor diet, for though on the whole the health of the camp remained fairly good, judged by prison camp standards, there were times when dysentery, beriberi, pellagra and semi-blindness affected a high proportion of the inmates. Even when not suffering from any apparent illness, prisoners' nerves were severely strained, and that too was an important factor. Still, the psychological moment was bound to come, and for that moment a number of prisoners waited and watched.

The constant nervous strain under which we lived caused normally rational beings to behave in curious ways. One lieutenant-commander, Royal Navy, had a number of small tins of food secreted in various parts of his hut, and every hour or two, when he thought no one was looking, he would take one down and with surreptitious ceremony extract a few grains of rice or a pinch of something else from his precious store.

One amusing feature was that strong animosities developed for no reason at all. A friend of mine was standing at the side of the parade ground one day, with clenched fists and a very belligerent expression on his face. He was muttering and swearing and making a show of really vile temper, and when asked what the trouble was he said, "Look at that blank blank blank", indicating an officer walking near the opposite fence. "I'd like to punch his blank face". I discovered that the object of all that disturbance was completely oblivious of my friend's feelings, for the two lived at opposite ends of the camp and they had never had any contact. The only reason given for those feelings was, "I just don't like the look of the bastard".

On another occasion an RNR lieutenant took a dislike to someone, and his hatred rose to such a pitch that one afternoon he hit a man a violent blow on the jaw.

Unfortunately the hate was so much a figment of imagination that the hater was not even certain of the man to whom his feelings were addressed, and he hit the wrong one.

Apart from those occasional little outbursts the temper of the camp was remarkably good, and there were plenty of amusing incidents to cheer us up. We had Lieutenant "Nobby" Clark, RNR, who was a famous raconteur of stories. One day he delivered the "Magic Touch", when he discovered that he could cure headaches by the laying-on of hands. This developed into quite a business, and a string of satisfied clients went away, vowing that their headaches had been miraculously cured in a few minutes. "Nobby" was painfully thin, his ragged clothes hung dismally on his gaunt frame, and when half an inch of stubble adorned his face he was a far from handsome sight. However, he developed a perfect bedside manner and a smooth patter which amused his hut-mates immensely, and his clientele grew rapidly. One day Lieutenant McNair, RNR, advised him to commercialise his talents.

"Look here Nobby", said Mac, "these majors and colonels have a lot more pay than you do, why don't you charge them a tin of herrings or some peanut oil when they come to be cured? Let me be your manager and we should make a good thing out of it."

"Nobby" was horrified, and turning a withering eye on his would-be partner he said in a most pious voice, "Mac, I couldn't do it. How could I prostitute God's gift in such a way?"

A roar of laughter followed that serious pronouncement, for it would be hard to imagine anything that looked less like a disciple of the Lord than "Nobby".

Then we had Lieutenant "Barney" Crowley, RE, who traded gold to the sentries. Where did he get the gold? That was easy. Barney went round the camp telling jokes. When his hearers were laughing heartily "Barney" could be seen peering into their mouths to see if they held any gold fillings. When he found what he wanted he would go to work on his victims until he persuaded them that they were practically criminals to be hoarding so much gold that could be translated into essential food. The conclusion of these efforts would often be long delayed, depending on the fortitude of the owner and the quality of his dentist's work, but sooner or later the deal would be completed.

We had a good laugh one day when a sentry took a dislike to Lieutenant Hutton-Potts, HKRNVR. The trouble started when he was out with a gardening party, and after they were dismissed the sentry came into camp looking for his victim. Potts was warned, and he jumped out the window of his hut as the sentry went in at the door. Then began a steeplechase, Potts going in and out through hut windows with the sentry after him. Everyone who could joined in to help Potts and delay the sentry, and the hunt was still on when he had to return to duty. When that spell was ended, back into camp he came, but he was beaten. In the meantime Potts had shaved off a big black beard that he had been cultivating, and the irate sentry looked straight at him without a spark of recognition.

One afternoon we of the RNVR had some very anxious moments. Twelve of us were living in a room partitioned off at one end of a hut, and there Dixon used to work on a new radio he was making. Whenever work was in progress our own men were placed to give warning of sentries entering the camp, but on this occasion the precaution had broken down because a sentry already inside a hut had not been noticed. The set was on the floor between Dixon's bunk and mine, and he was standing at the window filing some small part. Suddenly a shadow fell upon his work, and there was a Japanese standing facing him. Dixon went on filing, while the sentry, who knew few words of English, began to talk. The rest of us were stretched out either reading or dozing, and we froze to our bunks, almost painfully aware that the wireless was in full view of the intruder, and to our racing imaginations it assumed exaggerated proportions. After talking for a few minutes the sentry wandered off without asking what was being made, and without realising that he had been looking at a radio. We thanked our stars for the intelligence of our guards.

That wireless, in the making of which Dixon was ably assisted by Lieutenant Chown, RNVR, and Lieutenant Scott-Lindsley, RNVR, was a masterpiece of ingenuity, and when completed it kept us supplied with BBC news for several months. Then, one memorable morning in September 1943, while we were at morning muster, a large party of Japanese drove into the camp. With extra guards around us we were kept on the parade ground from 9 a.m. until 1.30 p.m., while a working-party went through the huts from end to end and from roof to floor. As they worked an amazing pile of electric wiring and gadgets grew up near the guardhouse. One wondered how on earth so much could have been smuggled into the camp, for there were hundreds of feet of wire and dozens of home-made water heaters. Only Dixon and one or two others knew that tragedy was in the air, for on that day the radio was in need of adjustment and it had not been returned to its usual hiding-place.

The set fitted into a five-gallon can that was usually kept in a hole beneath a small flower garden. That hiding-place had been brilliantly conceived by Dixon, and had the radio been there at the time its security would have been assured. The hole was covered by a wooden lid, on top of which was a brick border, and six inches of earth in which flowers were growing. The lid was hinged on one side, and on the other there were thin flexible wire handles. The whole garden swung up to allow the can to be lowered into position, and when it was down again the wire handles were tucked in, and loose earth was scraped back against the brick border. Except for those who knew, there was not a person in camp who suspected that Dixon's flower garden was anything more than it appeared to be.

If for any reason the set was out of the hole in the daytime, a tray of rice was fitted into the can above the set, and all that one saw was a perfectly innocent looking can of rice. That was what confronted the Japanese during their search. A sick officer lying in bunk saw five searchers lift the can to examine it, and not one had any suspicions. Then one clumsy oaf tripped and knocked it over in trying to recover his balance, and the tray was dislodged.

That was the end of Dixon's tireless and fearless efforts to outwit the Japanese, a task to which he had been devoted ever since that day, in March 1942, when he had stolen the necessary tools and equipment from the factory in Hong Kong.

The sequel to that discovery was that several officers were arrested and tortured. Dixon was given severe water torture, and together with Commander Craven, RN, Lieutenant-Commander Young, RN, and Major Boxer, he spent the remainder of the war years in prison. Luckily all survived, though when Hong Kong was relieved in August 1945 they were all in a bad way, and Dixon in particular was in a very low state through the ravages of dysentery, fever and beriberi.

After that raid the Argyle Street Camp was without any direct contact with the outside world. During the previous month, August 1943, the Japanese had broken up a complete network of land communications through which all camps were in touch with one another, and through which messages could be sent to, and received from, Army Headquarters in New Delhi. The ration trucks were the medium used to convey messages in and out of camp, and when the ring was broken the drivers were executed. More than thirty persons paid the extreme penalty for participation in that network, among them Colonel Lanceray Newnham from Argyle Street Camp. Everyone with whom he had been associated mourned the loss of a brave and gentlemanly soldier.

Thereafter continuous contact with the outside world was never again established, though occasional messages were received at Shamsuipo Camp from Indian troops who were employed as guards by the Japanese.

Chapter 3

Shamsuipo Camp

The discovery of the communication network and then of the radio caused our captors to intensify their security measures, and escape became more and more difficult. My plans were still only plans when, in May 1944, we were transferred to Shamsuipo.

After more than two years we had come to regard Argyle Street as a permanent home, and there was a feverish packing up of all our little bits and pieces. We knew that Shamsuipo would be just as bare as Argyle Street had been, and we were determined to take everything that could be moved.

Most of our party had spent some time in Shamsuipo shortly after the fall of Hong Kong, but it was entirely new to me, and it was therefore of the greatest interest. The first feature that sent my hopes bounding was that the camp was on the seafront. All my faith was in a departure by sea, for it was extremely difficult to leave any camp by road. From our exercise ground we could see that some roads were sealed off with wire barricades, while others appeared to be closed with brick walls. Once one was in the sea all those immediate dangers could be by-passed.

Shamsuipo Camp was built on a perfectly level area of reclaimed land which formed the eastern shore of Laichikok Bay, the southern and western boundaries being vertical retaining walls against the sea. Westward of the camp the bay was lined with boatbuilding yards, behind which ran the Castlepeak Road. Inside the road there was a narrow flat occupied by buildings, and from the back of those buildings ridges rose steeply to the Kowloon Range. Those hills were practically bare of trees and of habitations, many spurs showed big bald patches of reddish earth, while the remainder were sparsely covered with grass and short scrub. Deep narrow ravines fell steeply from the ridges, many of them containing swift tumultuous streams.

From the camp a small sandy beach could be seen near the western end of the bay, and from that a grassy bank seemed to rise directly to the road. That beach was to be my objective, and thence the open hills, and China. The problem was, how to start?

Reconnaissance began at once, and I attached myself to drain-cleaning parties since those sometimes worked right out to the sea-wall, and they provided an opportunity to study the nearer landscape. The main boundary fence had on the inside of the posts four electrified wires, while behind the posts there was barbed wire netting six feet six inches in height. Along the top of that netting there was a roll of barbed concertina wire two feet six in diameter, and altogether it formed a very nasty obstacle.

Beyond the main fence, across the northern boundary of the camp, there was a piece of open ground, fifty yards wide, and in the middle of that ground was a guardhouse in which the camp sentries were lodged. The outside fence of that area was not more than five feet high, and it had three electrified wires on the inside, heavy wire mesh on the outside, and a roll of concertina wire along the ground. Outside the fence there was a large area in which drums of petrol were stored in trenches, and adjoining the road there were large sheds in which the Japanese Army stored and maintained motor transport. Sentries were posted at intervals around that open ground, and each morning and evening, accompanied by a large dog, a corporal searched the trenches.

At first there seemed to be many obstacles to be overcome, but our arrival marked the beginning of a train of events which eventually cleared the way for my departure. First the concertina wire was removed from the base of the outside fence, and from that moment the fence ceased to be an obstacle. Earlier inspection had revealed a place where a short section of wire mesh had been removed, and at that place the lowest electric wire was high enough from the ground to allow a thin person to slide under. Next, some of the permanent sentries were replaced by a roving patrol, and an Alsatian dog took the place of one who had guarded the sea-wall beyond the electrified fence. Then a gang of men cleared the remaining petrol from the trenches, and everything of value was taken from that area, including wooden bridges from the drains. The situation was rapidly developing in my favour.

On a Saturday afternoon, while I tramped around alone in a drizzling rain that fell softly on a sodden exercise ground, the final scene was enacted. My curiosity was aroused by a party of Chinese workmen who were crossing the empty trenches, but the significance of their approach did not dawn upon me until they hoisted the dog kennel to their shoulders and made away with it.

Scarcely able to believe my eyes I was in a state of suppressed excitement, wondering how far they would go. It was not wise to display too much interest in the proceedings, and my walking continued, although it speeded up each time my back was turned. Right past the transport buildings they continued with their burden, nor did they put it down until they reached a small dump of fuel drums near the roadside. There was no doubt that that was to be the destination of the kennel, where the dog, in future, would take his nightly station.

My spirits were leaping and my heart was pounding unreasonably, and I could not prevent my features from expanding in a broad grin. At that moment I *knew* that the time was near. The dog, sole permanent guard outside, was so far away that his presence could be disregarded, and there was nothing between me and the sea except two fences and the regular camp guards. Once beyond those obstacles I felt that my chances of success would be good.

Shaking with excitement I almost ran back to the hut to tell my friends what had been happening, and though they guessed what was in my mind they all studiously avoided comment on my agitation. After all, such a prosaic event as the movement of a dog kennel from one place to another no more than one hundred and fifty yards distant did not call for much discussion, and in the event of interrogation the less one knew the better.

Within the past month whispers of escape plans had been rife in the camp, so much so that our senior officers became alarmed. A meeting of all unit commanders was called, and instructions were framed for promulgation. So anxious were some that they allowed their imaginations unlimited play in describing the terrors and dangers that lurked in the mountains surrounding Kowloon.

The senior naval officer present was Commander Crowther RN, and though an elderly man and frail from the privations of his interment, be it to his everlasting credit that he did *not* try to discourage anyone in his command. He merely pointed out the difficulties, and said that he considered that no one should attempt an escape unless he felt sure of at least a seventy-five per cent, chance of success. That was only sound common sense.

Those in camp who favoured attempts to escape were amazingly few, especially when one remembers that there were officers of the regular forces present. There were a number of reasons for that attitude, the strongest being the fear of reprisals. After the last successful escape from Shamsuipo in April 1942 several officers were interrogated, beaten, and given three weeks' confinement in a filthy jail where they all contracted malaria. After their release they were sent to Argyle Street Camp, where they arrived in a disgusting condition, their clothes full of filth and lice, their skins just yellow parchment drawn over protruding bones.

At that time all prisoners were ordered to sign a statement that they would not attempt to escape, although what the Japanese hoped to gain by forcing such action is hard to say. I don't think anyone regarded their signatures as being worth the ink they were written with.

No escape had been made since that time, although one attempt was made in October 1942, the party unfortunately being discovered and executed.

The immediate effect upon me of the latest scare tactics in Shamsuipo was that my last prospective partner dropped out. This was an officer of the RAF who, after his senior officer and the other occupants of his hut had had a long debate on the subject, felt that he could not reconcile his conscience to the sufferings that might be inflicted on those left behind. Although no better companion for such a venture could have been found, his decision lifted a weight from my shoulders, for I still felt that the dangers would be immeasurably increased by company. His withdrawal left me free for immediate action.

Careful study had convinced me that there were two possible routes out of the camp. One was by direct assault over the fences, the other was through the gate used by the sentries in passing to and from the guardhouse. There were serious disadvantages to both routes, and at the last moment I chose the fences.

Our section of the camp did not touch the sea-wall, for a hospital was situated at the north-west corner of the main enclosure. Between that hospital and our western boundary there was a vacant section on which were the concrete floors of two demolished huts. I decided to scale the fence opposite the end of that vacant section.

Let us now examine my immediate problem in a little more detail. A concrete path ran along the northern end of the huts, and outside that was a large drain, six feet wide and four feet deep. Along the outside edge of the drain was a roll of concertina wire. Beyond that again there was a narrow track between the wire and the fence. Fifty yards west of my hut there was a small bridge over the drain, and that was where I would cross. Along the fence at frequent intervals lamp-posts rose three feet above the concertina wire, and those were the only ones that it was possible to climb. On each alternate post there were two insulators, on one they would be on the bottom and third wires, on the next they would be on the second and top wires. I chose a post with insulators on the second and top wires, for once poised on the top insulator I would be clear of the fatal electric wires. Beyond the main fence there were the fifty yards of clear ground to cross to the second electrified fence, which, as stated previously, presented no great obstacle. Then there were one hundred yards of trenched ground to traverse to the sea-wall.

Special cables kept the electric fence alive all night, but owing to economy measures the fence lights were extinguished at midnight. No move could be made until the lights were out, so there would be, at most, six hours of darkness in which to gain distance from the camp. Once over the sea-wall it was my intention to swim across Laichikok Bay, and then travel north to Mirs Bay before striking west to Waichow on the East River. Unfortunately, except for the restricted portion in view from the camp, the country was completely unknown to me, for by land I had never been away from the immediate vicinity of the naval yard. However, study of maps and talks with those who knew the country had given me a fair idea of the salient features of the area, and while on patrol in Mirs Bay I had seen where the path to Waichow cut through the mountains.

Waichow was chosen as the goal because some objective within a reasonable distance had to be chosen, and Waichow, being about one hundred miles away, seemed to be the only logical place. We knew that the Japanese had occupied the town in 1942, but rumours had given me the feeling that they had since gone. That was something to be worried about in the future. One hundred miles does not sound far, but the country was rugged in the extreme, the disposition and numbers of the enemy were unknown, I knew nothing of the roads or tracks, and a European could move only at night. We knew that the Japanese had a strong defence line along the former boundary of the British territory, and also that they had a large camp in the Fanling area.

An escape from Hong Kong could be made only westwards across China into India, and at times the hazards to be overcome seemed to assume fantastic proportions. Once or twice during my captivity, at times of extreme mental and physical depression, my hopes sank to zero. Then, with returning strength the restless urge came back, and the constant watch went on.

At last, all unknowing, a few gaunt half-starved coolies carrying a dog kennel had brought me to a final decision.

In two and a half years we had grown accustomed to the miserable prison-camp existence, and, in comparative security, we could all make the best of it. We knew that the war was shaping to a successful end. The local Red Cross representative had been able to augment our rations, and at the beginning of 1944 conditions at Shamsuipo Camp were tolerably comfortable.

By trying to escape one might bring suffering on the heads of those left behind and, of course, one might die. The rewards for a successful break, against which the dice were heavily loaded, were freedom and a chance to hit back at a hated enemy.

What was the spur that drove me to take the chance? I believe it was fear itself; fear of my own conscience.

All through our captivity I had believed that everyone who could should escape. In innumerable arguments mine was one of the tongues that never failed to lash the protagonists of the non-escape theory. As time went on and those arguments recurred, it became increasingly difficult for me to speak convincingly, for two and a half years was a long time to hold a view without proving my sincerity. Still, there had to be a reasonable chance of success, and no such chance had come.

Now was the time to put my theories to the test, the time to take the plunge from which there could be no return. Once started on my way the end must be either freedom or death. Doubts assailed me. Why take the risk? It would be so easy to sit back and wait for the war to end, and certainly no one would cast any blame. Those fences looked extremely difficult, and the Japanese had nasty habits with swords and bayonets. Death at their hands would be horrible.

Then visions of the future would drift into my thoughts, and it seemed that an accusing spirit hovered on my shoulder, pointing a scornful finger. "You were afraid; your conscience was clear on every point, the way was open, and you were afraid to take the risk."

It was true. Given the right weather conditions there was nothing now to keep me in camp except fear of the consequences of failure. Therefore there was only one course open. If I failed I would be dead; but if I failed to try, that accusing devil would haunt my every waking moment, and I could never again look men clearly in the eyes. No; fear of my own soul was more powerful than any other. My mind was made up and at peace; I was determined to go.

Chapter 4

Escape

For weeks there had been electrical storms with constant rains, and Sunday the 16th of July 1944 was just another day of pouring rain, without, however, the usual display of lightning. In fact, when night fell, the rains came down with never a flash to break the darkness, a most unusual condition. Never before had there been such an opportunity.

Nothing could be done outside until after midnight, when the lights went out. Inside the huts all lights were switched off at 10 p.m., and after that my work began. With neighbours so close, there was only two feet between the bunks, I had to move with great care to avoid arousing suspicion. Mosquito-nets over the bunks hid me fairly well, and under my sheet I slipped on a shirt and shorts, and a pair of rubber-soled shoes.

Rain beat solidly on the roof and squalls whistled about the camp, making the interior of the hut seem wonderfully comfortable by comparison with conditions outside. It would be so easy to slip off my clothes, relax the nervous tension, and settle down to peaceful sleep. Outside there was nothing but streaming wet discomfort, unknown and unseen dangers, death lurking in every shadow.

Lying there, listening to the sounds of tempest, straining my ears for any sounds to indicate the proximity of guards, it was grimly amusing to think of what might happen in the next hour or two. Having seen the reactions of the Japanese to previous alarms, it was easy to imagine the scene should a false move cause me to short-circuit the electrified wires on the fence. Before my frizzled body hit the ground there would be guards yelling and rushing about the camp. Dozens of extra troops would be pouring in from Headquarters, and the whole camp would be paraded over and over again. There would be no more sleep for anyone that night because there had been caused so much inconvenience, so much loss of "face", and such a display of panic and stupidity as to feed anew the smouldering sense of inferiority in our captors. Anything in the nature of an alarm caused such a pandemonium, and such a display of ineffective effort, that it was a dismal commentary on the ease with which they conquered all our own positions in the East.

Suddenly the lights went out and the camp was plunged into intense gloom. There was no suspicious sound, only the noise of the wind and the rain. No one stirred inside the hut. Lifting the mosquito-net I slid silently off my bed, lifted my pack from underneath, and crept along to the door. There was no one in sight, and I passed safely through. To be seen fully dressed and with a large bundle in my arms at that hour of the night would have called for an awkward explanation, and I had a keen interest in avoiding everyone. There would be interrogations on the morrow, and it was better that nothing should be known.

Outside, a soft rain was falling and darkness spread an impenetrable cloak. A wayward squall whistled along the fence, rattled the lamp-shades, and was gone. No one was about. There might be sentries standing against the huts, they did that sometimes, but conditions were perfect and it was no time to hesitate. A few swift paces brought me to the bridge, and on the far side of that I dropped flat on my stomach to wriggle under the concertina wire. That was easy, for the wire had recently been raised a little by grass-cutters. By the time my pack had been pulled through, the rain had stopped, and just as I began to crawl towards the chosen lamp-post someone came to visit an open latrine that stood by the edge of the drain. From my position on the ground I could see him very clearly against the sky, but the darkness of the ground sheltered me. Then several more men came out to join the first, taking advantage of the lull between showers, and in spite of the dark it did not inspire me with any great confidence to be lying there, not more than twelve feet distant, with nothing but a few thin strands of wire to hide me. The intruders were much too clearly in view for my peace of mind, and valuable minutes were wasting.

When three or four of the nocturnal wanderers had returned to their huts I decided to wait no longer, and began to crawl cautiously along the narrow path between the wire and the fence. Then, having reached my post I was in the act of standing up, when approaching voices made me hug the ground again. This time it was the one o'clock change of guard going outwards, and it gave me a shock to know that already an hour of darkness had gone. Three soldiers filed past, ten feet distant on the other side of the drain, and I am afraid I took rather a morbid interest in their silhouettes, especially in their rifles and bayonets so clearly etched against the gloomy background. Rain was falling again, and lying there in the mud and water, scarcely breathing, it was not at all pleasant to think of the consequences should that party see me. I could do nothing until the relieved guards came in, and as it was a matter of only two or three minutes before they came trudging past, they were probably only too glad to return to the shelter of the guardhouse. It was then time for me to make the next move.

From long and close scrutiny I knew exactly what that fence was like, but in spite of all my study I had been unable to think of any way to pass the roll of concertina wire along the top. But the four electrified wires were my immediate danger, and I felt that if they could be successfully passed, the concertina wire would be beaten too.

Having carefully adjusted the pack on my back to give my arms greatest freedom, I lifted my right foot to the insulator, grasped the post above the top wire, and tried to climb. Imagine my dismay at finding that the step was too high and that my strength was unequal to the task. Here was a pretty dilemma. Rain was running down the post and wires, my shoes were wet and muddy, the insulator had only a very small cap above the wire, and it was imperative that my foot should remain firmly on that little piece of smooth porcelain. Several unsuccessful attempts to climb convinced me that it could not be done, and then I remembered that it was my right leg that had been injured. Though no weakness had been apparent when working about the camp it was possible that some infirmity remained, so, readjusting my balance I placed my left foot on the insulator. Then, using my arms to their utmost, I heaved myself upright.

That was an exhilarating moment, with the first really dangerous step successfully completed. I was off the ground, the insulator had not broken, I was not electrocuted. Now for the next step. It had to be my right foot this time, but the step was not so high. In poising for this step my bare leg pressed hard against the third electric wire. There was no insulator on that one, and it was standing out nine inches from the post. Those were moments of supreme danger. All my weight was concentrated on the small insulator top, little more than an inch in diameter, and my left foot was rapidly tiring. My bare leg was pressed hard against a live wire; my right foot was precariously poised on the top insulator, and my hands were grasping the post between strands of concertina wire. With my leg against the live wire one touch of those invisible strands above would have been fatal, and even without touching I was afraid that the running water would complete a circuit. The situation was one of great delicacy, and it seemed that Death looked on with more than passing interest the while I tried to adjust my balance. Then, summoning every ounce of strength, I straightened up and stood clear above the electric wires. As quickly as possible I stepped off the insulator on to the barbed wire fence behind the posts.

One major danger was passed, and then there began a most desperate struggle. Before I could stand up the roll of wire had to be forced outwards with all my strength, and it was pressing hard against me as I clung to the post. My only foothold was on top of the fence directly below the middle of the roll, and since half of it overhung either side of the fence my feet were resting under the middle of it, while my chin was resting on the top. I began a fierce struggle to transfer my body from the camp side to the outside of the roll. It was a war of attrition, won by pushing one leg down through the wire, then drawing the other one out and pushing it down again a few strands farther on. The hard steel wire was relentless, and it was an operation fraught with the utmost difficulty and pain.

The whole fence was swaying precariously, the lamp shade was rattling loudly, and the wires of the fence were slipping and squealing through their holding staples. I was doubled up over the roll of wire, with my shirt, shorts and flesh caught in a dozen places by barbs that sprang at me afresh with every movement. No matter how hard I pushed and trampled, the steel wire flew back to gain fresh grips the moment the pressure was released.

After several minutes of that exhausting fight I had to rest, and my heart sank for the first and only time on my journey. Would I never escape from that subtle enemy, which struck from every direction with a hundred invisible fangs? Where was the sentry who should have been at his post, twenty-five yards away at the end of the fence? At every moment I expected a torch to flash upon me, and to feel the thudding blows of bullets. It seemed impossible that he could not hear the noise, yet nothing happened.

Inside the camp another group had gathered at the latrine, and I felt certain from their animated voices that they could hear, and were discussing, the racket on the fence. That further added to my disquiet, for their talkative meeting at that hour of the night would be likely to attract the guards.

After a brief rest my struggles were resumed, the wires squealed again, and nothing less than a miracle could save me. Casting all caution to the winds I plunged and tore and strained with all my might, preferring to be shot struggling rather than just hanging limp in the wire. At last both legs were over the outside of the wire, and there I crouched with both feet on the top of the fence, my hands gripping the post, knees and chin almost touching, and with a dozen barbs gripping clothes and flesh with equal fervour.

My intention had been to climb down the outside of the fence, but I was quite unable to push the wire away to make that possible. The situation demanded a desperate remedy, so, straightening my knees, I let go with my hands, and hoped for the best. There was a tearing of cloth, the fence jerked violently, and I dropped seven feet to land with a tremendous thud on my back. Tins in my pack rattled loudly at that harsh treatment, and certain that an alarm *must* then be raised, I raced for the second fence. Finding the gap at once I dropped my pack and slid under the bottom electric wire, with my face scraping the mud and I know not what fraction of an inch between my back and eternity. I pulled my pack through and stood up, and then suddenly realised that my noisy though unceremonious departure had evidently passed unheeded.

How had it happened? The sentry could not have been asleep as the guards had just been changed, and my only thought is that he had left his post to yarn with one of the other sentries farther along the sea-wall. Whatever the reason, there I stood safely outside the two most dangerous fences, with comparatively easy going ahead.

To reach the sea-wall at a point beyond the electric fence I had to cross diagonally over that ground where petrol had been stored, and great care was needed to avoid its deep trenches. The intense darkness was my best friend, but it was also a great hindrance, for I had to feel for every step. The obstacles at the sea-wall were up to that time unknown, so it was with great satisfaction that I found nothing there but a broken barbed-wire fence with only three loose wires remaining between the posts.

Before leaving the hut I had stuffed a waterproof hat and a pair of stockings inside my shirt, and as it was raining heavily again I decided to put on the hat to keep my head warm. It gave me a rude shock to find that in falling from the fence my shirt had been ripped out, and the hat and stockings had gone. The discomfort which the loss would cause was nothing compared to the danger that the lost articles might indicate my route, for above all else the Japanese must be prevented from knowing the direction of my flight. Without that knowledge they must of necessity disperse their search over a wide area, and my chances of success would be so much better. My first impulse was to go back for the lost articles, but second thoughts convinced me that any such attempt would be foolish, since valuable time would be lost and the chance of finding them in the dark was remote.

Now for the last fence. Lying down I pressed the lowest wire into the grass and, as I started to roll through, my whole body contracted under the impact of a powerful electric shock. The current cut out immediately, and I was out on the top of the concrete wall, my mind racing with confused thoughts. Was it a trap wire? Had the shock recorded at the guardhouse? I remembered that at Argyle Street it had been said that tell-tale lights showed any interruption on the fence circuit. Haste to depart was my most urgent need, and I crawled along the top of the wall to a post which would serve as an anchor for a light rope. Below me was a black void in which was an unknown landing-ground. It might be rocks, it might be sampans with sleeping owners on board, or it might be just plain sand. The tide was out, so of one thing I was sure – there would be no water there. That much information had been gathered on one of the drain-cleaning expeditions.

Having made sure that the rope ran freely I dropped both ends over the wall and prepared to slide down. Accustomed as I had been all my life to rowing dinghies and climbing about the rigging of yachts, it had never entered my head that that would present any difficulty, but on trying to take my weight on the thin rope I was quickly disillusioned. My hand could not grip hard enough, so to hold on, while swinging my body over, I put a turn round my right hand, thinking that it would be a simple matter to take it off before starting to go down. Again, much to my surprise and discomfort, my strength failed and I had to slide down with the turn still round my hand. The result was inevitable, and I reached a beach of firm sand with the skin torn from both palm and back of the hand, an injury that gave me a great deal of pain in the days to come.

Matters of greater urgency left no time for regrets so, coiling my rope, I began walking towards the sea, keeping in deep shadow under the wall. Small waves were rolling on shore in bright lines of phosphorous, and when close to them I sat down to make ready for swimming. It took me two or three minutes to fasten one life-jacket on myself and one on the pack, and while I was engrossed in that job a sudden flashing of lights a few yards along the fence gave me a great fright. In a moment my fears were at rest, for the flashes were caused by a loose wire swinging in the wind against the electric fence. Every time the wires met sparks were flying, and there lay the explanation of the shock I had received. Each time the wires made contact a shock was sent along the barbed-wire fence, so my fears of a trap were unfounded. It was blowing hard and raining heavily again, so there was no danger of being heard. That was comforting knowledge, for in watching the flashing wires I had seen the sentry, who should have heard my departure, standing directly above me.

When the life-jackets had been inflated I tied my rope to the pack and set off towards the sea, passing close to grounded junks on the way. There were a great many craft in the bay, both ashore and afloat, and I had no wish to be seen by the people on board. In spite of the darkness there was a sheen on the water, and when looking seaward dark objects could be seen for some distance. It was not at all reassuring to know that while wading out through the shallow water I was plainly visible from junks on shore, for a person deliberately walking out to sea on a wet and stormy night could hardly fail to arouse comment, even in China.

The pack floated buoyantly, and when it had floated back clear of my feet I fastened the rope round my neck and started to swim. Brilliant phosphorous marked every movement with a trail of fire that made me proceed with care when passing close to anchored vessels. When viewed from the camp in daylight it did not seem to be far across the bay, but it seemed to be a long way then, with nothing but stormy night all about. Intense blackness hid the shore, and there was nothing to indicate my progress save junks that, as they swung towards me in eddying squalls, seemed bent on my destruction. The wind had its advantages, for besides covering my noise, by swimming almost at right angles to its direction I was able to keep to my course.

My sense of time had gone completely, and I had no idea how long it took me to cover the half mile to shore. At last my foot touched bottom, and I stood up to wade out on what looked like the beach. Fifty yards away a small sampan was high and dry, a small lamp burning beneath its matting cover. Nothing else could be distinguished, so turning my back to the sea I began to stumble up the sloping shore, making an inordinate amount of noise by tripping over empty tins and other rubbish lying there. I expected to find a bank sloping up directly to the road, but a few paces took me into a cultivated garden, with banked rows of sweet potatoes. That was not in my reckoning at all, and it made me think that the beach must be farther west.

Having returned to the sea I was wading past the stern of a junk on a slipway when I fell with a resounding splash into a hole of unknown depth. Bobbing to the surface it took me only a moment to reach the other side and scramble out, but after taking a dozen steps more the same thing happened again. That would not do, for there was no wind under the shore and there would be watchmen on the junks. A continuous noise like a porpoise floundering in the shallow water would be bound to attract attention, so I lay down to paddle and swim again. Soon the trend and nature of the shore convinced me that my first landing had been correct, so making out to deeper water I swam back to the beach, guided by the light still burning in the sampan. This time I continued across the potato patch, and soon reached the road.

Now what to do? The road was flanked on both sides by buildings, and directly behind those on the northern side steep hillsides rose to the Kowloon range. The salient features of those hills had been memorised, but how did one pass the buildings? I could see nothing and had no idea which way to go. My feet had been hardened by continuous barefoot walking while in camp, so, as my shoes were squelching loudly at every step, they were taken off and slung round my neck. I was still undecided which way to go when someone came clumping along the road in wooden clogs. As the walker approached I stood quite still, until he reached a point on the road directly opposite. Suddenly a brilliant torch-beam streamed from right alongside me, and it held a Chinese coolie for some distance, at the same time lighting up the buildings opposite. Among mingled feelings of surprise and fright came the realisation that I was standing within two feet of a Japanese sentry, and also that some thirty yards to the right a narrow lane ran in towards the hills. There was my route.

Chapter 5

Shamsuipo to Shatin

As soon as the torch was extinguished I edged silently sideways for ten feet, and then, under cover of an extra heavy deluge of rain, I dashed across the road, along the buildings and into the lane. Once there I felt reasonably secure since the torch could not reach me, but the lane was only fifty yards long and it ended against the face of a cliff. There was an opening just wide enough for me to squeeze through behind a building, so I went through to find myself in a courtyard that had been formed by excavating the hillside.

The face of the cutting was much too steep to give any foothold, and I began to feel my way along in the blackness, in the hope of finding some steps or pathway. In one place water flowing from above had cut a crevice which afforded some hope, but I went on in expectation of finding a better path. Nothing but sheer walls met my questing hands, and when a dog began to bark loudly close at hand I retreated to the watercourse and began to climb. Progress was slow, for every hand and foothold had to be gouged from the crumbling wall, and then, after climbing for eighty feet or more I almost went over into a black abyss. My position was not a happy one, for I found myself on a knife-edge of rotten laterite, so rotten that it crumbled beneath my feet at every step. Crawling on hands and knees I worked my way slowly up that treacherous ridge, until it rose steeply before me. My pack was greatly increased in weight since it had been thoroughly saturated, and I could go no farther.

Lying down, spread-eagled on that uneasy perch, I wondered if that was to be the end of my little adventure, for to try to descend would be to court almost certain disaster. My energy returned after a few minutes' rest, and I kicked out a niche in which to leave my pack. Then, after tying one end of my rope to it, I continued to climb. Relieved of that extra weight the climb was not so difficult, and suddenly my cheek pressed against a tussock of grass. A moment more and I was stretched out on an easy slope, thankful beyond measure to be past that hazardous ascent. It was then a simple matter to haul up the pack, and having emptied it of a quart of water that was greatly adding to its weight I started off quickly, feeling that the first round had been won.

A white building belonging to the waterworks showed up, but it was on the far side of a deep gully in which earthworks and landslides made a series of difficult obstacles. Clawing up steep banks, occasionally falling into unseen ditches and holes, sliding into deep ravines and pushing through stiff spiky scrub was hard slogging work. A concrete culvert gave me smoother going for a detour past the building, and then, after crossing a small stream I began to ascend the first open ridge.

Beyond that the view from the camp had led me to expect a shallow gully and then a rise to a much higher ridge, so it was disappointing to find myself going down into a deep ravine. I ran against a triple line of water-pipes, and I followed them down until they disappeared over what seemed to be a vertical cliff. From one hundred feet or more below came the roaring of a tumultuous stream. A track followed one side of the pipes, but that ended suddenly where a landslide had fallen to the stream below. In that narrow gorge I could see less than five feet, the sound of the torrent seemed to come from directly below me, and fearing that a false step might drop me over a precipice I clambered up to a path that ran along the hillside. That rough track hugged closely round the base of huge boulders, dropped suddenly into watercourses, and at times disappeared entirely where a landslide had swept it away. From its outside edge the ground fell vertically in places, and great care was needed. When heavy showers fell and dense cloud was overhead I could see absolutely nothing, not even the ground, and I was forced to feel every yard of the way with my feet. I was beginning to feel exhausted, and when heavier deluges fell I would rest for a time.

The track gradually became better defined and obviously more used, and I was making good progress when a house appeared, its open doorway just above me. Passing that with caution I was about to hurry on when other buildings came into view, and a dog began to bark. That was a bad locality with dawn so close at hand, so retracing my steps for four hundred yards I climbed from the track to seek a hiding-place. Grey light began to diffuse a little sodden visibility, and small trees and shrubs appeared on the slope about me. Several of those afforded no cover at all, and I was becoming alarmed at the increasing daylight when I found a clump of bushes that was just large enough for me to crawl inside. On that steep hillside, at an angle of about eighty degrees, it was hard to find any position of rest. Finally, I wedged my pack against the base of a small tree, and, seated on that, I could lean back against the streaming earth. Heavy rain continued to pour upon me, but it was forgotten in relaxation from the strain of the night.

Those moments afforded an opportunity for a little moist reflection on the relativity of comfort. There I was, with my seat resting on hard tins, my legs trailing downhill, my back and head resting against bare earth on which rivulets of rain were flowing, and yet that situation engendered a feeling of wonderful relief.

Rest was my most urgent need, and after that came food. It was important to retain strength during those first days, so in order to do that, and at the same time lighten my pack quickly, I had planned to use the heavy tinned foods first. For that reason my first breakfast in freedom consisted of an eight-ounce tin of beef. The meal was far from enjoyable for nervous tension had destroyed my appetite, and each little mouthful had to be chewed slowly and swallowed with great deliberation. At every swallow I was on the verge of being sick.

By the time that meal was finished it was full daylight, and my surroundings could be surveyed. The track passed one hundred and fifty feet below, and to the left it disappeared round a spur two hundred yards away. To the right my view was even more restricted, and with only isolated shrubs between me and that bare track it looked much too close. There could be no warning of anyone approaching: they would suddenly appear in full view, and the few leaves that hid me made me feel uncomfortably conspicuous. Every movement caused my shrub to jerk violently, so I made sure that no one was in sight before causing too much disturbance. Down the gorge to my left triple water-pipes crossed a bridge before climbing the far side, while to my right there were two single lines and one double line of pipes. Just visible beyond a turn in the valley was some unrecognisable concrete structure.

Out of sight down below, workmen were soon busy on the pipes. Voices, ringing blows from hammers and the barking of dogs came clearly to me above the noise of the rushing water, and although I saw no one those sounds continued all day. Opposite, above the initial steep side of the gorge, a ridge of completely bare laterite continued to rise at a more gradual angle. On a bare knoll at the top of the ridge there was a permanently manned guardhouse. That post, which had been visible from the camp, was the home of the sentries who guarded the reservoirs and other water-supply installations in that area.

Not a soul came near all day, and had it not been for the distant sounds of toil it might have been a deserted land. Time dragged heavily, for I could not sleep and aches and pains caused me to continually alter position in search of relief. It was amusing to guess at what was happening at the camp, but it was not so amusing to remember that I was no more than a mile away from it. My absence would be discovered at the nine o'clock muster, and allowing three hours for preparations to be made I guessed that a search would be in full swing by the afternoon. That guess proved to be wrong because the search of the camp went on until one o'clock, and the commandant was loth to report his loss of a prisoner.

My hat and stockings were found outside the fence, but since they were not marked in any way, and since they were saturated and dirty, the Japanese could not be sure that they were mine. Their lengthy efforts to find me in the camp were responsible for the quiet day I enjoyed so close at hand, and for that I was extremely grateful.

After studying the opposite side of the gorge I decided to cross by the triple pipes, for there the ascent seemed to be least difficult. My decision had to be made on the appearance of the other side, for I had no idea what difficulties there were on the near side of the gorge. There was nothing I could do to pass the time, and, being unable to sleep, I was very glad when fading light at last proclaimed the end of day. A tin of creamed rice formed my dinner, and after that was eaten I crawled out of my bushes to return to the pipeline. With the last of the daylight I safely reached the bridge and, crossing quickly, began a gruelling uphill fight against tangled undergrowth and rocks. Far too much energy and time were used in reaching the rim of the gorge, but once there I made good progress, for the rocky ground did not encourage growth and the ridges were quite bare.

While resting from my exertions I looked back and saw torches flashing on the slope I had just descended, and as there had been no rain for an hour or two I hoped that the searchers had no dogs with them. The sight spurred me to hasten, and the summit of the ridge was drawing close when

I went to earth as a searchlight swept along the hills. Several lights were directed from ships in harbour, and I lay low each time they passed over me. From the crest I looked down directly on to Shamsuipo Camp, almost gaily illumined with its closely spaced perimeter lights, while from beyond the camp brilliant blue fingers of the searchlights came probing through the darkness.

Before me, crossing at right angles, a path ran along the floor of a shallow valley, and beyond that rose the bare knoll on which the guardhouse stood. It was very good of the Japanese to bring the scene into relief with their searchlights, for until they were switched on I had seen neither the valley nor the house. Apparently a search had begun in earnest, for a patrol was coming up the path, combing both sides of the valley with torches. On the hill opposite sentries were shouting to one another as they spread out, conveniently disclosing their positions.

The patrol was not moving very fast, so, intending to hurry across ahead of it I began to slip down to the path, in my haste making much more noise than was wise. The last eight feet fell almost vertically, and I was about to go over that when someone who had been hiding against the bank rushed out from directly below my feet. He stopped no more than fifteen feet away, and I expected to be caught in the beam of a torch. But nothing happened, so I pressed my hands down on the earth and began to slide silently backwards up the steep slope. Still nothing happened, and having regained the ridge in safety I felt sure that whoever had been there was just as pleased as I was that there was no sequel to the encounter. Most likely he was a wood-thief or a Chinese guerilla, also bent on remaining out of sight. Somewhat shaken I sat down to rest and to decide on my next move, for whoever was down below was still there, and I had no wish to repeat the meeting. It was pouring with rain again, the searchlights had been extinguished, and everywhere was blackness.

Some distance away figures were moving about in the light of lanterns where part of the patrol had stopped, while a small party, talking in subdued voices, passed in single file along the path. When they had gone I moved off a little to my left, and there crossed over on to the bare ridge. A light was burning in the house, but neither seeing nor hearing the sentries I was soon past, and climbing up a steep spur. When the highest ridge was drawing close the clouds broke now and again, and at times even a few stars were visible. It was my belief that on the other side there would be a valley leading into Tolo Harbour, and after avoiding a building that might have been a guard-post I was deeply disappointed to see the water of a bay. That could only be an arm of Hong Kong Harbour, and I realised that my course had tended too far to the west. That meant that I still had the worst of the rough country to cross.

A path clung precariously to the base of rocky outcrops along the ridge, a narrow track with sheer walls of rock on one side and steep declivities on the other. To meet a patrol there would be fatal, and as there was every possibility that the path was guarded I decided against its use. A series of precipices precluded any possibility of following the ridge except by the one track, so I began to descend a spur tending generally eastwards. Occasionally I crossed shallow ravines to more favourable ridges, but in the intense dark that had settled down again I had little sense of direction. In one of those valleys I heard sounds of movement about me, and I stopped dead in my tracks. There were no voices or other human sounds, just a swish, swish in the grass, with an occasional noise of something being dragged over the ground.

That was a disquieting situation, and I lay down, straining eyes and ears in an effort to understand what was happening. My fears were at once dissipated when a figure, carrying two large bundles on a pole, passed a few feet from me. There was the explanation. Fuel was in very short supply, and every day in Kowloon we had seen lines of coolies jogging along with huge bundles of grass that they had brought down from the hills, grass with which to cook their miserable meals. Cutting from the areas round the reservoirs was forbidden, so the grass thieves were at work under cover of night. I felt that there was nothing to fear from them, but it was better not to be recognised as a stranger in their midst, in case they should be questioned. Rising to my feet I went on, passing silently between the workers.

Night was far advanced and a hideout for the day must be found. On a nearby spur small trees were growing, and I made my way there, clawing on hands and knees up a steep incline. The trees proved to be young pines of an afforestation scheme, but they were spaced widely and there was no undergrowth, so they did not meet my needs. When skirting the edge of the grove I almost collided with a man standing motionless in the blackness, and he made no move until I went off at a tangent, when he retreated beneath the trees. The situation made me chuckle inwardly, for each of us was creeping about in forbidden territory, each wondering who the other could be. An overgrown path led me in among the trees, and I followed that for some distance without finding any suitable hiding-place. Then I walked slap up against the side of a sentry-box, though whether it was manned or not I neither knew nor waited to find out. No advantage was to be gained by providing my head as a target, so I moved out to open ground again as quickly as silence would permit.

Sounds of a rushing torrent came from some distance, and I made my way towards that, expecting to find cover along its course. On the way I heard the last of the grass-cutters departing, and soon the first signs of daylight made me hurry. The stream seemed to be as distant as ever, no possible cover of any kind could be seen, and increasing light caused me considerable anxiety. At the junction of a number of valleys, all completely stripped of everything except short grass, I came out into a main defile and was greatly alarmed to see the guardhouse in full view above me. Something had to be done quickly, so, retreating up a side valley far enough to be out of sight of the lookouts, I found a narrow watercourse, just wide and deep enough in which to lie. Tall grasses and small shrubs on the banks gave some protection, but anyone on the hill above could look down on me, while I was in full view from the opposite side of the main valley.

That was the only place within reach to afford any reasonable degree of protection, so I settled down to make the best of it. The best was not very good either, for there were roots and stones that could not be moved, my clothes were saturated, and in a short time ants began to bite me unmercifully. My feet and legs were deeply scratched. Due to dermatitis there was no skin between my toes, and several toes had been split through striking rocks and stumps. To all of those injuries the ants went in droves, and their attentions were maddening as it was imperative that I remain lying down. In that position I could not reach them with my hands.

A drizzling rain fell during the first two hours of daylight, and then a blazing sun added its measure of discomfort to my lot. No breath of air could stir in that narrow bed, and the heat was stifling until clouds again happily covered the sky. Hardly had the sun gone when, more preoccupied with my immediate job of killing ants than with keeping out of sight, the sound of men's voices made me press down into the narrow ditch. The voices grew louder until the heads of the searchers must have been just below my line of vision, no more than thirty yards away, and then they receded into the distance again. At the same time several armed soldiers appeared on the other side of the main valley some four hundred yards distant, and they carried out a leisurely and seemingly not very enthusiastic search. Two of them remained seated on boulders for what must have been three hours, and if ever I wished anyone in hell it was those men. Big black ants were swarming on my sore feet, and their stinging bites had perforce to be endured, for any movements must have given me away.

It was a time for a little rueful and philosophic thought, and, subject to review as time went on, I decided that it was better to endure the biting of the ants than to attract the soldiers with their bayonets.

During the day my plan of escape was completely revised, owing to the difficulties of the terrain and my slow rate of progress. My original intention had been to swim across Tolo Harbour from a point near Shatin, travel north along the Saikung Peninsula, re-cross Tolo Harbour near its entrance in Mirs Bay, and finally reach the mainland at a point north of Shataokok. In that way all the main Japanese positions would have been avoided, but it was then clear to me that even with the aid of life-jackets I would be too weak to undertake those long swims. My heavy pack had to be lightened or I would never break out of that rugged country, and the jackets were quite a load in themselves. The rain and the intense darkness made cross-country travel too painfully slow, so I decided to find the road at Shatin and, chancing the guards, travel on the highway. When evening shadows filled the valleys I repacked my bag, after throwing out the life-jackets and other items which did not seem to justify their weight.

At dark on that third night I set off with a lighter load, and after traversing several steep ridges and gorges I decided that the only way to make any real progress was to climb the main range again. Several deep gorges had to be crossed, and it was most exhausting work climbing up and down their steep sides, on which tangled undergrowth and thorny creepers gripped me with malicious obstinacy. Showers fell with increasing frequency, but rain had ceased to trouble me except for the utter lack of visibility which accompanied it. A hard climb with frequent rests brought me at last to a lofty eminence from which ridges radiated on three sides, and unable to see anything but my immediate surroundings, I had to guess which one to take. It was a long, difficult, and painful descent, for my feet and hands were becoming ever more lacerated by thorns and jagged rocks. On reaching a track I followed that until it approached two houses, where I could hear voices and people moving about. A dog began to bark, so I left the track and continued down the stony ridge.

A lighter patch in the darkness down below appeared as a level field of grass, and in imagination I felt my burning feet resting in heavenly comfort on the cool soft sward. After another fifty feet of scrambling over steep sharp rocks I was at its very edge. At my feet a rounded tuft of grass offered a welcome invitation, and I stepped down with every confidence in its yielding surface. Alas for my hopes. The treacherous leaves allowed my foot to pass right through, and I pitched forward to fall with a resounding splash, full on my face, into eighteen inches of muddy water. The rounded tuft of grass, so fondly imagined, was in reality a small shrub growing on the edge of a vertical bank six feet high, and it was over that that I pitched to my filthy fate. Too utterly disgusted to extricate myself, I just lay where I had fallen and cursed volubly until my temper and disappointment had subsided. Then, gathering myself up I splashed across the swamp into the entrance to a valley, where my spirits rose rapidly as I found a much-used path.

That track followed the floor of the valley up a slight ascent, crossed a low saddle, and then travelled down another valley which must surely emerge on some part of Tolo Harbour. At last it seemed that the wilderness of ridges and valleys would soon be left behind, but after continuing for perhaps a mile the path disappeared into what might be the results of an earthquake. Black chasms split the ground, landslides had fallen to the floor of the valley, and masses of broken concrete were piled up in confusion. In those conditions my progress became slow and hazardous. Then a darker shadow on a face of rock resolved itself into the entrance to a tunnel, and I realised that the upheaval had been caused by the collapse of a mine.

The path ended in that ruin, and I could find no way of exit. An attempt to work my way along the side of the valley very nearly ended my career. Unable to see anything, and probably giddy with fatigue, I suddenly fell out into space. Obstructions dealt me violent blows as I went hurtling down, but I had no recollection of striking the bottom. My returning senses first became aware of babbling water. A tinkling stream was within a foot of my ear, and there was an overpowering weight pressing on my neck. Full consciousness returned suddenly, and I realised what had happened. The end of the fall had taken me head first down between some large boulders, and there I had come to rest on the back of my neck in the gravel of a stream bed, with my feet pointing skywards through the hole above. The weight on my neck was my own.

It was with some trepidation that I began to extricate myself from that position, and I was very pleased to find that no bones had been broken. During previous nights I had had other falls of less severity, any one of which might have ended disastrously, and I was thinking that my luck could not hold indefinitely. Each fall had been caused through lack of care in placing my feet, with the result that instead of going round sharp corners I had stepped straight ahead into space. In such circumstances any fall could easily have marked the end of my journey.

Dawn could not be far off, so carefully picking my way between yawning chasms of unknown depth, I regained my original path. I had had enough of that valley of trouble, so, returning for some hundreds of yards, I then climbed a hill on which was a pylon carrying electric power lines. Patrols might pass that way in daylight, so I continued for a little way before settling down to await the day, very curious to find out where I was. It was essential to remain in a position from which there was a good view, but there was practically no cover on the ridges, and increasing light caused me some anxiety. I moved swiftly from one small bush to another without finding a suitable hiding-place, until I came upon a shallow excavation that had been made inside a fringe of grass and scrub. The previous occupant must have been very short for my feet poked out into the open when I tried to lie at full length, but the view from that position was very extensive, so I decided to remain.

Leaving my pack out of sight I went out again to reconnoitre the position. A quarter of a mile to the eastward, round a spur and out of sight from my nest, were two powerful pillboxes. Although no one was in sight they would certainly be manned, so memorising their positions I retired out of sight.

My chosen lookout could not have been better placed and, as growing light dispersed the gloom of the deep valley below, I saw the whole length of the Shingmun River, from the dam to Shatin. Another pillbox was in sight farther eastwards, and though it seemed to be deserted, that appearance might have been imparted by camouflage.

Nothing more could be done at the moment, so hoping to be able to sleep I crawled into my shelter. Although it was three days and nights since I had had a wink, physical and nervous strain had taken me beyond the possibility of sleep, and after an hour of rest I made a leisurely survey of my surroundings. In the full light of day a manned watch-tower on Shingmun Dam was clearly visible, and eight hundred feet below me the river was foaming on its way to Tolo Harbour. The road and rail bridges at Shatin were in sight, but the country between me and those bridges was far from encouraging. On the other side of the valley an endless series of ridges fell steeply from Mount Tai Mo Shan to the river, and it might take two more nights of hard work to reach the road at Shatin.

Already three nights and a great deal of energy had been expended on part of a journey that I had expected to complete in one night, and my food was rapidly dwindling. With those considerations in view I was toying with the idea of wriggling down a small valley that would hide me from the pillboxes, and of working my way along the river in daylight. Those deliberations were rudely interrupted by a clamour of talk that arose nearby, and I was surprised to see about thirty Chinese men and women come over the ridge one hundred and fifty yards west of the spur on which I lay. They spread out and began to work systematically, shaving all grass and brushwood from the hillside.

The advent of the Chinese was an added incentive for leaving, for they might work towards me. Taking great care not to rise into view I fastened on my pack, and I was ready to slide out of cover when a sentry, fifty yards above me, fired his rifle. That the shot was not aimed at me was apparent from the sound, but I flattened to the ground again, very thankful for the warning. In another moment I would have crawled out into full view, to be a perfect sitting shot. Overhead a hawk made several leisurely circuits, and possibly the sentry, in his boredom, had fired at that.

My position was hardly one to inspire confidence, lying as I was with only a few blades of grass between me, the sentry and the Chinese, and with absolutely no cover over me at all. However, nothing further happened just then, so I settled down to rest.

While thinking over the events of the morning I remembered the words of a fortune-teller who had made some amazingly accurate forecasts of my life. She had said, "I don't know how this can be, but a bird is going to save your life." Could it be that that hawk, circling over a barren Kowloon range, had attracted the sentry's bullet and thus fulfilled a prediction made so long ago? Be that as it may; I shall always hold feelings of high regard towards that bird.

The sentry remained behind me all day, frequently talking to the Chinese who at one time were no more than thirty yards away. Had he walked only twenty-five yards forward he could not have failed to see me, but evening shadows began to lengthen, the Chinese departed, and silence settled down once more. Mingled with feelings of relief was one of growing confidence in my luck.

On the opposite side of the Shingmun River there was a poorly defined track close down to the water, so I would follow that. As soon as it was dark enough I broke cover and scrambled down the deceptively steep and long descent, waded along in the river for some distance, and then climbed the bank to make two or three false starts before finding the right track. At first a few stars were shining, and I covered two miles on a reasonably smooth path, until it turned inland where a stream joined the river. There I took to the water, wading or stumbling over shingle banks, for rain was falling again and it was intensely dark.

I continued until the bank rose to a vertical cliff, and the river became a deep wide stream that could be followed only by swimming. Unable to see anything, and not knowing what lay beyond, it did not seem wise to embark on what might prove to be a long swim, so I retraced my steps to a place where a watercourse gave access to a hill above. On that knoll fairly large trees were growing, and I knew that Shatin was very near, for the grove had been in sight from my vantage-point of the previous day. Also on that hill there was a Chinese grave distinguished by a tall flagpole, and having reached that I expected to find the road in a few moments. Another disappointment was in store, for on following a path it seemed to come to an end at the river bank.

My next move was to climb over the hill and try to find an exit on the other side, but large areas of rice paddy came right to the edge of the trees and I could not find a track anywhere. I had no wish to be caught in daylight wading about in open flooded fields surrounded by villages, so I climbed up near the top of the hill to gain such shelter as was possible in the prevailing miserable conditions. While rain fell in torrents a gale was roaring through the trees, and after sitting for a time I was feeling very cold and dejected. Lack of sleep, an extremely meagre diet, and the desperate physical effort of the journey were beginning to take their toll.

There was possibly an hour to wait for daylight, and that night gave me a bitter taste of a feeling that persisted throughout my escape, when every day became an agony waiting for the night, and every night became an agony waiting for the day.

Growing light revealed a dismal scene of flooded fields, from the far side of which a metalled road climbed steeply. That was of no use to me, for the one I sought followed the foreshore, and I turned back towards the river to examine prospects on that side. There was no undergrowth at all and I was feeling much too conspicuous in the rapidly growing daylight, so I hurried down the path that had led me, some hours before, to what I thought was the river.

A bamboo thicket offered very good cover, and in making towards it I topped a rise to step out into full view of an open window in a house one hundred feet away. Luckily no one was in sight, and I disappeared inside the thicket without arousing any undue interest.

The bamboo stems were three-quarters of an inch thick and seven or eight feet high, and being very closely grown they afforded a perfect hiding-place. My first concern was to make a space in which to lie before people began to stir, and it was a slow job since my only tool was a small pocket-knife. The stems proved to be very hard and tough, and the result of my labours was a far from comfortable bed, for uneven knobs and spikes made a harsh resting-place. While trying to ease myself down between sharp stakes it ran through my mind that a prospective escaper could profit by a course of training in the Indian fakir's art of sleeping on a bed of nails.

Having settled down gently into that sodden couch I became aware of an increasing throng of people passing, and there, only a few yards away, was the road, my goal of the past four nights. Its smooth tar-sealed surface looked wonderfully inviting, and it was a tremendous relief to see it so close. In the darkness that level surface shining with water had misled me into thinking that it was the river, and after so much anxiety the certainty of its nearness seemed to relax all my tension. There would be a definite route to follow after the heartbreaking cross-country struggle, in which I had maintained little sense of direction, and throughout which, even in the daytime, I had had little idea of my exact location.

The thicket was so dense that there seemed to be no danger of being discovered, and I soon settled down to obtain what little rest was possible. It was still drizzling slightly, sleep seemed to have deserted me entirely, and with dull eyes I was watching the people passing when a Chinese woman left the road and came straight towards me. What was to happen? She was carrying the inevitable pole, some lengths of thin rope and a heavy reaping-knife, and she came right up to my thicket to begin chopping away at the outside stems. She was visible to me with an exaggerated clarity and I expected her to see me at any moment, but she was concentrated on her work and her eyes were focused at the distance of her flashing knife.

After the first alarm had passed, the situation struck me as having its grimly humorous side. There was nothing I could do, for had I started up she must have seen me and would most likely have cried out with fright. In any case there was nowhere for me to go except out into the open, to certain discovery. My only course was to lie still and hope that she would desist before she became aware of my presence.

But the lady's need of bamboo was evidently as great as mine, and she kept on chopping away with an Oriental persistence that in the circumstances amused me intensely. I had ample opportunity to study her as she worked only a few feet away; a strong healthy coolie woman of a good type. In a full rounded face her big brown eyes set wide apart were calm and placid, seeming unconcerned with anything but her immediate task. Cutting steadily she came nearer and nearer until only a few stems and scanty leaves intervened between us, and I could scarcely believe that she could still be unconscious of my presence.

With eyes glued on hers and fingers pressed to my lips to enjoin silence at the moment of recognition, I watched her every glance intently. Not until she swept away the very last row of stems did she see me. Then she received a terrific fright. Her eyes opened like saucers and she sprang away, throwing her pole and reaping-knife before her as she rushed out on to the road.

She had friends at a small roadside stall, and it was obvious that they asked her what was the matter. My fate was in the hands of that frightened woman. Standing there in full view, without once glancing in my direction, she gave some little laughing reply and then picked up her belongings. My gratitude can be imagined.

It was no wonder she received a fright, for my appearance could hardly have been reassuring. Dressed only in tattered shirt and shorts, wet through and covered with mud, with tousled hair and eyes sunken with exhaustion, I must have been a sight to startle stouter nerves than hers when encountered suddenly in that land of violence. For that was territory occupied by Japan, and the Chinese, poor devils, had learned by bitter experience what it meant to be ruled by the sword.

I had to make a quick decision, for with the front of the thicket gone I was exposed to view from the road, and some move must be made. The only other cover near was a similar thicket sixty feet away, so I dashed across and dived inside. A quick glance at the open window satisfied me that I had not been seen from the house, and I settled down again, wondering if my discoverer would keep silent or bring out the guards. If she talked the game was up, for there was nowhere else for me to hide.

Only fifteen feet from that new position a track passed, and frequently men and animals went by, much too close for my peace of mind. However, no one noticed me, and even a fossicking terrier snuffled round the thicket without scenting my presence.

At some time during the previous night the cork had gone from my water-bottle, so I spent some time in fashioning one from a small pine cone. Otherwise there was nothing to relieve the tedium of waiting. Endlessly the long day passed, while I turned continuously from one position to another, trying to find some comfort on the knobbly roots and sodden ground.

I crawled out of the bamboo to make my way nearer to the road at dusk, and sat down beside a small bush to await full darkness. Too late to move I heard heavy footsteps padding down the track, and a barefooted Chinese passed, carrying some heavy poles on his shoulder. Whether he saw me or not I do not know, but just as he came alongside he dropped his load and bolted down to the road. He certainly gave me a fright for I had not expected anyone from that direction so late, but no doubt he had been stealing firewood and his guilty conscience would cause the fright to be mutual.

Chapter 6

Shatin to Shataokok

Traffic on the road became very spasmodic, and finally stopped altogether. Then, when all was quiet, I stepped on to that perfect highway and set off at a fast pace, revelling in the speed and the smooth comfort. Almost at once there were houses at the edge of the road, and I stepped lightly, making no sound with my bare feet. This was the village of Shatin.

Buildings crowded close along the roadside and lights shone from open doors and windows, but not a soul was stirring outside and I took a chance that in retrospect seemed to be the height of folly. Stepping swiftly and silently I walked straight through the village, through the beams of light from the doorways, looking in at Chinese families busy at their household chores. A few short minutes took me through, and I was swinging along a silent deserted road, my spirits bubbling over with the pleasure of this easy progress after the pain and effort of the four previous nights. The alternative to passing through Shatin was to make a detour of perhaps a mile over unknown terrain, and the temptation of the road was too strong to resist.

A slight delay occurred at the railway station. Bright lights covered the road from a veranda on which sentries were stationed, so I climbed to the tracks, hoping to be able to pass on that side. But lights flooded the railway lines too, so I crept up to the end of the station to listen to what was being said. Several Indian guards were inside, and someone was speaking in English. Unfortunately the voice was too muffled for me to follow, the only words that came to me clearly being "Shamsuipo ... Japanese ... fifty yen." The mention of Shamsuipo made me wonder if they were discussing my escape, but my ego would not allow me to believe that a reward of only fifty yen, about £3, 10s., was being offered for my capture.

Moving away beyond the range of lights I crossed the road climbed down a bank and passed the station over the paddy fields. Then I enjoyed a splendid walk of several miles over a perfectly level highway that followed the shore. Where this road turned inland it crossed the railway lines, and there a sentry was on guard. It was one of the rare times when stars were shining; as he was visible for some distance there was no chance of slipping past unseen. Leaving the road I intended to climb over a ridge and so pass the crossing, but the track became more and more difficult and I could find no way down the steep banks. I went back across the road, scrambled down to the sea, and waded for some distance before deeming it safe to return to the road. Heavy showers fell with increasing frequency, but I was enjoying the smooth going and when the road began to rise inland I climbed and climbed until it seemed my heart must burst. What felt like violent explosions took place inside my head, and after the second one, which almost made me fall, I stopped to rest beneath a large tree.

From that vantage point I had an extensive view across Tolo Harbour, and the lights of the fishing fleet made a most pleasing picture, especially to eyes so long confined to the limited scene from the camp. Hundreds of craft were there with one or two bright incandescent lamps on each, and, with reflections added, the whole made up a fairy city twinkling in the black expanse of the bay.

Starting off again I soon topped the rise, and began a long easy descent. The slopes of Tai Mo Shan rose steeply from the left of the road, and many streams came tumbling down to afford a plentiful supply of drinking-water. My water-bottle was nearly empty, so I decided to fill it at the next accessible place. It was then that the fireflies gave me their first assistance, the first of three encounters with those brilliant little creatures, which are events bordering on the realms of fantasy.

No access could be found to the next two streams, and then I came to one which tumbled down some distance from the road. That one was guarded by thick scrub and tangled thorn-bush, and, while seeking an entrance I noticed many fireflies passing me, going a short distance along the road, and then turning in towards the water. So many were flying the same course that I decided to follow them, and sure enough, they were turning in over a track that led to a waterfall. Having filled my bottle I went on my way, musing over the usefulness of those unexpected allies, for as it happened, that was the last place at which water could be had.

Continuing on my way I came to a railway crossing, and beyond that there was a long bridge that ran directly seaward. There was no indication of any such bridge on my map, and since the night was far spent I turned back and climbed to a ridge from which to view the scene by daylight. Perfect cover was available on a level spur two hundred feet above the road, and I settled down there, feeling very satisfied with the night's work.

Full day brought a very pleasing view, but it was bad luck that the road disappeared behind a high headland no more than half a mile distant. After the railway line crossed the road at the intersection reached on the previous night, it immediately plunged into a deep cutting and also disappeared from sight. Directly before me, perhaps four hundred yards from the railway embankment, there was a small island from which a causeway ran westwards. The road was carried on a long bridge to that causeway, and at the junction there was a Japanese guard-post, where all vehicles and pedestrians were being stopped and searched. There was no sentry at the rail crossing.

Taipo Market was not in sight, but I knew that it must be very close and could only assume that it lay directly behind the hill that blocked my view. The island and causeway formed a sheltered bay into which all day long there came a stream of junks and sampans, the smaller vessels lowering their masts and proceeding under the bridge to a more sheltered haven inside. It was while watching those little ships coming to anchor that I decided to steal a sampan that night and proceed across Mirs Bay by sea, and so cut out many miles of dangerous travel. Most of the junks had a sampan towing astern, and there were several others hauled out on the island.

My pocket-knife was too blunt to cut a rope swiftly, so I bound a razor-blade into a split stick. That occupied an hour or more, and then there was nothing more to do except wait for night. Traffic was constantly moving on the road, chiefly coolies with heavy loads on their shoulder poles, and it did not cease until it was fully dark. Occasional late-comers passed, so it was not until another hour had gone by that it was safe to move. Then I went down the road to the railway crossing, and walked back along the lines to put my plans into operation.

A smooth concrete wall sloped steeply to the sea, so, when opposite the junks which were anchored farthest out, I passed my rope round a telegraph pole and slid down to black rocks below. No thought of having to regain the road entered my head at that time, so I pulled my rope down. Stripping off my clothes I left them with pack, water-bottle and rope, and swam out into the bay. The razor-blade knife was between my teeth. Not one of those sampans held an oar or anything else that could be used as a paddle. One after another yielded the same result, so I continued to the island to carry out another fruitless search there. There was not a stick or board anywhere in sight.

By that time it must have been near eleven o'clock. It was raining steadily, a fresh wind was blowing, and I started to shiver violently. There was only one way to cure that, so finding a sheltered place I indulged in a few minutes of strenuous physical exercises to start my blood flowing again.

The search for a sampan having failed, I then decided to try to beg a passage across Mirs Bay in one of the junks. They were all vessels that plied about Hong Kong, and I hoped that someone on board would understand at least a smattering of English. Wading into the sea again I swam quietly to the junk farthest out, and consequently farthest from the guard-post, and floating close alongside I began to call softly to the owner. At last a sleepy voice made some reply, and a figure rose in dim silhouette against the dark sky. While I stated my needs as simply as possible the owner was peering down at me, but before I had finished he suddenly began to shout, to jump up and down, and to shake his fist at me with every indication of fierce hostility. In my most persuasive tones I tried to quiet him, but my efforts only increased his agitation, and an attempt to climb on board brought me a narrow escape when he made a vicious crack at my head with a piece of timber.

The increasing clamour made me fearful that the guard on shore would be roused, so I had to go. Brilliant phosphorus lit me like a flame as I swam, and, when passing close to another junk her crew opened an attack upon me with chunks of wood. Four or five men on board had been roused by the shouting of the first junk owner, and in addition to their bombardment they also raised their voices with threatening shouts. The situation was becoming serious, and I was torn between the desire to get out of range and the need to slow down so that the phosphorus would not disclose my position. Any one of those heavy blocks could have knocked me out, but, after being straddled several times without suffering a direct hit the ammunition all fell behind me, and I went as hard as I could for the railway embankment.

Luckily my sense of direction had been fairly good in the dark, and I soon found my gear. By great good fortune there was a wire-stay from the pole to a bolt embedded near sea-level, and using that to haul myself to the top of the embankment I stopped only long enough to realise that a great deal of shouting was arising from the bay, and bolted along the railway to cross the road before the guards were roused.

Almost at once I plunged into the impenetrable gloom of a deep cutting, and, hearing someone approaching, I pressed hard against the bank. The man collided with me as he passed, and he rushed off, evidently receiving as big a fright as I. He was probably a smuggler using the railway to dodge the guards on the road, and he would certainly have been shot had he been found there by the Japanese.

On rounding a bend I had a clear view back over the bay of my unsuccessful adventure, and there was a great uproar in progress, with lanterns flashing everywhere. My nocturnal visit had certainly started something, and vowing never again to seek assistance as long as I could still walk, I hurried on my way.

A high bridge carried the railway over an arm of sea, and my first few careful steps on that structure, not being quite careful enough, almost ended in disaster. The footways had been removed from alongside the rails, and a pedestrian had to step over the sleepers. Occasionally a sleeper was missing, and suddenly there appeared a space where not one but two sleepers were missing. My weight was already going forward, and, not being prepared for such a wide gap I just managed to throw myself sideways and grab a rail in falling.

The experience gave an added jolt to my already somewhat tattered nerves, and from then on I proceeded warily on hands and knees, for the water seemed to be a long way below and gaps in the sleepers were both frequent and irregular. On looking down I thought that there was a straight canal there, separated from the sea by only a narrow bank with a row of trees on it, but on taking a second look in a lighter period between showers I saw that it was a road, not a canal, that lay there. Once again a wet and shiny surface was giving the illusion of water. That being so I erroneously reasoned that the bridge would take me to the wrong side of the estuary, and I began a laborious return.

Once back on solid ground it did not take long to find a track leading down to the road, but that was no highway, for it soon narrowed to little more than a track beside the sea. That was very disappointing, and I made my way back to the railway. My mind seemed to be fixed on the idea that the road should be on that side of the estuary, so instead of making another attempt to cross the bridge I walked back along the lines. There the railway was carried on a high embankment, and I could find no way down until fireflies again came to my assistance. Many of those bright little sparks began dancing along, following the same course, and after going some yards ahead of me they dipped suddenly down over the edge of the bank. It was a real game of follow my leader, and, having joined in, I found that they were turning off at the start of a narrow track. It was no more than nine inches wide and barely discernible on the hard ground, so it was a mystery why the flies should choose to wing their way directly above it.

Reaching a tarred road of good surface I soon passed an archway through the embankment, noting it in case of future need, and continued until hemmed in by buildings. A narrow path lay alongside a large brick or concrete structure, and I advanced with the utmost caution, my bare feet making not a sound. At the top of the lane there was a wide roadway, and turning left I climbed carefully but quickly up a steady incline. Just as the road levelled off I stopped stock still, every nerve in my body tingling, for not more than eight feet to my right the luminous face of a wrist-watch was glowing.

A moment later a man on my left began to speak softly, and there, about twelve feet away, was the faint silhouette of a sentry. My first thought was that he must have been speaking to me, but apparently he was addressing the man with the watch. Slowly I began to back out from between the two guards, expecting at every moment that a torch would flash upon me. Nothing happened, the voice continued steadily, and as soon as I was well clear I turned and bolted down the narrow lane from which I had so recently emerged.

In my official report that incident was described as having taken place at a crossroad, but after the war I saw that I had actually walked up to the entrance of Taipo railway station. The sentry with the watch was posted near the top of a narrow flight of steps, the talkative one was posted at the gate. The Taipo station at that time was occupied by the Gendarmerie, so my luck may be imagined when it is remembered that I had already passed it twice on the railway, before making my frontal assault on the building. All of that folly was occasioned by the intense darkness and my complete ignorance of the locality.

My next adventure occurred when, having returned to the archway through the embankment, I decided to go through and try my luck on the other side. Exactly what happened next will never be known to me. My belief was that the arch opened out into a large storage space, that I could smell rubber and petrol, and that people or animals were there, breathing and moving in their sleep. That was my impression. Sounds of loud breathing made me stop dead, not knowing what to do. Behind me every avenue of escape seemed to be blocked, so believing that it was no more dangerous to proceed than to retreat I went on again, and shortly emerged among the buildings of a village. My next clear impression is of climbing up a steep concrete road thinking that at last I was on the highway, only to find that it was leading to a private estate which was closed to prowlers by large and handsome iron gates. Nothing could be gained by climbing in there, so I descended the road for a little way and then climbed to a ridge, where, feeling utterly exhausted, I sank down to await the dawn.

It had been a night crammed with adventure. First there was the abortive swim among the junks which almost ended in disaster; then there were the dangers on the bridge, the escape from the sentries, and the eerie passage through the railway arch. It was no wonder that I was feeling haggard and worn.

When I tried to go over my route in September 1945 I could not learn what had happened in my wanderings about Taipo. The arch through the embankment was just a plain bare archway, but directly opposite it across a very narrow lane there was the permanently open entrance to a large house. My conclusion is that I must have walked through the arch and continued straight through the house, there hearing the people breathing and moving restlessly. Be that as it may, the fact remains that I could not find the roadway up the hill or the large iron gates, nor could I discover where I had climbed to the ridge above. What is more, although there is no doubt that I went through the arch and into the village, during my later inspection I could find no possible route from the village to the position on the ridge where I found myself the next morning. That is a small section of my life on which my mind is a complete blank.

Mercifully the day was not long in coming, for fierce squalls roared through the bushes about me, torrential showers were falling, and in spite of the high summer temperature I was shivering with cold. Full daylight revealed the road on the far side of the estuary, so most of my troubles had been caused through returning from the bridge instead of crossing over. Three or four miles away a spur running down from Tai Mo Shan cut across the head of the estuary, and as there could be only a narrow stream at that point I decided that a crossing there should be easy.

A full typhoon was blowing, and squalls of wind and rain were driving across the landscape with all the ferocity that such storms can bring. A hurtling sky dragged tenuous grey veils low down across the mountains, and all normal work was suspended. The paddy fields in sight were deserted, and no one was abroad. I was on a ridge devoid of habitation or cultivation, and in the circumstances it seemed to be safe enough to go on my way, using the contour of the land to shield me from houses and villages. My intention was to go down the spur which ended near the road, and to reach that objective I had to climb high up the side of Tai Mo Shan, above the villages and paddy, and there cross several intervening valleys and ridges.

The wind was terrific, and clouds of small pine tufts, torn from a grove on the lower slopes, went flying across the ridges. Squalls drove me running in efforts to keep my balance. It was tiring work climbing and fighting the wind, and I was very glad to rest in the shelter of some large rocks which offered a haven of refuge in the driving onslaught of the storm. Not a soul was in sight anywhere, and after resting for a few minutes I set off again in a lull between showers, and climbed steadily until the highest of the paddy was a long way below.

As I climbed, the valleys became narrower and the traverse shorter, and soon I began to look for the right place to cross – the point at which farther climbing would entail more effort than the crossing.

There were fierce little torrents rushing down the mountain, and the gullies in which they ran were filled with small bushes. Those gullies were deceiving, for, having started to cross the mountain-side I found them to be much tougher obstacles than I expected. A space from fifty to one hundred and fifty yards wide was filled with dense growth, thickly tangled with thorny creepers. It was very slow work pushing through those barriers, and when I did reach the rushing streams I jumped in and let the solid water pour over me.

For six days and nights rain had been pattering almost constantly on my bare head, and it was with feelings of exultation that I held my breath and buried my head in the water. It was grand to feel the torrent roaring over me, and the stream felt much warmer than the wind and the rain.

There were three such valleys to be crossed, and it was late afternoon before the last of the clinging vines had been left behind and I began a long descent. The storm had subsided, and, as there were tracks to follow most of the way, progress was swift and easy. Of course my feet always pained more going down hill, for there was no skin left under or between my toes, and almost half the ball of each foot was devoid of skin also. However, the pain from those merged in the general ache and pain which signified my feet, and it did not unduly delay me.

Half-way down, the track began to skirt the top edge of pineapple plantations, and though it was too early in the season, the sight of freshly peeled skins made me keep a sharp lookout for fruit. Nearly a mile of those plants yielded nothing, and then, just before dusk, I saw a small green pineapple, not far in from the edge. Although it was a very immature specimen it tasted remarkably sweet, and to my disordered palate it was delicious.

Having quickly disposed of that all too meagre meal I continued to the rim of the final declivity, and saw a most satisfactory scene below. Beyond a flat of paddy a track led from a village to a narrow unguarded bridge across the river, and there was my road, hard by the far end of the bridge. The day's work had been well worth while, and I lay back to rest until evening shadows deepened. Before it was quite dark I went down and across one of the irregular winding tracks that led across the fields. The main path leading from the village to the bridge should have been easy to find, but the fields were very much wider than they had appeared to be from my resting-place on the hill, and when I finally reached the other side it was to emerge right in the village itself.

I tried several paths, each of which entered a labyrinth of buildings, and my position was not a happy one for many people were moving about, and several times I was forced to step aside to let someone pass. It was intensely dark beneath large trees which grew about the village, and after trying one path after another without success, I realised that my sense of direction was rapidly going astray. That was no place in which to be lost, so returning quickly to the open paddy I retraced my steps while there was still enough light to see the outline of the hill previously descended.

Greatly relieved to be back in comparative safety I forsook the track and skirted the foot of the hill, ploughing along through knee-deep mud and water. It was hard walking, and the paddy went on endlessly. I seemed to be in the midst of a boundless morass, and then, suddenly, I was up on a stone pathway and almost at the bridge.

No one was in sight, and a few swift steps took me across to the smooth level surface of the road. What a wonderful feeling it was, to be able to step out freely along the clear highway after the heartbreaking struggle on the mountain. My spirits rose tremendously as I set off at a steady pace along the road towards Fanling, and I am afraid that I was filled with more elation than care. So much so that, when trees along the roadside began to take on a pale ghostly light the reason did not dawn on me at once. When it did finally register I felt terribly conspicuous in the headlights of a car that was coming along behind me. Military vehicles were the only ones running, so I was very pleased to see it turn into a drive leading to a large house some distance off the road. The occupants had not noticed me, but it was with a more wary eye that I emerged from a hiding-place and resumed my journey.

Light showers were falling, but the wind had died away and soon stars were shining between the clouds. It was then possible to see much farther, and the sheen on the wet road brought trees and occasional buildings into dark relief. Old trees had originally formed an avenue along the road, but many of them were missing, and the gaps formed long stretches where there was no shadow. On glancing back at one of those open spaces I saw a stump standing in very clear silhouette, and thereafter I crossed to whichever side of the road offered the best background. When approaching the clear patches I had a good view of what was ahead, but where trees grew nothing at all could be seen, and it was not comforting to know that I would be in full view of anyone in the shadows. No doubt my fears were exaggerated through strain, but to travel at all on the only road was a very hazardous procedure, and there would be no second chance if I were once seen.

A shower passed; then the clouds broke and all the sky was studded with brilliant stars. There was nothing on the road, and I stepped along at a steady pace, highly pleased at the ease with which the miles went by. On the left of the road a clump of big trees made a black patch against the sky, and as I neared them a group of people came along. They were talking cheerfully and had obviously been making a social call, and I stepped among the trees while they passed. Almost at once the headlights of a car came streaming down the road. I stepped back behind a tree, and as the car went by I saw that it was filled with Japanese officers. When all was quiet again I went on until some buildings appeared a little distance to the right of the road. Several soldiers with lanterns were moving about, voices were raised, and someone was shouting orders. Very much on the alert I kept moving cautiously, and soon saw the railway lines crossing the road ahead of me. That was a point that might be guarded, and there was a small building that might be a sentry-box standing by the crossing.

The road ran along the top of an embankment raised eight feet above level fields on either side, and, slipping over the edge, I worked along the sloping bank until I reached the railway. That too was running on an embankment of the same height as the road, and the only way past was over the top. The sentry-box looked menacing, so moving away out of sight I went swiftly over the rails and down the other side. It took only a few minutes to regain the road, and my steady pace was resumed.

Intense darkness had settled down, rain was falling, and shortly there occurred an incident which savours of the miraculous. Did some movement catch my eye? Was there a slight sound? Nothing recorded on my memory except a sudden feeling that imminent danger lay ahead. I grabbed the base of a small shrub growing at the roadside and threw myself over the bank, holding on with my face on a level with the road surface. My feet had scarcely stopped sliding and crackling in the grass and shrubs, when the legs of a soldier went past only three feet from my face. He was the first of a patrol of six who filed silently by. They were wearing soft rubber-soled shoes that made no sound, and, as they were walking on my side of the road, had I continued for a few more paces we must have collided. The last man went past, and close on his heels was a large Alsatian dog.

There was intensity of drama, with my life hanging on the outcome. I neither moved nor breathed, and yet had a curious feeling of detachment as if my mind, removed to a safe distance, was able to concentrate its whole attention on the scene to be enacted. I felt no fear at all, but every sense was tuned to its ultimate degree of tension on what was about to happen.

The dog turned towards me, sniffing the air inquiringly. His nose was less than two feet from mine, yet he seemed to be at a loss what to do. There was only the darkness between us so surely he must have been able to see me. He was only too clearly visible to me.

He lifted his nose, laid his ears back, and there was a strange expression in his eyes as if he were trying to recall something from a long way off. His ears pricked forward again, and he seemed to be looking directly into my eyes. Then his head went down slowly, and he turned without a sound. With his tail drooping to the ground he loped off after the patrol, a picture of utter dejection. The men began to speak softly, and when their voices grew a little louder I thought they were coming back. But the sounds faded again, and all was silent.

Why did the dog neither growl nor bark? Did he know I was there, or did my presence fail to register on his senses? Some of my friends suggest that I was probably so dirty that the dog was mystified; others, of a more serious bent, suggest that a higher Power was guarding me. I leave it to you to ascribe your own reason, for my part I am content with the event. One thing is certain; and that is that prior to that experience no one could have made me believe that any dog, confronted with a similar situation, would have failed to make some demonstration.

It was my belief that the road should then be safe for some distance, so I set off at a good pace and soon came to a concrete road leading off at a right angle to the main road. On my very meagre map there was only one road going off to the right, and that was the road to Shataokok. However, that would be a very old road, whereas this one looked new and it was spanned by some ornamental archway. The Japanese had large camps in the Fanling area, and it was my guess that this was the entrance to one of them, and that it was from there that the patrol had issued.

Acting on that assumption I went on, and soon a road fork came in sight. There were white railings round the corner, and large trees on both sides of the road threw the whole area into deep gloom. Walking as silently as a cat I took the right-hand road. This went off at an angle of forty-five degrees, not at right angles as shown on the map, but after going some distance I felt sure that it was the right one, for thick old trees lined the sides.

Afterwards I learned that a guardhouse was located at the fork, but I walked right past without even knowing that it was there.

The night was far advanced and, though occasional buildings appeared, no lights were showing and no one was astir. Then the road ran along an embankment across miles of flooded paddy. It seemed to go on endlessly, and I was beginning to fear that dawn would find me out in that wide expanse, when the outline of hills came into view. Soon they were close about me, and thinking that Shataokok must be near I decided to climb a hill from which to view my surroundings in daylight. A hillside thickly grown with small trees offered a good prospect of cover, but there was no undergrowth so I kept on climbing to the top. There I found a clump of bushes large enough to crawl inside, and the sky was already growing lighter by the time my hideout had been made a little more comfortable. The rain had stopped, and it was a pleasure to be able to lie down at full length, for I had then been walking more or less continuously for two full nights and a day.

That was the seventh night of my journey, my clothes had been soaked the whole time, and sleep persistently eluded me. Never had I had more than half an hour of oblivion in any twenty-four hours since leaving camp. My tinned food, mostly used in the first few days to keep up my strength at that critical time, had all been consumed except for one tin of condensed milk. The remainder of my supplies consisted of soya bean powder, a tin of a heart of wheat cereal, a small bottle of peanut oil, and a small tin of black pepper. The pepper had been taken to drop along my tracks to discourage dogs from following me, but the continuous rain had made its use unnecessary. Instead of deterring dogs it was put to good use in flavouring my scanty meals.

Those were eaten twice a day, breakfast about sunrise, dinner just before dark, and each meal consisted of three dessert spoonsful of soya bean flour, two spoonsful of cereal, half a spoonful of peanut oil, a little water, and a flavouring of pepper. That mess was mixed diligently into a smooth paste, and it was surprising how appetising it seemed. The full meal occupied only about one inch of depth in a very small tin, so it was eaten slowly and with great deliberation.

I enjoyed those meals immensely, while any addition to my diet, such as the pineapple, was extremely welcome, yet I had never at any time felt hungry. Presumably the stress of nervous tension in which I constantly travelled had ruined both my appetite and my ability to sleep.

A disappointment was in store, for with the coming of full day no trace of Shataokok was to be seen. A range of hills stood between me and the sea, so it was obvious that I had stopped some miles short of my objective. No more than half a mile away the road disappeared round a bend, my view was hemmed in by mountains, and as nothing could be done until night came I settled down to rest. A much higher hill rose steeply from immediately behind me and I kept watch for people moving there, but the whole place seemed to be deserted and I saw no one, either in the fields or on the road.

Towards noon the sun was breaking through, and it was most comforting to be really warm again. It was a good chance to dry my clothes, so I stripped and hung them out of sight among the bushes. Then my papers and diaries were spread about, and though they had been soaked for a week, the ink with which some of the papers were written had suffered remarkably little damage. Everything from which water could evaporate was hung out to dry, and even my current diary was brought out to air. That was carried in a plastic shaving-soap container, one which had originally been retrieved from a Canadian's pack on the battlefield high up on Hong Kong's Mount Cameron. In it were my watch, three razor blades, a short pencil, and several small sheets of writing-paper. The watch had a broken spring, but it was a gift of some sentimental value and I did not want to lose it.

Sleep would not be coaxed, and the day passed in a wakeful quietude so profound that I seemed to be alone in a deserted world. No sound of man or beast disturbed the silence, only occasional butterflies darted in swift flight, with flashes of brilliant wings. My sole tormentors were the pestiferous ants, which made every day a misery with their vicious stinging bites.

A survey of my feet and legs showed them to be in a sorry state. Every toe was burst, and the balls of my feet were almost devoid of skin. That condition was brought about partly by dermatitis, "athlete's foot", or any other name which indicates that virulent fungoid growth that eats its way between the skin and the flesh, causing the outer layers to peel off. In addition there were several deep holes caused by sharp stakes, there were cuts and scratches of varying size and depth, and there was scarcely any skin left on my shins. Thorny trailers were responsible for that. I do not know what the plant was, but it grew like a blackberry, the trailers running for yards through the grass. I was everlastingly sliding my feet under those in the darkness, with the result that their savage thorns tore across my shins, taking skin and flesh with them. Just for good measure my right hand was very sore and stiff. That was the result of the injury received when sliding down my rope over the sea-wall at Shamsuipo, and during the past nights the wounds had been aggravated by continued stabs from sharp branches and stiff grasses.

My only ointment was a small box of dubbin which was one of a consignment that the Japanese had for some unknown reason sent into the camp. Each morning I covered the sores with a thick coating of that grease, and apparently it was clean enough, for none of the injuries ever turned septic.

I still had my shoes, although most of the time they had been slung round my neck. I had worn them for only brief periods in the rough country behind Kowloon, and again when I waded in the sea past the sentry on the railway line beyond Shatin. On wet roads they would squelch loudly at every step and it was quite impossible to wear them there, for by going barefoot I could walk in complete silence. In that way I had passed close to many large houses and villages without once rousing a dog, in spite of the fact that every

Chinese village is alive with curs of every breed and temper, mostly bad.

In the late afternoon I gathered my belongings and, after a meal, went down through the trees to a spot near to, though hidden from, the road. There some dry straw made a most comfortable bed, and a sound sleep claimed me for about half an hour. On waking I found that it was nearly dark, so, after waiting for another ten minutes I crossed to the road and went on my way again. The clouds had cleared away, and a bright new crescent moon shone in the western sky. The sight cheered me beyond measure, for a new moon shining in a clear sky is a most passionately optimistic symbol. Nothing transcends the promise diffused by the bright silver crescent, for each night it will grow larger and more luminously beautiful, more powerful to weave its magic spell.

The road turned in among steep hills, the moon sank out of sight, clouds obscured the stars again, and intense darkness engulfed me. Trudging steadily along it was difficult to concentrate on the road. In fact, my legs seemed to move automatically, and my mind wandered off at all manner of strange tangents, so completely detached from the immediate scene that I was walking as if in a dream.

Fireflies began to dance across the road, and soon they gave me their third and final help. Penetrating the mists that shrouded my mind there came the realisation that one of those bright little sparks was coming straight towards me. Glowing brighter as it came it headed straight for the middle of my forehead, and then, at the moment before impact, it skimmed up and away. Soon another followed the first, coming directly towards me up the road. This one seemed to glow brighter as it came, and at the last moment it too skimmed up and away.

Hazily I thought it strange that they should both follow exactly the same course, but they made no further impression until a third fly came bearing down towards me. I saw this one a long way off, and as it approached it grew in size and brilliance until it seemed that a blazing meteor was about to strike my forehead. At the last moment that one also skimmed up and over, but the repetition of the act, together with the amazing brilliance of this last visitor, shook me into consciousness. I felt it was a warning, not to be ignored, of some danger threatening from straight ahead. Concentrating all my faculties on the road I soon became aware of a luminous glow on bushes a little distance off on the right-hand side of the road. It was very faint, fading and growing brighter, and I was wondering what could be causing it when the bushes suddenly stood out in sharp relief. A car was swinging out of a concealed drive, and just as I flung myself full length into a ditch all my surroundings were flooded with brilliant light.

Had I been too late? The car approached rapidly, and, feeling extremely conspicuous on the snow, I kept my face buried in the mud as the vehicle went by. It had been a miss by a split second, and had the fireflies not brought me back to consciousness it is certain that I would have blundered on, full into those lights.

The road was descending, and soon occasional buildings showed. These became more frequent, and it was obvious that a settlement was near. I noted a worn path that left the road to disappear into fields, thinking that it might be useful later, and soon came to a picket fence. Beyond that there were solid two-storey buildings on either side of the road, the space between them intensely black. With all my senses alert I moved in between the buildings, but I had advanced only two or three yards into the dark when there came again that urgent feeling of danger. There was absolute and utter silence, and I stopped still in my tracks, straining eyes and ears for some hostile movement. Suddenly, with a crash, a rifle fell to the ground immediately in front of me, and the sentry was muttering as he picked it up. Once again some sixth sense had saved me, and, after backing away for several yards I turned and made for the track, previously noted, which led to the fields. That brought me to a village nestling at the foot of a steep rise, and I emerged on to a narrow pathway that ran along the fronts of the houses. Turning right I soon came to the end of the path, where there was a steep wooded bank on my left and paddy fields on my right. Across the fields lanterns were moving and torches flashing, and I knew that there lay the important market and fishing village of Shataokok. That was right on the boundary between China and the New Territories, and before the Japanese occupation one side of a long street had been under Chinese control, while the other was under British.

Since the roads were guarded I decided to skirt Shataokok, and, hoping to find a path that would lead inland I returned along the fronts of the houses. Extreme care was needed, for just inside several open doorways I saw the heads of people asleep. After one excursion up an alley which ended in a courtyard, I continued to the end of the village without finding any outlet. Somewhere among the buildings a dog began to bark in increasing agitation. Had he heard me? Was I the cause of his alarm? It might have been so, and since other dogs would soon be roused I must go quickly.

The dog was growing more and more excited, so I took to the paddy and waded silently away. Had he come after me my discovery must have been certain, and I was very glad when a safe distance lay between us and the barking died down. Making a wide detour I finally found another track which took me to a narrow, though well-formed road. As that led away from Shataokok and began to rise inland I knew that it must be a road, shown on my map, which followed closely the boundary of the New Territories.

From careful scrutiny of contour plans of this area I knew that the land rose steeply from the shores of Mirs Bay to the highest ridge, and then fell away in a gradual slope westwards. I decided to follow this road up to the ridge, and there cross the frontier into China before returning to the coast north of the village. All reports and rumours had indicated that Shataokok was heavily garrisoned, and I had no wish to approach it too closely.

Although wide enough for small cars or pony carts the road was very narrow, and as it climbed it wound along the side of a steep gorge, twisting and turning tortuously, at times going through deep cuttings. There was plenty of evidence that mule traffic had been heavy, but there was no sign of either troops or of human habitation. Approaching the summit I moved with care, for that seemed a likely place for a road-block, but I reached the saddle and there was nothing but silence all about; an eerie menacing silence as if something evil lurked in the gloom beyond the narrow circle of my vision. High banks of a steep cutting hemmed me in, and I had to go on for some distance before the side could be scaled.

From the roadside a level area of grass and bracken stretched to a hill on which small trees were growing, and beyond that lay China and my way to freedom. It looked as if my worst troubles would soon be over, but Hong Kong was not going to let me go so easily. The grass was almost waist high, and I had gone only a few paces when thorns tore deep scratches up my legs. But were those hard stiff trailers the usual flexible stems of thorn bush? They were not. Those were the vicious coils of barbed-wire entanglements, and the whole field of wire was buried in grass. The coils had been laid densely and with purposeful efficiency and, as the wire was galvanised and still in perfect order, I presumed that it had been laid by British troops.

No matter who was responsible for it being there it formed a difficult hazard, and my progress was slow and painful. So much so that I was afraid that daylight would find me a helpless target in the open, and being unable to gain any idea of the extent of this trap I decided to return to the road before it was too late. It was decidedly unpleasant to feel that whatever happened it was impossible to take any avoiding action. I could not even lie down, so my nerves were very much on edge by the time the road was regained. Half a mile on the Shataokok side of the ridge a small torrent rushed headlong down the mountain-side, and, making my way to that, I went over the edge of the road and slipped and slithered down to a secluded resting-place. The side of the gorge was very steep, and I had to wedge myself in among some large boulders, which looked as if they themselves might take to flight at any moment.

There was no comfort to be had, and once more I was glad when daylight diffused the eastern sky. Cold greys gave place to warmly glowing hues, until, in a rising crescendo of colour, there unfolded before me a most glorious masterpiece. The whole canopy of sky, flecked and streaked with cirrus clouds and level bars of haze, glowed and pulsed with a flood of light that mirrored and magnified on the glassy surface of Mirs Bay. Nature, in a mood of passionate inspiration, poured colours on the sky until it held a miracle of composition, overpowering in its prodigality. There indeed was inspiration for a Turner.

I watched spell-bound until the rising sun itself dispelled that marvel of its own creation, and then began to contemplate anew the problems immediately confronting me. The torrent tumbled steeply to a considerable stream which flowed along the bed of the gorge, and though the coast was invisible from my position, I knew that stream entered the sea at Shataokok. On the other side of the gorge a pathway followed the stream, and, while I watched, some Chinese came into view, carrying to the village their baskets and bundles of produce. Down near the stream, on my side, there was a patch of level ground with trees and bushes that would afford good cover, so I climbed down there, deciding to use the track to travel on after dark.

Not far from the confluence of the streams there was a perfect lair with nice soft grass on which to lie, but sleep had never been farther from me, and, after resting for some time, I cleared the stones from a pool and had a lazy, if not luxurious, bath. My clothes were almost dry, and in that warm sheltered place a sense of well-being came to me, though heaven knows there was little enough to give me any sense of comfort.

There were fat prawns in the stream, but in spite of every trick to snare them they always escaped from the most impossible situations, and at last I tired of the fruitless sport and returned to my soft couch. It was a delightful place, with many wild flowers in bloom, while birds and beautiful butterflies were my constant companions. There were prawns and small trout in the small stream, while in the larger one there were many fresh-water snails. Unfortunately those were beyond my sphere of movement, for that area was in full view of people walking on the track.

During one of my tours I saw some ripe pandanus fruit, most of them completely spoiled by birds or animals, but one was of such a rich ripeness that I determined to gather it. The fruit was high up, in sight from only a short section of the track, so as soon as a group of people had passed I sprang up the palm, secured the prize and successfully made off with it. From a distance it looked exactly like a four-pound pineapple, but closer inspection showed the core of the fruit to be surrounded by an outer casing of roughly hexagonal knobs, some three-quarters of an inch in diameter and about one and a half inches long. Those knobs felt as hard as wood and made a stout protective covering, but when two or three had been broken off, the others followed more easily. All that was left was a round kernel about the size of a cricket ball, of the texture of a potato. There was no flavour in it at all, but as it appeared to be quite innocuous I ate and hoped for the best.

An entry in my diary, written that afternoon, reads: "Am feeling rather weak; a good sleep would make a lot of difference. With any luck this should be the last of my most anxious nights, though do not know how far the 'Nips' hold."

During the early afternoon huge billowing masses of cloud were piling up around the mountains, and thunder was rolling and muttering incessantly. The storm moved northward inside the coastal range and then it rolled out over Mirs Bay before turning inland again up the valley in which lay my pleasant little retreat.

It was a most awe-inspiring spectacle, tier upon tier of huge cumulus cloud rising to a tremendous height, intense indigo running into sulphurous high-lights, lightning streaming in all directions and stabbing viciously at the earth. After moving very slowly all afternoon the storm then came on at a great pace, and the cloud was swiftly overhead. Lightning struck at both sides of the narrow gorge, which was filled at once with a terrific throbbing roar, as burst after burst of thunder echoed and re-echoed between the steep mountain-sides. In a moment a deluge of rain came down, and for more than an hour that disturbance continued at its full power, after which the thunder lessened and gradually muttered away inland. Alas! for my brief comfort. Everything was completely saturated again, and my only wish was that darkness would come quickly.

After the storm had gone there was little traffic on the track, and by the time daylight had completely faded it had ceased altogether. The stream had been greatly swollen by the afternoon storm, so while there was still a little light left I made my way to the other side, climbed to the track and set off on another night's adventures. That was the ninth since my departure from camp.

Soon the gorge was dark as in the uttermost pit. The track was very rough, it was washed out at innumerable places, and as there were vertical drops over the side I had again to feel for every foothold. It was very slow going until the valley opened out a little, when the track became much better. The lights of Shataokok came into view, and I pursued my way, very much on the alert.

Houses appeared on both sides of the path, and after warily passing several of them I came to a full stop when a sentry flashed his torch, perhaps fifty yards ahead of me. The way was too narrow and the fences too unknown to risk an encounter there, so retreating hurriedly I searched for a way down to the paddy. There were thick hedges and barbed wire along the sides of the fields, and it was some time before I could find a path leading from the road. Where it passed through the hedge it had been very effectively wired up, but the track was obviously one that had been extensively used, so reckoning that that would be as good as any other I worked my way under the wire. It was soon evident that Shataokok was a heavily guarded place for, along the road which I had left, sentries were stationed at intervals of little more than fifty yards. They continually flashed their torches across the flooded paddy, and I made a wide detour, for the lights shining on the glassy water made objects stand out in black silhouette.

Frequent delays were caused by rolls of concertina wire laid across the paddy, wire which had to be crawled through or under. I ploughed along through mud and water for an hour, and then a solid mass of buildings stretched right across my line of advance. Hoping to find a road that would take me through I advanced cautiously, but when one did eventually open up, instead of taking me to safety it brought me to a scene of uproar. Torches were flashing, lanterns hurrying about, orders were being shouted, and much commotion and unusual activity was afoot. That was very disappointing, for it meant that all the guards would be roused to the alert, and it would be foolish to a degree to try to pass through those streets.

The only way open was through the paddy on my right, so, although that meant going south instead of north, I had no option. For some distance I kept walking parallel to the buildings, and then veered away to gauge the width of the paddy and try to find out what lay beyond. Much sooner than I expected the ground suddenly fell in a vertical drop to a river below. There was no safe way down that cliff, and I sheered off to follow the flooded fields. These were narrowing rapidly, and rapidly too was my strength failing. Soon I could go no farther, and I sank down in the mud to rest and to try to decide on a course of action.

There seemed to be no way out of this impasse, and I was feeling very exhausted and low spirited. Suddenly it dawned upon me that there were no longer any buildings near. On the side where they had been there was only a bank about eight feet high. That proved to be a forbidding obstacle in the dark, for it was covered with a dense growth of thorn bush. Vicious spikes and barbs tore at my flesh as I pushed through to the top of the bank, but there, much to my surprise, I found myself standing on firm sand. There at last was the coast, and after crossing a hundred yards of dunes I saw surf breaking on shore. Again the sea was to befriend me.

Chapter 7

Shataokok to end of Solo Journey

My spirits rose like a rocket in flight and I could scarcely refrain from cheering, for until that moment I had no idea that the sea was so close. A little sober reflection would have made me realise that it must be very near, but by that time I was beyond the stage of reflection of any kind.

A sentry flashed his torch as he patrolled between a road and the sea, and I stepped out towards him, travelling on firm sand. There was no chance of going past on the beach, so, having approached as close as safety would permit, I sat down and went through the painful and laborious performance of putting on my shoes. They were very necessary when wading in the sea, for razor sharp shells and coral growths made cuts and scratches that readily turned septic, and I had no wish to add poisoned feet to my other ailments.

Hoisting my pack to my shoulder I waded out, up to my neck in the sea. All was quiet ashore, but the sentry kept swinging his torch about and it was by no means certain that I could wade far enough out to be beyond his range of vision. The pack on my left shoulder, carried there in case someone opened fire on me from the shore, completely hid my head; and had the sentry seen it I fancy he would have been greatly surprised to see a square bag gliding silently and smoothly along over a glassy tide.

To seaward several boats were fishing, all using brilliant lamps which carried a long way over the mirror of the water.

Other boats between me and the lights showed in black relief, and that meant that anyone looking from the beach could also see me if he were observant. There was little I could do except move slowly and make as little wake as possible. Everything went well until I was almost a hundred yards past the critical point where the guard was stationed, and then one of the sampans with its vivid light came working towards me. There was a pretty situation, for every moment made my pack more conspicuous from the shore, and my only chance of escape from this new danger was to make for shallow water. Wading as far as possible, stooping as the water shallowed, crawling on hands and knees and finally lying full length in the small surf breaking on shore, I kept ahead of the sampan which followed with uncanny accuracy.

Had they seen me? The light came closer until my sur-roundings seemed as bright as if lit by the sun. The features of the rower were clearly visible as he swayed forward on his oars, as were those of the man who stood motionless in the bows, his eyes intent on the water, seeking fish.

For a tense moment I thought the sampan was going to run ashore right on top of me, but when a few yards off it turned sharply and headed out to sea again. The experience put me in a very bad temper, for the situation seemed to be fraught with an amplitude of difficulties and dangers without those perfectly innocent intruders coming along to scare me so unnecessarily.

When the sampan had gone I crawled out in its wake, and then waded parallel to the shore until it was safe to leave the sea and again use the beach as a highway. Heavy showers commenced, and a rising wind sent shivers through my bones. Scarcely had I begun to walk on shore when the sole came completely off my right shoe due to sand having cut the stitching. The heel still held firm, so that each time my foot was lifted the sole flapped back. It was impossible to continue walking in that way, so the shoes were removed and carried in their usual position round my neck.

Increasing squalls of wind and rain drove me before them along the level sand, and dawn found me where a long low point jutted out to sea. There I found a sheltered place in the lee of a steep bank, where small trees and bushes afforded good protection from the wind and from prying eyes. No one was about, so to make my bed a little more comfortable I gathered armfuls of rice-straw.

This proved to be a terrible day, for another typhoon was soon in full blast and a torrent of rain poured down. Fortunately the bank gave me protection from the wind, but it roared through the trees overhead, tore away leaves and branches, and whirled them off along the beach. In lighter intervals a little of Mirs Bay was visible, and beyond the boiling surf there was a mass of flying foam and spindrift, rising to mingle with the rain and mist in a smothering cloud of driving spray. Rain poured in a deluge and my bed was three inches deep in water, but nothing was to be gained by moving, for the part of me that was submerged was actually warmer than the rest.

The day dragged on interminably, for sleep was beyond me, and I felt low-spirited, miserable, and utterly worn out. My only job was a little shoemaking, the sole being fastened on again by the very primitive method of boring a number of holes through the sole and insole, and tying the pair together with strong hempen cord. That operation had to be repeated on later days, for sand and grit quickly cut through the cord between the leather.

Late afternoon saw the squalls abating and coming at less frequent intervals, and during a lull several men went past on a track running parallel to the shore. That would be my route, and as the storm had blown itself out by nightfall I set off in a little brighter mood. But my progress was slow and difficult, for in many places the track was washed away or broken down, and, unable to see anything, I continually stumbled and fell. Where a high point fell steeply to the sea the track turned inland. There was no path continuing towards the headland, so I assumed that the original track would climb over a ridge and descend to the coast on the other side. That reasoning proved to be fallacious, but, as usual, the knowledge was gained by hard experience.

It was gruelling work clambering up the steep, damaged path, and I was very glad to reach the summit and begin, at first, a gradual descent. When the track forked I rested for a time before taking the right-hand path, which descended steeply, as I fondly imagined, to the shore. But when I reached level ground there was no friendly beach in sight, there was only a wide expanse of paddy stretching out into the blackness.

Behind me was a very hard climb, while in front the way was at least level and, thinking that I would eventually reach the shore, I started off across the fields. Time and distance no longer had any meaning and I had not the vaguest idea how far I had gone since dark or how near to dawn it might be. A large village on rising ground came in sight, and as I walked warily through a narrow alley a watchman with a lantern passed along the central roadway. Avoiding him I walked right through the village, hearing the occupants of the houses moving in their sleep, and several times seeing the heads of people asleep just inside open doorways. My bare feet made no sound, so I explored one alley after another in an effort to find some way out of that frightening place. At any moment some cur might hear me and give tongue in such a way that the whole village would be roused, and my anxiety was growing each time I failed to find an exit.

This was like the majority of Chinese villages. One marvelled at the difficulties with which they surrounded their everyday movements, until one remembered that in that land of pirates and bandits the villages were havens of refuge as well as places in which to live.

As far as I could see there was no way out of that village save the one by which I had entered, so, retracing my steps, I skirted the buildings and then climbed a steep hill which was closely grown with small trees and thorn bush. It was too difficult to go far, and on reaching the foot of three very big trees I settled down to await the day. To say settled down is to give a grossly erroneous impression, for the steeply sloping ground was saturated, there was no place in which even a modicum of comfort could be found, and I endured a most distressing hour or more before the grey daylight came.

The strain of the journey was making itself increasingly felt. The constant wet, the desperate struggling over rugged terrain in the intense darkness and the almost total lack of food were rapidly wearing me down. It was obvious that my solo effort could not last much longer.

Daylight brought a bitter disappointment, for not only was there no coast in sight, there was a range of hills, almost mountains, lying in the direction in which I had expected to find the sea. For the first time I had no idea how to proceed, and the only way out was to retrace my steps to the coast. The village below was on a point of land that jutted out into a sea of paddy fields, and in order to extricate myself from that position I decided to skirt the fields in daylight, and return to the ridge which had been so laboriously and needlessly surmounted during the night.

That decision was no sooner made than the plan was put into execution, for every moment of delay increased the chances of discovery. It had been hard work climbing to my hiding-place in the dark, and even then, when it was light, it was far from easy to descend. A painful struggle through the usual thorns brought me to the top of a terrace of gardens descending to the paddy, and that looked like an easy way down until I found that each terrace was guarded by a hedge of thorn. Also, every path was blocked by barricades of the same vicious branches. These were different from the usual trailing thorns, being more like hawthorn trees with hard needle-sharp spikes up to two inches in length that seemed to have been deliberately designed by the Devil to cause me more hindrance and pain. At last the final barrier was passed and I reached a track which followed the edge of the fields. A quick glance showed that no one was yet at work, so I set off at a fast pace to leave the village behind.

The going was very good indeed and by the time workers were beginning to dot the fields I had gained the shelter of a valley which fell directly from the ridge which was my goal. This valley had very steep sides, it was thickly grown with trees, a sizeable stream flowed along its bed and there were many comfortable resting-places completely concealed from every direction. At the confluence of two streams there was a level point and, as the morning was calm and fine, I lay down there to rest, thinking that these first pleasant conditions would quickly send me to a much-needed sleep.

Alas for those hopes. Sleep steadfastly avoided me, and I knew the full significance of those lines of Shakespeare's:

"Oh! Sleep, oh! gentle Sleep, how have I frightened thee,
That thou no more wilt weigh my eyelids down,
And steep my senses in forgetfulness."

Sleep was out of the question, I had never felt wider awake, so after resting for half an hour I was up and doing. Sunshine was streaming into the valley, and its generous warmth made me feel immeasurably better. An entry in my diary on that day read: "Beautiful sunny day, hope there are more of them. Another wet one would have finished me."

I soon collected a small pile of fresh-water snails, of which there were many in the stream. Also during the previous night I had collected some rice, so deciding that a little smoke would not arouse unwelcome interest in such a place, I proceeded to light a fire and try my hand at cooking. When my pack was opened, the first thing to emerge was a large land-snail, a creature about two inches in diameter that must have crawled inside during my early morning rest near the village. It seemed to be a perfectly healthy snail, and having long since ceased to be fastidious I added that to the pile of water-snails waiting to be cooked.

My matches had been carried in a watertight container, but instead of striking, the heads disintegrated into wet mush. That caused a temporary setback, but after they had dried in the hot sun for half an hour they flared as if they had just come from their original drying-rack. A fire was soon crackling merrily, and since the dry bracken and twigs made very little smoke I had no worry on that score.

The big snail had a horrible flavour but the water-snails were very palatable, their worst feature being that they were so small that to eat them only made me hungrier. The rice was a failure for the husks did not burst in cooking and there was no way of extracting the grain. By chewing it the pulp was squeezed out, but those husks had serrated edges of sharp teeth, and my tongue and mouth were soon severely lacerated.

When that experiment was over a feeling of exhaustion gripped me and I stretched out again, this time settling to a better rest. But rest was all that could be had, for sleep still steadfastly eluded me. Everything I had was scattered about to dry, and it was simply marvellous to feel warm, dry and comfortable after ten days of constant saturation, of chilling gales, and an extreme of physical depression.

After several hours in that pleasant place I gathered my belongings, then only half the weight, and started to climb. The only way out of that place was to go right over the top of the ridge, and I had to rest frequently on the steep ascent. The sun was half-way down the western sky by the time I reached the top and there I found myself near the end of a spur which fell directly to the shore. There was not a tree for miles on those ridges: they were covered with short grass which offered no cover at all. However, my khaki clothes and brown skin blended with the grass to form good camouflage, so, using the contour of the ground to conceal me as much as possible, I proceeded right to the very edge of the spur. There I lay down, flat on my face.

Never had any scene appeared lovelier than that which lay below. A light easterly breeze was blowing with just sufficient strength to put tiny white caps on a gloriously blue sea, and round the splendid sweep of Mirs Bay a white ribbon of surf separated the blue from a series of golden beaches.

Close inshore, looking very near though not at all alarming, a Japanese patrol launch idled along, and a wave of anger passed over me to think that my enemies on board could enjoy such beautiful conditions. The sight was a reminder that any carelessness on my part could easily end in disaster, and it was a warning against standing up or making myself conspicuous by movement. On such a day it was no hardship to remain quietly resting, and my whole being drank in that most enchanting and extensive vista.

For two and a half years my eyes had been denied any outlook save through barbed-wire fences, and the view at all times had been strictly circumscribed. Here at last was a scene such as my imagination had often pictured, for Mirs Bay is very similar in size and features to the Bay of Islands on the north-east coast of New Zealand. In that other far-off bay I had spent many delightful cruising holidays, and the present peaceful scene recalled them vividly to mind.

From the foot of my hill a wide beach curved away to a headland on the near-side of the village of Shatau. Behind that headland there was a narrow neck of flat land and beyond that again there was a wide estuary about which were embankments and other complications of harbour or river works, too dim to be observed in any detail. Although the estuary could not have been more than three miles away it appeared to be at least twelve miles off, so dimly was it visible, and although I was not aware of it at the time, the reason for that dimness was that my eyesight was rapidly failing. That condition was brought about by diet deficiency, and at a later date I was reduced at times to almost total blindness. There was no doubt about the route to follow after dark. The beach offered a perfect highway, so, when the seaward slope was buried in deep evening shadow, I descended to a Chinese grave not far behind the sand. It was very painful, slipping and sliding down the steep incline, for the rest and comfort of the day had made my injured feet more sensitive. A level concrete platform at the grave gave very welcome relief, and I lay down there to await full darkness, thanking the legitimate occupant for considerately placing his grave in such a convenient place, but fervently wishing that he had exorcised the ants before he had finally settled down.

A small stream made a convenient pathway to the beach, and I was soon stepping out under a starry sky, feeling that every yard gained took me from my greatest danger of recapture. That was very pleasant going indeed, and I was sorry when the beach gave way to rocks at the base of a cliff which obviously skirted the headland I had seen during daylight. Returning a little way I began to search for a track that might lead across the flat, and soon found a clearly defined path.

After my experience of the previous night I had decided to stick to the coast in future and avoid all paddy fields as I would the plague, but on reaching the northern shore of the flat my resolution was somewhat shaken. A main track turned slightly left and obviously followed the contour of the shore round the estuary, while a very small path turned right and just as obviously led down to the sea. What to do? The night was overcast and very dark again, but I stuck to my decision and turned right. In a short time I came to a patch of soft mud on which were piles of large squared stones. There was timber about too as if some work were in progress, but it was too dark for me to discern any plan in all that mess. Ploughing along, sinking to my knees in the soft clinging mud, I came to an erection of scaffolding which rose from the face of the sea-wall. Down below were several large sampans and lighters and it seemed that a door opened into a building below my feet. Before me was a mound of mud, shaped over in a curve, and this made me think that it was the thatch and mud roof of a low dwelling whose entrance for some unknown reason was halfway down to the sea.

I was extremely nervous, not being able to understand the structure, and it was some time before I decided to climb on to the "roof" and explore further. This audacity brought its just reward, for after crawling a few yards I realised that my "roof" was the top of an embankment about ten feet wide. The whole confusing situation was immediately explained. Evidently the sea-wall had been breached in the corner during one of the recent typhoons, a river of mud and slush had poured down from the fields, and gangs were at work repairing the damage.

The top of the wall had been kept cleared of bushes, and soft grasses growing there made a perfect roadway which curved away round the estuary. At the end of a mile the wall was running straight inland, and the water was little more than one hundred yards wide. I decided to try to cross and was overjoyed to find that the water reached no higher than my waist, the bottom being composed of firm sand. A similar wall flanked the northern side of the estuary and, mounting that, I was soon on my way to the sea again. That wall also was broken down in places, but I passed the breaches by wading in the sea, and made rapid progress until the compact mass of Shatau village lay directly before me.

More caution was needed, for there were sounds of movement among sampans nearby, and occasional lights were flashing. Then my wall took a turn sharp left and followed another arm of sea which ran in behind the village. The buildings were no more than one hundred yards away on the other side of the water and there were dozens of sampans at anchor, so I stepped along quickly, keeping a sharp lookout. Suddenly there were no more buildings opposite and clear sky was visible right down to the horizon. I kept on going for a few minutes, with no apparent change on the opposite shore, and then decided to cross over. Again my luck held, for the water was no more than three and a half feet deep, and I was soon out on a level flat of sand.

Lights were flashing among the buildings of Shatau, which village was evidently located at the end of a long sand spit, but, too good to be true, there were no houses at all in my immediate vicinity. That looked suspiciously easy and I expected to run into barbed wire or some other obstruction at every step, but to my great surprise and pleasure I soon saw surf breaking. Another splendid beach then provided a highway on which to continue my merry way, until it finally ended at a high rocky point. There I lay down to await the coming day. A cold wind was sweeping along the shore, and there was no shelter to be had from the wayward gusts and "willywaws" that swirled about and around the rocks, driving sleep away and making me shiver violently. I was feeling dreadfully exhausted.

In the first grey light I caught a large crab, and then climbed up a watercourse in search of cover for the day. There were snails in the stream, so gathering a number of those I boiled them together with the crab, and then tried to cook some more rice. This attempt was no more successful than the first, and the best I could do was to drink the water in which the rice was boiled. The snails were tiny, and altogether they made no more than a comfortable mouthful.

Falling steeply as it did, the stream was rather exposed to view from seaward, and when a number of sampans came past close in I felt rather guilty at having built a fire there. However they all went by on their lawful occasions, until one appeared coming directly towards me from Shatau. On it came, approaching rapidly with two men rowing. Had they seen the smoke, and were they coming to investigate? I am afraid it was a case of nerve complex with me, but if they were really looking for me there was no chance of escape. To attempt to run would cause me to fall in my tracks.

On came the sampan, never deviating from its course, and my heart was beating faster as it neared the shore. Straight on to the beach it came, and a man jumped out to hurry towards me. It looked as if the game were up; but what was that he was carrying? Yes, sure enough he had a wooden pail, and stopping at a clear pool thirty yards below me he filled his container, returned to the sampan, and off they went again. Well! it was all very innocent in its design and execution, but my nerves were in no condition to stand shocks of that nature.

Farther west the shore became very steep and rugged, with high cliffs falling to the sea, so some way had to be found on which to continue my journey that night. A number of people had passed on a track which wound along the hillside five hundred feet above, and I decided to explore that route. It was a much harder climb than I had expected, and it was a miracle that my career did not come to a full stop then and there. In jumping from one large boulder to another my judgment was at fault, my foot skidded off the smooth surface and I sailed out into space to land with a loud smack on my left thigh. So loud was the crack that I felt certain that the bone had snapped, but I gathered myself up to find that no damage had been done at all. That steadied me down somewhat, and the track was reached without further mishap.

Following it for a little way I soon saw that it could not be used at night, for washouts and landslides had carried it away in many places, and even the best of it was obstructed by boulders and holes which were bad enough to negotiate in daylight. Feeling disappointed and dejected I returned to my camp near the beach, and tried to rest.

A long reef ran out from the shore nearby, and at low tide that might possibly yield some fish or shellfish. Unfortunately, my intention to carry out a search was frustrated by a Chinese fisherman who came to the reef with his circular net. He remained motionless on a rock directly below me for at least an hour and then he moved about two hundred yards to a more prominent position. There he remained upwards of two hours. The tide was right out and, as it was possible to slip down among the rocks out of his sight, I took a chance as it was imperative to find some food.

The fisherman stood like a bronze statue watching the water, and it looked as if he might remain there all day. Several times during my search a quick glance assured me that he still remained impassive. Not a thing was to be found among the rocks, which were cleaned bare of everything large enough to be edible. A big population lives around Mirs Bay, harvests are often poor, and it was clear that the shore had been thoroughly searched. Down in a crevice there were three oysters that had been overlooked, and I set to work to open those with a small pocket-knife.

It was while I was struggling with the last one that a slight movement made me look up, and there was my fisherman, staring down at me. He stood motionless, intent, staring at me just as he had stared at the sea, searching for fish. He was not armed but he looked as tough as teak and I pursued the only course possible in the circumstances – nodded my head, smiled, and wished him good day – knowing full well that he would not understand a word. Luckily for me he acknowledged the salutation, smiled back, and greeted me in turn. I climbed up beside him and began by speech and pantomime to ask if he had any fish. He in turn indicated that he had none, but he kept on smiling and saying unintelligible things. That was all very well, but as he showed no inclination to go I began to grow anxious, and moved off on my own account.

The fisherman then continued his way also, walking quickly in the direction of Shatau, and since I was discovered I had to go too. He might be going to report my presence and it would not do to remain longer in the vicinity.

No sampans were near, so packing hurriedly I started off along the shore, for by taking that route it would be possible to keep out of sight from the occasional wayfarers still passing on the path above. After climbing round the rocks of one point, I crossed a small bay and then began to traverse a stretch of steep rugged cliffs. Progress became slow and painful in the extreme, for the rock strata was composed of sharp flints standing vertically, intensely painful to walk or sit upon. Then sheer crevasses with smooth granite walls barred my way, the only route past those being over the top, eighty to one hundred feet up the cliff. Two such crevasses were passed successfully, though while standing on a precarious foothold high above the second one, I almost lost consciousness. Unable to move I could only lean against the cliff, in imminent danger of being precipitated into the sea. My strength soon returned, and having completed the crossing I descended to a spot where there were some smoother rocks on which to rest. There my present situation and future possibilities were surveyed.

The cliff along which I was struggling continued round a headland one and half miles long, and my rate of progress was so slow that it seemed that I might never reach the other side. Even if the effort succeeded I would have made a real advance of little more than half a mile, and the fact had to be faced that my strength was all used up. I was continually light headed, with prolonged periods of semi-consciousness, and it was practically certain that very soon I would fall into the sea or to the rocks below. In that extremity there was little choice left, so I decided to climb up and proceed along the track, keeping a sharp lookout for anyone in uniform.

It was a stiff climb even for a fit person and I was forced to rest many times on the way. Once, while lying in a bed of soft bracken, bathed in warm sunshine, my thoughts ran on the theme that it would be infinitely more sensible to remain there in comfort and let my bones whiten on the hillside. *Why* go to all that desperate effort when it would be so much easier to die than to go on living? I believe the only thing that roused me to further effort was a fierce determination to deny the Japanese the satisfaction of knowing that they had encompassed my death.

The first persons encountered were several women, walking with an easy speed that only the Chinese can attain, with poles over their shoulders and heavy loads of merchandise. They came singly, some distance apart, and though they saw me coming they did not hesitate, they just kept on going with eyes averted as they brushed past on the narrow track.

From the summit of the ridge a beautiful view of sea and beaches was disclosed, while near at hand, nestling on flat ground close behind the sand, was a sizeable village.

Something strange was happening to my eyes, and three black objects began to dance in my vision. After some difficulty in bringing them into focus, I saw that they were men coming towards me. As they came closer I felt certain that they were Chinese, and it was obvious that they were very interested in *me*.

Chapter 8

The East River Striking Force, Kwangtung Peoples' Anti-Japanese Guerrilla Unit

The critical moment of my escape had arrived. Were they friends? The next few minutes would decide my fate. I had no regrets, for I knew that everything possible had been done to the utmost of my powers. It was hopeless to continue alone any longer, and should those men prove to be enemies, well – death would come a little sooner, that was all.

I kept on walking straight towards them and they, very much on their guard, separated as I approached. Certainly my appearance can hardly have been reassuring, for my shirt and shorts were in filthy tatters, while a ten-days' growth of beard covered my gaunt and haggard face.

We stopped and greeted one another, and to come at once to the main point I stretched my hand towards the village and said, "Any Japanese down there?"

One of the men gave the answer: "No; no Japanese long time."

What a relief. Then we began a long and difficult conversation from which neither side gained much satisfaction, for though my original question had been understood and answered, not one more word of English could my informant understand.

However, we carried on an animated pantomime by which they were informed that I had come from Kowloon, which they understood, and they conveyed to me that I should proceed to the village. Its name was Taimuisha. By dint of much more chatter and gesticulation I made it clear that I wanted one of them to go with me, whereupon they became very voluble and dramatic, imitating explosions and the throwing of missiles. Finally one of them opened his jacket to disclose half a dozen grenades slung round his chest. Apparently those men were guerrillas bent on some mission, so bidding them good-bye I continued on my way alone.

Although my recent companions had appeared to be friendly enough I could by no means be certain that my future reception would be the same, and it was with feelings of some excitement that I walked steadily along the main pathway, right into the village. A number of women and children bolted indoors at sight of me, but in a central square where a large old tree threw generous shade, a number of men began to gather round. We smiled at one another and they spoke a lot of Chinese which conveyed nothing at all to me, and, feeling that I could stand no longer, I subsided on a wooden bench beneath the tree.

News of my arrival spread rapidly and in a short time the entire population had gathered round. Someone said in English: "Where you go?"

I replied: "Waichow."

Someone else heard the "chow", meaning food in Chinese, and he called out, "Wantchee chow?" I nodded vigorously, for there was nothing I needed more than some "chow" to sustain me.

Immediately they escorted me across the street to a small teashop, and while all those who could not enter gathered round outside, I was given a pot of Chinese tea and four sweet scones. It was the most delicious food one could possibly imagine. Thinking that the shopkeeper might object to my continued presence, for no one could possibly approach to buy anything, I decided to return to my seat beneath the tree. Then it became evident that, though these people were disposed to be friendly, I was, nevertheless, their prisoner. They tried to bar my exit from the shop, but when it was conveyed to them that my only wish was to return to the seat, they readily agreed.

Fresh batches of people were arriving every minute to inspect this bedraggled intruder, and then someone of importance was seen approaching, for everyone made way for him. This man had a limited English vocabulary, and after asking a number of questions as to who I was, where I was from, where I was going to, he said that he must take me along to the next village. Excitement was buoying me up, and after perhaps half an hour's rest we set off across a level path to a village on the far side of the beach. There my man handed me over to what he described as "the Chinese policeman".

This was a colourful character, good looking, well built, about twenty-two years of age, and he wore a military uniform with a broad-brimmed hat with the brim on the left side fastened up to the crown. He carried a whistle, a length of cord, a knife in his belt and a heavy pistol on his hip, and altogether he appeared to be a very efficient upholder of the law. He soon let me see that he was not prepared to accept my story as related to him by my guide and he started off on a long cross-examination on his own account, rather overacting his part, giving the impression that he would much prefer to be ventilating my body with his gun than listening to my replies.

At last he was satisfied that he could drag no more information from me, and in a few minutes another man came along to say that I must go with him to the next village of Siumuisha.

My new guide set off at a pace that was quite beyond my powers, and when we had to surmount a low ridge he became very agitated at the slowness of our progress. He was extremely nervous about something, and most anxious to push on. Something he was trying to convey to me regarding my behaviour should we meet anyone completely eluded me, and I have never been able to fathom what he meant. The conversation would go something like this.

Guide: "If someone ask, You know me! you with me."

Me: "Yes; if we are stopped I say I am going with you, that I know you."

Guide: "No, no. You know me; you know me."

Me: "Yes I understand, I say that I know you."

Guide: "No, no. You know me."

So it went on until I was fed up with arriving at no conclusion, but every little while he would return to the same theme and we would repeat the performance with the same negative result. Perhaps he wanted me to say that I did not know him, but my grip on life itself was far too feeble to enable me to enter into the realms of abstract speculation, and I lapsed into silence, hoping that the need for explanations would not arise.

Near the top of the hill a small stream crossed our path, and requesting time for a drink I lay down to suck up a few mouthfuls of water, more from sheer exhaustion than from any great need of a drink. I remained on the ground for a few minutes, but my guide was growing increasingly agitated and he urged me to go on as the daylight was rapidly fading. So on we went again and soon descended to a richly fertile flat, on the other side of which was the village of Siumuisha.

There, with unfeigned relief, my guide handed me over to a Mr. Cheung, an officer of the Guerrilla Army who spoke fairly good English, and who soon set himself out to attend to my comfort. A local command of guerrillas was stationed at Siumuisha, and a fine looking bunch of men they were. Lookouts were stationed on the surrounding hills, and all approaches were guarded at night, so that the possibility of any surprise attack was remote. The men were wearing civilian clothes, but they each carried an assortment of weapons ranging from knives to light automatic rifles, practically all of which had been captured from the Japanese.

A tremendous meal was prepared for me, the basis consisting of two fried eggs, some sweet and sour pork, and a large bowl of rice. Mr. Cheung detailed a small boy to attend to my wants, and during the next four days that lad looked after me with an absolutely uncanny anticipation of my every wish. His consideration and thoughtfulness might have been expected from a mother's selfless devotion, but it was simply amazing in a boy of ten who had never seen me in his life before.

After the meal I did my best to recount the story of my escape, but distressing exhaustion overcame me and my hosts soon showed me to a primitive house where I was to spend the night. This place had an earthen floor on which fowls and animals roamed at will and where farm tools and cooking-utensils were strewn about. There was a large bench built to accommodate several sleepers, but little else could be seen for the rest of the room was in a deep gloom which the small light of an oil lamp failed to dissipate.

Blankets were brought, and I turned in on the smooth level bed, among friends, with a roof over my head, and feeling that life could hold little more. It was wonderful to feel warm and dry and to know that no matter how it rained it would cause me no discomfort. Eleven days had passed since I had left the camp, and for nine of those days and ten nights my clothes had been saturated with rain or sea water. I had been constantly under severe nervous and physical strain, my diet had been ridiculously low, and I had not had more than half an hour's sleep in any one twenty-four hour day. It was no wonder that sleep still eluded me but, even so, it was unbelievably peaceful to be lying there in such surroundings, and wakefulness was pleasant.

The night soon passed in waking and dozing, and morning found me much refreshed. Hardly had the sun risen when my boy brought in a clean suit of Chinese clothes, while he took mine away to be washed. That made me feel that it was time for me to be washed too, and in order to make myself a little more presentable I emptied my pack in search of shaving-gear. During my captivity I had been using a Rolls razor that it had been my good fortune to retain, but that was much too heavy to carry out with me, and I had taken an old Gillette. I had three blades in the container with my watch and diary.

When my small mirror had been set up the only reflection it produced was an indistinct blur, so, thinking that it had been ruined by water, I asked for another. That yielded the same result, and when I complained that I could see nothing in either mirror, my friends assured me that both of them were perfectly clear. The knowledge gave me quite a shock, for I realised then that my sight was only twenty-five per cent, effective. Certain perplexing features of the latter part of my journey were at once made clear. Earlier that morning the fields had appeared to be buried in a thick white mist, and when I had asked Mr. Cheung if it were usual to have such heavy fog at that time of year, he had looked strangely at me and murmured something about there being no fog. I had assumed that the question was not clearly understood, and did not press it further. Failing sight was the reason why distances had appeared to be much greater than they were, why I had repeatedly tripped and fallen over obstacles in my path, and why I could see absolutely nothing at night. It also explained why I could walk about in brilliant sunshine, without a hat or dark glasses, and suffer no inconvenience at all. In camp, and prior to the war, it had been painful for me to be out in the full glare of day without my eyes being shaded, and that was one of the reasons why the loss of my hat at the first fence had seemed at the time to be so serious.

The state to which I had been reduced was due to diet deficiency. Many of the prisoners had suffered from partial blindness, some went almost totally blind, but my sight had not been affected until the added strain of escaping had further weakened my reserves.

By dint of close concentration I managed to shave, and when that painful operation was over, feeling much better, I made my way to a stream for a thorough rub down with soap. Then, having donned a clean cotton Chinese suit, I was almost beside myself with feelings of pleasurable well-being, and I lazed luxuriously after spreading all my belongings and papers to dry in a hot sheltered place.

The head man of the village, Mr. Chin, invited me to have the morning meal with him, and I sat down to my first Chinese "chow" in a real Chinese setting. One could scarcely call the apartment sumptuous, and it rather surprised me to find the head man living in such poor conditions. A square wooden table that had never been washed stood on an earthen floor showing unmistakable signs of many previous meals, and the seats were narrow wooden forms like carpenters' sawing-horses. A pig, so hollow-backed that its belly touched the ground, snuffled about in its search for scraps, and a dog or two curled up in the dust. Hens pecked inquisitively around our seats and beneath the table. Sanitary arrangements were of the most primitive kind, and the whole place was rich in a variety of smells.

When the food was ready Mrs. Chin and two daughters joined us, and an excellent meal was served. There was fish soup, boiled fish with soya sauce, chopped pork fried to a rich brown and served with a sweet sauce, curried fish, sweet potato and dry rice, all of it helped down with a very pleasant rice wine. After he had watched my ineffective struggling with chopsticks my host kindly suggested that I use a spoon, a concession for which I was exceedingly grateful, for my fingers and brain were in no condition to achieve the finesse of co-ordination necessary for handling the sticks. The delicious food was irresistible, and, though I knew it was foolish to be eating such rich fare, it must be admitted that the quantity I consumed could not fail to satisfy the most fastidious Chinese host.

The good food and the comfort proved too much for me

and in a very short time sleep laid his gentle hands upon me and I sank into blissful oblivion. That happy state did not last long, and on waking again I busied myself with repairs. There were a number of major rents in my shirt and shorts to be mended, and what repairs were possible were made to my shoes.

Mr. Cheung came along to tell me that it was too dangerous for me to remain here, and that I must be ready at four o'clock to go to another village, five miles distant. My heart sank at the thought of having to make that journey on my battered feet, but my fears were quickly dispelled when I learned that we were to sail there. Mr. Chin came to invite me to have the afternoon meal with him before we left, and it is to be regretted that I did not recognise my visitor. He was a very thin little man, no more than five feet two in height, of insignificant appearance, and he arrived almost completely submerged under an enormous topee. My head was not at all receptive, and I cannot recall how it happened that I did eventually become aware that this man was my host of the morning. Conversation between us was limited to smiles, nods and gesticulations with the hands, so I was very pleased when Mr. Cheung arrived with news that the sampan was ready. I was sorry that my appreciation could not be more tangibly expressed, for my new-found friends had done everything possible to make my brief stay pleasant and comfortable.

We set out for the beach, the vividly intelligent little boy, who was by then my constant attendant, marching along with my pack. That arrangement did not altogether please me, for all my papers were in it and I was afraid that they might be lost. However, he was very upset at thought of losing his most important assignment, and I did not have the heart to refuse him.

A group of sampans lay in a small cove at the eastern end of the beach, and in making towards them we passed a row of broken-down huts, outside of which we stopped for some time while Mr. Cheung and others of the party held animated conversation within. Suddenly I noticed a pair of eyes watching me through a hole in a wall, and then it dawned on me that there were many peep-holes in the walls, that occasional rifle muzzles protruded, and that many eyes were watching. The dilapidated huts were housing many armed men, for that was the main defence-post on that side of the village, the side from which Japanese patrols could be expected.

Three armed soldiers came out to join us as an escort, and they were as tough a looking trio as one could wish to see.

The sampans were much nicer looking than the type used in Hong Kong, for these had less beam, they had longer and finer sailing lines, and their bows were nearly as high as their sterns. They were designed to sail well, and to be able to go to windward in rough water. At a guess our craft was about twenty-five feet long, and after we had embarked a dozen passengers, including four women, our journey began. An appreciable surge was running into the anchorage, and when one of the mooring lines carried away, we swung on to other boats alongside. It was just such a situation as the Chinese revel in, and, with everyone shouting directions and lending a willing hand, we were quickly pushed clear.

At first the sheet was hard aboard as we beat to windward out of the bay, but once clear of the western point we could comfortably lay our destination on the starboard tack. It was late afternoon of a glorious day, with a light sea breeze blowing over a bright blue bay, and with the sampan gliding smoothly along over low swells, the whole scene seemed to be too ethereally lovely to be true. I slid down to leeward and let the salt water flow over my burning feet as the rail dipped under, feeling an almost irresistible urge to jump over into the warm translucent sea.

Going aft I took the tiller from our one-armed master, and he was highly amused to see that I could sail his vessel by the wind. However, that pastime quickly palled, for there was no pleasure in it at all. Although the hulls are fairly deep, all sampans and junks are flat bottomed, and a very large rudder raked forward acts as rudder and centreboard combined. The result is that they are very hard on the helm, and even in the light breeze then blowing a tiller-line was constantly in use. Being accustomed all my life to sailing finely balanced racing yachts, there was no more pleasure in that than in steering a barge, and I soon gave it up.

One of the girls and one of the soldiers succumbed to the gentle motion and gave their last meal to the fishes, but the others relaxed in comfort.

My main interest was centred in one of the guards who lay sleeping on the weather-deck, with an ancient rifle by his side. In his belt was a wicked-looking dagger, its handle gaily ornamented with coloured cords plaited into patterns, and those were frayed out into a plume at the top of the haft. His appearance held me fascinated, for there was something indestructible about that short stocky figure, of the colour and texture of weathered bronze. He was wearing the poorest of grey cotton civilian clothes, jacket and trousers, and his cartridge-belt was of the same material. There were thin cotton braces over his shoulders, to give the belt support. All the guerrillas had that same poverty-stricken equipment, much of it fastened together with tapes, string, pieces of wire and safety-pins. They were a sorry army as far as arms and harness were concerned, but what they lacked in material wealth they made up for with tremendous spirit and morale.

Mr. Cheung saw me gazing at that rugged soldier, and, divining my thoughts, said: "Yes; he does look tough, doesn't he? He has been with the armies in the north and has been fighting the Japanese for ten years. Before ever he acquired a firearm he killed two Japanese with that knife in his belt."

No wonder he looked hard. It was difficult to visualise a life such as he had led, drifting about for ten years with the Communist armies, living off the land through summer days and bitter northern winters, his entire possessions on his back, living frugally, advancing, retreating, always fighting, always in danger, with nothing to gain and nothing to lose but a life that was barely worth living.

I thought back to the many discussions we had had in camp, to the derogatory terms in which some of those who had lived in the East referred to the Chinese as soldiers, and looking at that block of bronze I vowed that I would trust my life to him through heaven and hell. It was the leadership, not the soldier, which was at fault.

We reached our destination at dusk, with a brilliant half-moon shedding its soft light on the placid waters, and all I wanted was to lie there and sleep on that cool deck beneath the stars.

Suddenly a challenge rang out from an anchored sampan, and our master was soon in vigorous discourse with the men aboard. The craft at anchor had a small sampan on its deck for use as a dinghy, and our crew was evidently bargaining for its hire. A satisfactory price having been agreed to, the dinghy was hoisted overboard, and it was sculled across to pick up what seemed to me to be a heavy overload of our passengers. Very thankful not to be in the first party, I watched them approach the lines of surf, expecting every moment to see them overwhelmed. But, skilfully awaiting his chance, the sculler landed his cargo with no more damage than a thorough soaking. He then returned for the remainder of us, a much lighter party, and we too successfully shot through the surf.

When all were assembled on shore a guide took station ahead, and led the party for about one mile to the village of Toyeung. We quickly learned that the provision of a guide was necessary, for challenges rang out at frequent intervals. On every little footbridge a lad was ostensibly fishing; in narrow paths girls or men appeared with their inevitable bundles, and everywhere alongside their stations rifles protruded menacingly from the bushes. Toyeung was evidently a heavily guarded village.

Other members of the party scattered to their various destinations, while Mr. Cheung, the boy and I called at several sizeable houses where my guardian talked volubly with the occupants. I fancy he was not having much success in finding me accommodation, in spite of his salesmanship, but we shortly found an obliging landlord who showed me to an upstairs room. The window looked out over the village, over fields of paddy, and beyond to the open bay where a cluster of fishing-lights gave the appearance of a floating village.

A tiny oil lamp threw a faint and wavering light within this spacious room, which, to my distorted vision seemed furnished in a most luxurious manner. There was a large mirror on a wall above a handsome dressing-table, a large wardrobe, a neat occasional table, various chairs, and last but not least, a level bed with a straw mat and blanket complete. Of course there was no mattress, just bare boards with a thin piece of matting over them, but one would expect to find nothing else in China, for that is the national bed.

Various visitors came to see me, to hear my story and ask many questions, Mr. Cheung acting as interpreter and obviously enjoying his role. As time went on it was becoming increasingly difficult to give coherent answers, for the room was swaying about, my visitors were taking on enlarged and distorted shapes, and at last I had to excuse myself and lie down, feeling quite incapable of either sitting up or continuing the conversation any longer.

It was quiet after the guests had gone, but severe aching pains in my ankles and knees prevented me from sleeping. There seemed to be no more elasticity left in my muscles, and during the last few days, whenever I fell or tripped, the sinews tugged directly at their anchorages on the bones. Now they were beginning to swell and register their complaints in no uncertain manner, and the night passed in restless tossings.

I was glad when a new day drove darkness from the eastern sky, and scarcely was the sun risen before my diminutive valet came in to ascertain my wants. Of course a wash and shave were the first things, and he led me out on to a level roof platform, where preparations had already been made. Words cannot adequately convey the mingled feelings of astonishment and pleasure which were constantly brought to me by that little heathen with the vividly intelligent black eyes.

On the parapet awaiting my use were a mug of clean water with a toothbrush ready spread with toothpaste, a face cloth, soap, a clean towel and a basin of water. Simple enough, perhaps, but at such a time and in such circumstances that thoughtfulness seemed to touch the zenith of hospitality, and I was deeply moved. The toothbrush was particularly surprising, until I learned that a mug and toothbrush formed part of the regular equipment of all guerrillas, and whenever they were leaving for an outpost those accessories were usually to be seen dangling from a piece of tape fastened to some part of their harness.

Someone had presented me with a small tin of ointment, and I had just finished doctoring my injuries when breakfast arrived. Three ten-inch plates were placed on a table. The first was filled with rice, the second held three large fried eggs and some green beans, while the third was laden with four large pieces of fish, beautifully browned. I looked at that stack of food, scarcely able to believe my eyes, and then it occurred to me that others must be joining me for breakfast.

Pointing to the table, I asked: "For how many?"

I was quickly made to understand that it was all mine.

After the large meals of the previous day I did not feel at all hungry, in fact I scarcely knew how to begin on such a colossal repast. That would not do at all – some effort must be made to do justice to my host's generosity – so I began slowly on the eggs. The first mouthfuls whipped my appetite into acute appreciation, and my jaws worked steadily through those dishes until not a grain of rice was left. Never had food tasted so delicious, never had fish melted so easily in the mouth. It had been steeped in batter, fried in oil, and served with a slightly sour sauce which lent an exquisite flavour.

No sooner were the dishes cleared away than the lad appeared again, this time with a clean suit of long thin cotton trousers and a striped cotton shirt. A cool breeze blew directly in my window from the lovely blue waters of Mirs Bay, and lying down once more I thought, just before lapsing into a sound sleep, that life could grant no greater favours.

That perfect rest lasted for almost three hours, and then the boy awakened me to ask what I wanted for tiffin. Eggs were suggested, but I could not face any more, and countered with a request for some fruit and some very weak tea. This request caused consternation and long parleys downstairs. Apparently fruit was very scarce, but they would do their best. Had I known, nothing would have induced me to ask for fruit, but once the wish had been expressed there was no way of stopping my friends from trying to satisfy it. At some time on the previous day I had mentioned how short of sugar we had been in camp, and how we had missed sweet things, so when my tea arrived it was accompanied by a pound of raw brown sugar in slabs. Another thing I noticed was that a bottle of wine had appeared on my dressing-table, and it seemed that, did they but own it, these people would have given me the world.

Occasionally men who could speak a little English came in to talk to me, and I gathered that it was intended to keep me there for perhaps two days, and then set me on my way again. Just then I felt that were it not for my anxiety to send news home, a stay of two months would be more to my liking. Actually there was another reason for wanting to push on quickly, and that was the expectation of an attack of fever.

During talks in the camp with men who knew this country well, it had always been said that anyone passing through it without the protection of a net would be certain to become infected with malaria, unless he happened to belong to that small and fortunate group which is immune from fevers.

Malaria was very prevalent in all the villages I had visited, and it could be safely assumed that the anopheles mosquitoes had been present in force in all the country I had traversed.

From the date of infection malaria takes nine days to develop, and as it was then thirteen days since I had left the camp an attack could be expected at any time. I had no wish to be laid up there, so close to the Japanese lines.

While looking about the room I suddenly caught a glimpse of myself in a mirror, and, on going closer, I could scarcely believe that that sunken cheeked, haggard-looking visage was mine. The sight caused me to sample the wine, and while it was quite pleasant to the palate it seemed to be very strong, and I deemed it wiser to reserve my drinking till the evening.

A messenger arrived with a basket of pears, and though they were rather hard and woody they were at least fruit, something for which my system was crying out. Then a Chinese nurse came to see me, and she bathed my feet in hot water before treating the cuts with ointment. My feet and ankles had swelled to twice their normal size since I had stopped walking, but the attention eased the pain considerably, and I soon fell asleep again. That happy state was disturbed by the advent of another meal, a quart of rich soup made from chicken livers, eggs and bean sprouts, followed by three large pieces of beautifully roasted fat chicken served with rice. Unable to resist such appetising fare I cleared everything from the table, albeit there were serious misgivings about the wisdom of eating so much unaccustomed food.

Mr. Cheung had been very ill during the previous night, and all that day he was suffering from severe diarrhoea and weakness. When I paid him a visit he said that many people were suffering from the same complaint, and as he was in no mood for conversation I soon left him alone with his pains.

A heavy storm of rain and thunder swept over the village in the late afternoon, and it gave me the utmost satisfaction to remain perfectly dry and comfortable while watching the

Lieutenant-Commander Ralph Burton Goodwin OBE, RNZNVR.

Above: Japanese troops march on to Hong Kong Island, December 1941. (Historic Military Press)

Below: A clip from a news reel showing Japanese troops in action during the fighting for Hong Kong. (Critical Past)

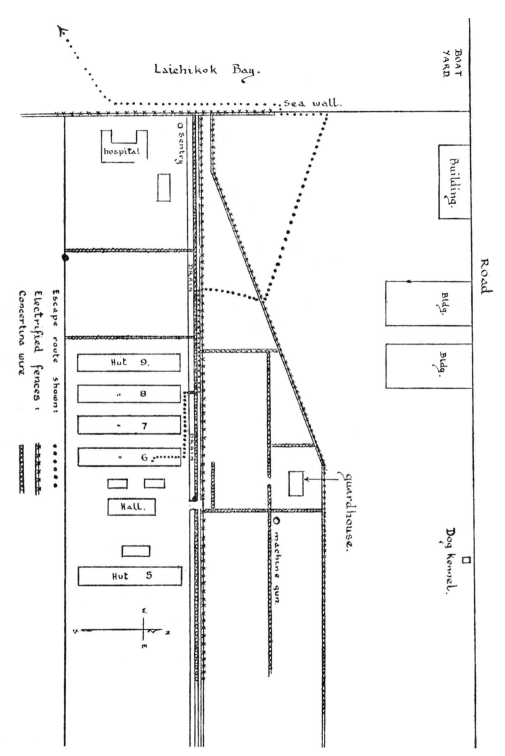

A plan drawing of Shamsuipo Camp.

Above: Another clip from a wartime Japanese news reel, this time showing Allied naval personnel pictured in the immediate aftermath of their capture at the dockyard in Hong Kong. (Critical Past)

Below: From film footage, this image depicts victorious Japanese troops posing for the camera after the fall of Hong Kong. (Critical Past)

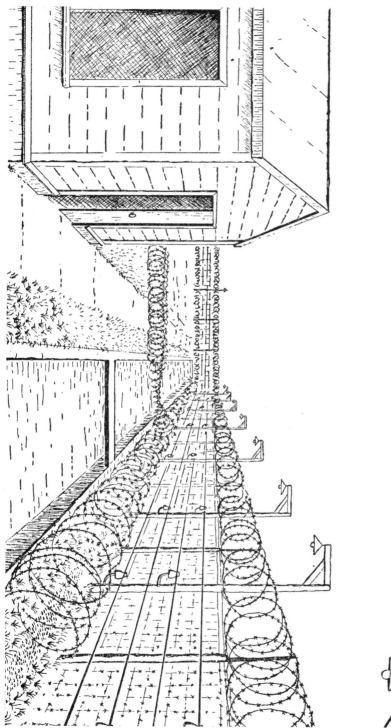

A drawing depicting the north-west corner of Shamsuipo Camp.

Above: Taken from a news reel, this picture shows Japanese troops awaiting an inspection having participated in a victory parade down Hong Kong's Queen Street. (Critical Past)

Below: Commander Peter MacRitchie with liberated Canadian prisoners of war at Shamsuipo Camp, Hong Kong, in September 1945. (Library and Archives Canada; MIKAN 3617924)

Above: Major General Umekichi signing the Japanese surrender of Hong Kong on 16 September 1945. Rear Admiral Cecil Harcourt (C-in-C Hong Kong) signed the document in the presence Admiral Sir Bruce Fraser (C-in-C British Pacific Fleet).

Below: Colonel Tokunaga under guard having been arrested as a war criminal in Hong Kong.

The memorial statue in Hong Kong Park which commemorates the defenders of Hong Kong in 1941.

rain streaming down outside. The misery caused by constant saturation so recently endured, was one of my bitterest memories.

My knees and ankles were aching severely in the evening, and their increasing size was causing me some concern. However, that was only the prelude to a most uncomfortable night, for my stomach at last rebelled against the treatment it had received. From dark to dawn violent pains and diarrhoea assailed me, until I was hardly able to stagger up the steep stairs after my frequent excursions in search of relief. Daylight caught me looking like a perfect subject for a famine picture, with cheeks sunken into deep hollows, and yellow skin drawn over protruding bones.

Offers of breakfast could not tempt me. During the morning the nurse again came to tend my feet, and on hearing of my condition she brought and administered some white powder, which gave almost immediate relief. By lunch-time I was so much better that I thoroughly enjoyed three lightly boiled eggs, but although my appetite was ravenous again, I did not risk eating anything more.

Mr. Cheung had recovered too, and much to my regret he and the boy returned to Siumuisha, after they had introduced me to a new guardian, Mr. Raymond Wong. This officer, who had come from guerrilla headquarters to look after me, spoke English very well; and he informed me that, prior to the outbreak of war, he had been employed for two and a half years in an office in the Hong Kong naval dockyard. He gave me a great deal of interesting information about the disposition and work of the guerrillas, and he, in common with all others I had spoken to, found it very difficult to believe that I had been able to travel so far without being reported by their lookouts.

Guerrillas were holding the country north and east of Shatau, and they were operating all through the Japanese-occupied territory, right into Kowloon City itself. It was they who had blown up the railway bridge over Waterloo Road.

That was a well-conceived and executed piece of sabotage, which failed to achieve the full measure of success it deserved only through the pitifully small amount of explosive which they could afford to use. We heard the boom of that explosion in Argyle Street Camp, and though the attempt failed in its main design of material damage, it shattered the Japanese morale to such an extent that for nearly a week all work and traffic in Kowloon was brought to a standstill. At that time some hundreds of coolies were levelling a hill at the foot of Argyle Street to make room for extensions to Kaitak Airfield, and for five days not a pound of earth was moved. Lorry loads of troops were racing about at high speed, with machine-guns mounted on the cabs, and as none of the culprits could be found the soldiers vented their anger in a festival of brutality against the populace. Many civilians were interrogated, and several were dragged from the street into Argyle Street Camp, where they were severely beaten. In the guardhouse one man had a wooden chair smashed to pieces over his head before he fell insensible.

A spectacular rescue claimed for the guerrillas was that of Lieutenant Donald W. Kerr of the 32nd Fighter Squadron, USAAF. Shot down in a dogfight over Hong Kong on the 11th February 1944, the officer landed by parachute near the crest of the main ridge above Kaitak, very close to a guard station on the Customs Pass Road. From our camp we had watched that parachute float gracefully down, but we did not know whether it was American or Japanese. Wong gave me the following story:

As soon as the parachutist hit the ground a Chinese boy raced up and guided him to a small cave. While the American crawled inside, the lad walked away and soon met a party of Japanese troops. He denied any knowledge of the aviator, and the party continued their search farther afield. After nightfall friends were taken to the cave, friends who escorted the airman to a house on the shore of Tolo Harbour. There he was safely concealed for a week while a thousand troops combed the area, and when the search had died down he was successfully smuggled across Mirs Bay. From there he returned through China to his unit in Kweilin. Having watched the parachute gracefully descend, I found that account of the sequel to be full of interest.

Guerrillas were also operating along the Kowloon-Canton railway, and we had frequently read about the total annihilation of those forces by heroic Japanese troops. Unfortunately for the authenticity of those accounts, no sooner had complete disintegration been announced, than a fresh wave of interruptions to traffic would occur. The menace became so serious that the Japanese were forced to stage a major offensive against the saboteurs, and while, according to their own reports, their battles ended without fail in the total destruction of the enemy, Wong gave a different version of at least one attack.

One thousand guerrillas had been driven up the slopes of a hill by encircling Japanese troops, and, expecting an easy victory the Japanese were deployed for a dawn attack. It was just bad luck for them that one unknown path had been left unguarded, for during the night the entire guerrilla force melted away. At dawn the hill was taken with great gallantry, and also with some casualties, caused by enthusiastic troops hurling hand-grenades among their own men advancing from the opposite direction, but not a Chinese was discovered. To cover his discomfiture the Japanese commander wrote a lurid account of the slaughter his men had done, and the Press blazoned forth another successful campaign of annihilation.

According to Wong, two nights after I had passed Shataokok, guerrillas stormed the police station there, killed the guards, and made off with all the arms, ammunition and cash. Whether the tales were true or not did not greatly matter, just to hear those exploits recounted gave me tremendous satisfaction, for there was a burning hatred within me for my recent captors.

Besides waging constant war against Japan, the guerrillas also had to withstand blockade and attack by Nationalist troops. An area along the East River was held by a Government army, and as recently as May 1944, only two months previously, fighting between the two factions had occurred inland from Toyeung. A number of villages had been occupied and ransacked by the troops, while certain persons had been arrested on charges of assisting the Communists. All those villagers who were fit enough disappeared into the hills with the possessions they could carry, and there they remained until the troops had departed.

It was a great pity that the internecine strife had to continue, for had there been mutual assistance a much greater effort could have been directed against the Japanese. All arms and ammunition used by the Communists were captured from the Japanese or smuggled precariously through the Government blockade. Wong was of opinion that the blockade was quite effective, for he said that it would be of no use for me to try to send any gifts back to the people who had assisted me. He had heard that several Americans who had been escorted back had sent parcels, but none had ever been received.

Explosives were the greatest need of the guerrillas, and Wong thought his men might be able to recover some mines from the fields about Hong Kong. He was given all the information in my possession of their location, but his chances of success were remote. The mines had been laid at the beginning of the war in Europe, and even by the end of 1941 large numbers had broken adrift. It was certain that two and a half years later it would be difficult to find any active mines still afloat.

My friends had had several encounters with armed Japanese trawlers, and they flattered me by asking my opinion on the best methods of attacking those vessels with two or three armed junks. With pieces of wood for ships we worked out several plans according to the relative direction of the wind, all very entertaining in the safety of the house, but the best of them would have been desperate adventures and I was in no mood to be putting my theories into practice.

That these men were popular with the villagers was beyond doubt, for I had watched the friendly greetings, had seen them laughing and joking together, and had watched them at village sing-songs in the evenings. One reason perhaps was that the troops had a very strict discipline and high morale, and another was that a large part of their time was spent in helping the people to improve and extend their rice fields and gardens. Those regions had restricted growing areas due to the mountainous nature of the country, and with the normal trade channels completely disrupted they had to rely largely on their own efforts. In 1943, due to failure of the local crops, it was said that some villages lost from forty to fifty per cent, of their populations, starvation being the cause of death. This was primitive China where famine, disease and death hovered closely day by day, where the people lived close to the earth and by the products of the earth, where an intense vitality surmounted every calamity and where the mortality-rate was alarming by European standards.

Yet life surged along in an atmosphere of great friendliness. Through all their trials these people retained an irrepressible sense of humour and a buoyant philosophy which death alone could destroy. Primitive in their homes, utterly devoid of any knowledge of hygiene, living in conditions that would appal our pampered trade unionists, those peasant peoples and fisherfolk looked at one with smiling, friendly eyes. They had no axe to grind, no hate instilled by propaganda, they accepted a person as they found him, and a happy comfortable atmosphere reaching everywhere made it a pleasure just to be among them. At that time the Communists had not achieved domination of the country, they were just cultivating the confidence of the people.

I was very anxious to contact our own forces, and information was passed to me that there was, or had been, a

British officer stationed at Waichow. Liaison had been maintained with the guerrillas until political pressure had caused the contact to be broken, and apparently there were some difficulties to be overcome in handing me over to the Government troops. Mr. Wong said that he could go only a certain distance with me and he would then hand me over to a gentleman who acted as a go-between. That worthy would see that I proceeded safely.

Although he talked a great deal, my interpreter was really very hazy when it came to discussing my future movements, and the situation was not altogether reassuring, for in the early days of our captivity we had heard rumours of a strong leader in the region of Tamsui who would, as likely as not, hand a European back to the Japanese. That I was a virtual prisoner, in spite of the generous treatment accorded me, was made very obvious whenever I suggested taking a walk to look about the village. Any such request met with evasive expressions of doubt as to its wisdom, unless a "guide" went with me. Naturally in such a small place one could not possibly go astray, but perhaps there were good reasons why I should remain out of sight. In any case I was much too weak to want to go far, and certainly much too weak to try to break through any local "Iron Curtains".

The distance from Toyeung to Tamsui was described as a walk of six hours, and from there I could go by motor-boat to Waichow. That was a very pleasing thought, for my legs were still badly swollen and my left ankle was very strained and weak.

It was then Sunday, the 30th of July, only fifteen days since my departure from the camp, yet my nerves were in such a state that it seemed an age since I had been wrestling with the wire on that first fence. I felt that a lifetime had passed in the last two weeks.

Wong told me that they were able to operate a black market with Hong Kong dollars, and as I had HK$180 with me it seemed that they would now come in useful to pay for the food and shelter provided. But my hosts would not hear of it; everything that they possessed was at my disposal, and they refused to accept any payment.

The nurse came again to tend my feet, and they were healing rapidly under the combined influence of attention and rest. Not so my stomach, which had been so shocked by the sudden flush of rich food that it was quite unable to cope with the prodigality of its fuel. A return to a full diet should have been much more gradual.

There was more thunder about in the afternoon, and it still gave me great satisfaction to lie and watch the rain streaming past the window, revelling in my dry comfort. Next morning was fine and calm and I felt so much better after a restful night that I asked to be allowed to continue my journey. My stomach was still upset, but I felt that it would be well worth while to try to reach Tamsui, after which, with the river to travel on, it would not matter if weakness did again overcome me.

My shoes were virtual wrecks, and after wasting two hours in vain efforts to fasten the soles and heels to the uppers, my friends brought a pair of canvas sandshoes, size seven. As my size is nine and a half some adjustments were required, but after the shoes had been split from tongue to toe, and windows had been cut for my big and little toes, they were much more comfortable than my old ones.

What those people were doing for me was becoming more fantastic as time went on. That day started at 5.45 a.m. with an early morning tea consisting of two soft-boiled eggs and a bunch of fruit called "lung-an". At 8 a.m. breakfast proper appeared, three fried eggs, two slabs of fish and a bowl of rice. It was no good, stomach trouble or no stomach trouble, the temptation was too great and I polished off everything in sight. Lunch consisted of two enormous omelettes, delicious but running with oil, and in deference to my tortured intestines I made a great effort and sent one back. On waking from a fitful doze at three o'clock I saw a boy leave half a pound of Indian tea and a cake of carbolic soap on my table, while half an hour later another lad came in with a tin of pineapple, a tin of water-chestnuts, a huge papaia, and six very large and perfectly ripe bananas.

The afternoon was sultry and thunderous again, and suddenly it seemed that everything was unreal. How could these things be? Was I still a prisoner and were all these past experiences and emotions but the fevered ramblings of a mind in torment? Had there been any symptoms of a coming illness to account for these unbelievable happenings? Were my last recollections of the camp quite normal?

On thinking back over past events everything seemed to have occurred in proper sequence, and I concentrated once again on the table near me. This was a poor Chinese village where people died of starvation, yet those tins and fruit looked real enough, and, unable to continue longer in doubt, I went over to touch them, and to verify their solidity. It really was not fair. Here were things that I had been craving for years, and now that they were available my system was too upset to be able to cope with them. How I longed for a stomach like a mincing machine. Resisting all the other good things, I ate half the papaia and in the evening an excellent custard and a small tin of pineapple rounded off a day of feeding that should have satisfied the most fastidious gourmet. At least, those were my thoughts at the time. No one who has been subjected to long months of systematic starvation should be called upon to face such temptation, especially when to refuse would be to offend the hospitality of his host, and I paid for my frailty by having violent pains all night.

On Tuesday, the 1st of August, the question of my departure was raised again, and I was told that all arrangements had been made for me to leave next day, when coolies would bring a chair in which to carry me.

On the strength of that promise I wrote a letter of thanks for all that had been done for me, and my hosts were so pleased with it that they said that it must be published in their news sheet. We fell to discussing the war and other things, among which were many thrilling stories of the exploits of the guerrillas in their constant raids on Japanese posts and communication lines. No doubt Wong embellished them with everything that his imagination could conjure up in extolling the virtues of his men, and in decrying the stupidity of the Japanese, but it made extremely good entertainment and the time passed pleasantly.

He also painted a revealing picture of the Nationalist troops, who were described as being of very low morale and of no use at all as fighting troops, largely owing to corruption among the officers. He said that the soldiers were half starved and so pitifully equipped that they offered practically no resistance to the Japanese, but they frequently suffered heavy casualties owing to hopeless leadership and the work of traitors.

Remembering that Chiang's men were enemies of the guerrillas I tried to strike a happy medium between the virtues of Wong's men and the faults of the others, but in the light of subsequent experience, I found that he was only too correct in his assertions.

The latest news and rumours were that the Russians were within twenty miles of Warsaw, Hitler was wounded, and Tojo had resigned from the Premiership of Japan. All very cheering news, even though it was highly inaccurate. The worst feature of the news was that the Japanese were staging another offensive south from Changsha, down the Hankow-Canton Railway, and that proved to be the start of their last big drive in China. Should they continue they would sever my escape route from East to West China, and I was particularly anxious to avoid being cut off.

My eyes were causing me considerable pain and inconvenience. Sometimes for most of the day I could see only as if looking through a dense white smoke, and then my eyes would grow fairly clear for a short time before they clouded over again. Then, after responding well to bathing and ointment, my feet and legs swelled up to a great size again, and this time they showed all the symptoms of beriberi. My loss of vision too was just another sign of vitamin deficiency, and though I had kept clear of those complaints while in camp the strain and hunger of the escape had turned the scales against me.

Late in the afternoon there occurred one of those little incidents that make a lasting impression on the mind. Somewhere on the outskirts of the village a meeting was being held. Groups of people – men, women and children – were all converging towards the one spot, and I was watching them passing from my upstairs window, when a party approached that immediately gripped my attention. Dressed in the conventional Chinese suit of black jacket and trousers, the jacket buttoned to a level neck band, twelve men came down a path, walking two by two. They were pale, small-boned, almost effeminate in their slim lightness of build, and as they wore no hats I could study their calm expressionless faces. At a first glance they could be shop assistants, clerks, or any one of a dozen similar classes, yet as they came nearer, talking softly among themselves, there was something terrible in their appearance. An aura of horror surrounded this silent moving group that roused every nerve within me to a pitch of suppressed excitement, and I watched them, fascinated, as one would watch a snake about to strike. Without observing me they passed some twenty yards away, and I felt my scalp creep, and the hair seemed literally to rise on my neck as that sinister and terrifying party went to join the gathered throng.

My first reaction when they had gone was to thank Heaven that they were on my side and not against me, for never had anything appeared to carry so much of the relentless inevitability of doom.

They were no mere shop assistants or clerks, those loose-limbed striplings who had passed, they belonged to that class from which the assassins are recruited. Utterly devoid of fear, regardless of their personal safety, taking the most appalling chances, the paid agents and assassins of China had plied an enormous trade in the days since Japan had first attacked their country. Perhaps it would be learned that some official was trading secretly with the enemy, and once the moving finger pointed in his direction he could surround himself with an army of guards and a hundred safety devices, but one day the house-boy would go out on some errand never to return, and the master would be found in his own bedroom with his head split by a cleaver. Or the victim would drive out with two of his trusted guards on a journey which would end at some isolated spot where his bullet-riddled body would be found slumped down in a mess of blood. They had one trait in common; those men who carried out the political murders of China, and that was one of utterly relentless tenacity of purpose to which every other consideration was subjugated.

I had been as close to some of them as ever I wished to be, and the sight had made me feel how utterly helpless was I, and how completely dependent on the goodwill of the people.

Later a reporter came to take down my story and to ask a great many questions, but concentration quickly exhausted me and it is quite possible that much more was said than was really wise at the time. However, as far as I know there were no repercussions, so probably the guerrillas themselves exercised a strict censorship on everything that appeared in their little news-sheet.

After the departure of my guests I could not sleep, and among the racing tumult in my brain was a growing anxiety that nothing should delay our journey on the morrow. The night dragged on interminably, and soon after daylight my disordered fancy was rudely shocked by hearing a high-pitched, unmistakably Chinese voice singing. A youth about eighteen years of age was putting all his power into a spirited rendering of the *Marseillaise*, and it struck me as the height of incongruity to hear that martial strain being mangled in such a setting. I could well imagine the skeleton of De Lisle sitting bolt upright in its grave, could it but hear such a version of his immortal song.

Breakfast consisted of four fried and three boiled eggs followed by bananas and chestnuts, so I was very well fortified in case there should be a long wait for the next meal. Wong brought me $2,000 in Chinese National Currency, a sum that sounded colossal, but which had a value that was rather hard to assess. At black-market rates it had a value of thirty shillings, at the official rate it was worth £10. What it would buy was the only real test of its value, and that was not very much. After promising to do my best to have compensation paid for all that had been done for me, I was given three copies of the guerrilla newspaper and also a letter from their commanding officer.

Following is a translation of the letter made by a Chinese interpreter in Waichow, and it is reproduced in its original form:

H.Q. EAST RIVER STRICKING FORCE,
KWANGTUNG PEOPLES'
ANTI-JAPANESE GUERILLA UNIT.

30th July 1944.

OUR BELOVED AND RESPECTED LIEUT. GOODWIN. – We thank God that you have safely arrived in our Guerilla area in Free China.

On hearing the story of your dangerous escape we beg to express our high respect and deep sympathy towards your great spirit by which you have conquered all difficulties.

The brutality which the Japanese Militarism has employed in harassing the human race has been experienced by all human beings throughout the world, and it is important that the Japanese Military High Command should be wiped out. The Japanese

Militarism in the East and Hitler and his gang of bandits in the West should both be penalised with the most drastic punishment.

As regards to those Allied friends who are still interned in the Japanese Internment Camps, they are leading a slavish life, like millions of our fellow countrymen in China, to all of whom we feel the greatest concern. Your escape is an explicit manifestation of your strong will in your struggle with and hatred towards the Japanese, and your freedom will increase the strength of the Anti Fascist Party and will enhance the relationship between the Chinese and British peoples.

Although the East River Striking Force of our Kwangtung People's Anti Japanese Guerrillas helped quite a great number of our Allied friends to escape from the Internment Camps shortly after the fall of Hong Kong – such work is a sort of obligation that should be fulfilled by our Hong-Kong-Kowloon Guerrilla Unit – yet, with the strict supervision and blockade and the improved administration in the camps, our work cannot be carried out successfully, and, in this case, we beg to tender our humble apologies. But we hope to renew our contact with our Allied friends in the camps and, should there be any possibility, we will do our utmost to pursue this objective.

If the Kuomintang Authorities in China can change their policy to stop their Anti-Red civil war and to adopt a democratic government, then China will undoubtedly show a vast improvement in her war against Japan. Such co-ordination will greatly lessen the difficulties of the British and American Allies in their counter-offensive against the Japanese and will bring far better and unexpected results. If our East River Striking Force can be relieved of our present situation earlier, which has been made by the Kuomintang Party and in which we are attacked on two sides, then our co-operation with the Allies in our war efforts will make greater progress. But, up to the present date, the political situation in China has produced nothing that would inspire us, while the Kuomintang troops along the East River have never stopped their attacks on us.

However the Fascism of the whole world will probably vanish with this war, and China will get their ultimate victory in their war of resistance. China must become a democratic nation. No efforts can revert the course of the wheel in history. We, of the Communist Party in China, all hope that when our hard struggle has ended, there will be a new programme to maintain permanent peace in the world, and that democratic and Free China will join the company of and unite together with Britain, America and Soviet Russia to march on the road which leads to financial prosperity and blessings of the human race.

We beg to tender you our salute,
H.Q. EAST RIVER STRICKING FORCE,
KWANGTUNG PEOPLE'S
ANTI-JAPANESE GUERILLA UNIT.

Of course the above letter was handed to me in Chinese characters and I was unaware of its contents until a later date, but the original forms a very interesting souvenir, being a curious mixture as it is of a little praise for me and a lot of propaganda for the Communists.

Next morning was cloudy, still and very warm, and I dressed again in my old shirt and shorts in preparation for the journey. A light bamboo chair with poles twelve feet long for handles arrived at 8.15 a.m., and we were soon ready to go. It was quite a cavalcade, for besides Mr. Wong there were the two bearers and a guard of fourteen soldiers, one armed with a light Browning automatic rifle, the others with an assortment of rifles, pistols and hand grenades. Hoisting me to their shoulders the two coolies set off across half a mile of level ground, behind a headland which shut off all view of the sea. On the way we passed a number of people returning to the village with bundles of fish, among them a number of snapper of a shape and colour similar to those we used to catch on the New Zealand coast. I felt very tempted to sample them. We soon saw where they were coming from, for we came to a sizeable tidal stream in which there were many fishing sampans, both at anchor and on the move. This stream lay athwart our path, and we were ferried across to the other side where, winding inland, a track followed close along the water.

The tide was in and it was very pleasant skirting that lovely placid stream, where trees lining the banks were reflected perfectly on its shining surface. Perhaps a mile had been covered when the roar of falling water filled the air, and on rounding a bend we came into full view of a tumbling mountain torrent, which spent its force in a final plunge to the headwaters of the tidal stream. From that point the track began to climb steeply, following the bank of the torrent, and at one place I could scarcely allow my bearers to proceed. On the far side of the valley there was a large pandanus palm, and hanging from its branches there were at least a dozen ripe fruit, richly golden. In spite of the fact that I had recently had a surfeit of food, and that future supplies were almost assured, hunger had for so long been my companion that it seemed to be a crime of the first magnitude to leave that practically worthless fare behind. It was only the difficulty of approaching them that prevented me from gathering one or two.

In spite of the steepness of the path an amazingly steady pace was maintained by my bearers, one of whom was a very small man. He had had so much difficulty in lifting the chair to his shoulders that I had expected him to soon give up, but his appearance was deceiving. Once the balance had been adjusted there seemed to be no end to the endurance of those men, who plodded on with sweat running from them until their clothes were saturated, clinging rags.

Several times we stopped for a spell at some wayside tea-house, where the inevitable pot of very weak tea was served in its tiny cone-shaped cups. Along thousands of miles of China's tracks, over which the merchandise goes on the backs of coolies, tea-houses stand at intervals to refresh the weary traveller and thirsty bearer. Rest is rationed on those ways of toil, and one can assume that that is the reason for the small cups with their wide mouths and narrow bottoms, cups that present the maximum cooling surface in relation to the contents. The wayfarer with a set distance to cover in a day has no time to dawdle while large cups of tea cool, and the problem has been admirably solved.

Used cups were swilled in a pail in which hundreds of cups had been swilled before, and looking at those lip-stained edges, about which dozens of flies were settling, I thought that it was no wonder that disease spread like wildfire in this land of teeming millions, ignorant as they were of the most elementary principles of cleanliness. These tracks, these tea-houses, had been used by countless hordes for centuries; and who was I to criticise and be fastidious of customs so long established? No; I cast my qualms into the nether regions and enjoyed the hospitality provided, myself an object of great interest to all and sundry. Europeans were rare indeed in that area in those days of war and turmoil, and it was increasingly apparent that news of my coming was preceding us. Curious groups were waiting at the tea-houses, and they watched my movements with candid interest.

The bamboo chair was hard and uncomfortable to my still rather bruised and battered body, so when the path began to climb steeply to the head of the pass I dismounted and walked for half an hour. Steps were formed of smooth flagstones in good repair, and in spite of the effort it was a welcome change to be out of the chair until we had descended to more level ground on the inland side of the range. There the track had been washed away in parts by flooded streams, it was rough and difficult, and I was very glad indeed to be carried again, to ease the pain in my feet.

So well had my heralds carried their message that in two or three villages the local troops were drawn up for my inspection, and I had to say a few words of praise. I could not help smiling at these little gestures of respect, for having said my few brief words the interpreter produced a harangue that lasted fully five minutes, and he astonished me with his invention, evidently using me as a pretext for a pep talk. It would have pleased me very much to know what he was saying on those occasions.

After travelling thus for four hours we came to the outskirts of a small village somewhere near Pingshan, and there we met a man who was to conduct me to the Government forces. A long parley ensued between this man and Mr. Wong, after which my escort was drawn up and I bid them good-bye. A few words of praise from me spurred Wong to greater heights of oratory, and even after hearing his previous performances I was astonished at the length and variety of the discourse that my speech had inspired. When he had finished I shook hands all round and departed with my new guide. Four of my guards stayed with me for another mile, and then we were met by a man dressed all in black who had come from Pingshan to escort me to Waichow. After a brief exchange of talk the four guards disappeared towards Toyeung, and when they were out of sight three men with bicycles emerged from some nearby bushes. My new guide was wasting no time, and mounting the carrier of one bicycle he motioned me to climb on another.

Chapter 9

Pingshan to Waichow: The British Army Aid Group

The road from Pingshan to Tamsui, a distance of ten miles, had been described as being very good, so I assumed that our narrow path would shortly join it. My rider was a lad of eighteen who had a mania for ringing a loud bell mounted on the handlebar, a bell that nearly drove me to distraction before we reached Tamsui.

The "good road" proved to be a myth and a delusion, for most of it was no more than an ordinary foot-track across the paddy fields. Every hundred yards there was a stone channel through which water flowed from a higher field to the one below, and at each of those channels we had to dismount. How I longed to reach that good road; but for at least five miles there was no relief from the endless climbing on and off the bicycles, while the track itself was fiendishly rough. My cushion was of the scantiest material and barely dulled the edges of the iron frame, so that from pain and exhaustion I was soon only barely conscious.

At one sizeable village the head man came to greet me and to present me with a beautiful bouquet of sweet-scented white flowers. He also had a company of troops lined up for my inspection, and I somehow hobbled through that ordeal. Then on we went again, my rider ringing his bell with the persistence of a child with a new toy, while all three riders charged their mounts at the most difficult obstacles with the reckless abandon of youth.

My guide, with a stiff-brimmed straw hat set squarely on his head and a neatly rolled black umbrella hanging from his left arm, rode his steed as if he had been born on the carrier of a bicycle. He sat there, stiff-backed, legs hanging limply, his black attire neat and proper, looking more like a Lutheran pastor on his way to prayer than a man who was playing a game that might separate his head from his shoulders should he make one false move. As he was leading the way I had ample opportunity for observing him, and I was contrasting his easy posture with my own agonised feelings when we descended into a shallow gully. There the path had been washed out and broken so that only a narrow ridge remained, with a drop of three feet to a flooded field below. With more confidence than judgment the leading rider charged full speed at that hazardous crossing, with the result that his wheels skidded over the side. Bicycle, rider and passenger landed with a mighty splash in a foot of mud and water and the convulsive flounderings that ensued reminded me of the sea lions at the zoo.

That misadventure rather spoiled the spiritual appearance of my guide, but he had no word of complaint to make; he just remounted and continued the journey as if one could expect that sort of thing to happen at any time. Needless to say I walked over the broken track, feeling that the hardship of being *on* the bicycle was enough to endure without suffering further damage by being flung off into the mud.

Heavy showers began to fall, and at the next village an umbrella was presented to me, a gift that I tried hard to refuse because of the difficulty of carrying it on my present journey. However, my benefactor insisted, and I rode off carrying the umbrella in one hand and the bouquet in the other.

Our path then left the fields and we were able to proceed for long distances without dismounting, a fact that spurred our riders to greater speeds, and mine in particular to greater efforts with his bell. Speed had got into their blood and there was no stopping them, not for ceremonies or anything else as long as the road was clear. When we were entering a village I saw the chief waiting to greet me, with a file of troops lined up in honour of my passing, but my steed had gone berserk and I was completely out of control. Gathering speed as we went down the street, with the bell ringing continuously, we charged between the head man and his troops while I made frantic efforts to stop my rider, retain my balance, umbrella, and bouquet, acknowledge the greetings of the chief on one side and salute the troops on the other. Everything happened so suddenly that I am not sure how much of that was accomplished, but by the time I was conscious of still being on the bicycle, we were through the village and going across country again.

A similar thing happened once again before we reached our destination, and every time we went through villages or past buildings it was to tear along at full speed, with the bell ringing furiously. We certainly attracted attention, and our riders seemed to be revelling in their unaccustomed importance.

Twice I made surreptitious efforts to lose my bouquet, for as the journey progressed I was having increasing difficulty in keeping my balance. Holding the flowers imposed an added strain that could very well be done without, but it was not to be; those flowers simply could not be lost. Each time I dropped them someone brought them back, and though none of the Chinese could speak more than a word or two of English I was made to understand that it would be very bad luck if they were not taken at least as far as Tamsui.

The last part of the journey was just a fight against insensibility, and I have no recollection of how, or at what time, we entered Tamsui. But I do remember being met by a Portuguese who spoke fluent English, and who informed me that he was an agent of the British Army Aid Group. He insisted that I should dine with him and spend the night at his house, and after some argument with my "Lutheran" guide, that worthy consented to allow me out of his sight for the night.

After a rest I enjoyed the luxury of my first hot bath for more than two years, a luxury we had dreamed about in camp, especially during the winter months when we endured the icy morning showers, and when a biting north-east monsoon whistled around us in the open bath-house. An excellent meal followed, much too excellent for me in my weak state, and that was topped off by a large cup of very strong black coffee. After having eaten so much that coffee was the last thing I should have taken, but my host put me in a defenceless position. He told the story of how a small packet of coffee had recently been delivered to him, the first he had had since the war started, and he had been saving it for a special occasion. He considered that no better occasion than this could arise. So down went the coffee on top of the dinner, and shortly, feeling that my eyes were completely glazed over, I retired to bed. My body was aching in every joint, my brain was racing, and without any way of obtaining relief my stomach was in violent turmoil. The night went by on leaden feet, and I was very pleased indeed when the world about me was once more spinning into dawn.

Arrangements had been made for me to travel to Waichow in a river launch leaving at 9 a.m., and I have little recollection of the journey since I was lying down all the way, incapable of recording any impressions. One fellow-passenger who spoke a little English plied me with interminable questions that were beyond my strength to answer, and he seemed to grow very annoyed at my continuing silence.

We arrived at Waichow at 2.30 p.m., and my guide insisted that I should go with him to the district magistrate. That entailed a walk that lasted fully thirty minutes, and I could have killed that heathen for making me travel so far. Considerable discussion was going on over the disposal of my body, when in came Lieutenant Thomas and a doctor of the British Army Aid Group. Never could anyone have been more pleased to see friends than was I at that moment. They soon brought me to a house that they occupied in a church mission compound, and after having a wash and another overdose of food I was shown to a bed with a spring mattress in the mission hospital. In spite of the marvellous luxury of that mattress I could not sleep, and I remained on my bed all next day, feeling very ill indeed.

The doctor gave me an injection of Vitamin B and also some vitamin pills to swallow, and I settled down for a stay of several days. During that time my health, or at least my feelings, fluctuated in a most astonishing way. One day I saw myself in a mirror and the sight gave me quite a shock, for anything that looked so much like a dead body had no right to be still walking about. My head was filled with turmoil and I was unable to concentrate on anything, so my friends generously refrained from pressing immediately for details of my escape.

The Compound was a most delightful place, with lawns shaded by huge old trees, with flower gardens and a lake on which ducks swam in leisurely contentment. The whole atmosphere of the garden was one of peace and repose, yet when earlier escapers had sheltered there the Japanese had attacked it with their bombers. Every afternoon a reconnaissance plane came over, but apparently the bombers had more important business elsewhere, and they left us alone.

A rumour came through that seven more officers had escaped during the second typhoon after my departure from camp, and thinking that they might belong to a party which I had been invited to join, I was looking forward keenly to seeing them. Days passed and no more word came through, and it proved to be just one more of those mysterious reports which originated out of nothing, spread with amazing rapidity to astonishing distances, and then disappeared to give place to more rumours of equally baseless origin.

The following entry was made in my diary on Sunday the 6th of August. "Lay down all day feeling very ill. Diarrhoea still persists and there is something seriously the matter with my head. Unable to focus my eyes." That followed a night in which a violent shuddering had seized me for more than two hours, a condition which I erroneously attributed to complete nervous exhaustion, but which was in reality the beginning of an attack of malaria. Possibly because of my low state, the fever did not follow its normal course. There was no high temperature and sweating, there were no cold shivers, only at irregular intervals those violent shudders would seize me, shudders that seemed to originate in the uttermost depths of my being, and which left me completely exhausted when they had ceased.

The doctor failed to recognise the symptoms and was encouraging me to go for long walks, at the same time pressing me to eat all manner of rich and indigestible food, such as fat pork chops. I rebelled against those and asked to be able to order my own food from the cook. This he agreed to, and I found a diet of light custards and soups much more suited to my needs. My feet and legs were still far too painful to invite much walking, and as I was quite unable to stand up for an hour or more after each attack of shudders I did not want to roam far for fear of being unable to return home. One night the doctor gave me a sleeping-draught which had a magical effect. After sleeping soundly for three hours I woke up feeling wonderfully refreshed, and wondering what had happened. A profound silence engulfed me, and it was some time before I realised that all the pain and turmoil had gone from my head. It was a marvellous feeling, and it was a pity that it did not last.

Major Cooper, in charge of the British post at Waichow, was doing his best to make me comfortable. His agents produced a supply of toilet requisites, and then they came along with a new shirt and a pair of shorts. They were British Army issue, purchased in a Chinese shop in Waichow. Strange as it may seem, my most prized gift was a small face-towel, for I had been constantly in need of something on which to dry my hands or to wipe my face.

A signal arrived from Kweilin congratulating me on my escape, and informing me that a truck would be sent from there to pick me up at Laolung, which was the terminal for the larger boats that plied up the East River. Plans were made for me to rest for eight days at Waichow, and then travel for four days on the river to Laolung, after which farther progress would depend largely on my health and the state of the war. That at least was a concrete scheme with a reasonably definite schedule, and although the prospect of remaining at Waichow for eight days was irksome, I was very glad to know that I would be soon moving again. The Japanese were still driving south from Hengyang towards Pingshek, and it was through that town that I must pass if my journey was to be continued by road. I was in no condition to attempt any long cross-country trek.

A day or two passed pleasantly enough, and then a little too much concentration brought me down. Major Cooper came in with a collection of photographs that had been on exhibition, pictures from illustrated papers, and I began to look through them. Suddenly a most excruciating pain struck my eyes, a pain that completely blinded me and laid me helpless on the floor. This continued for four hours before it eased off, to leave me limp and exhausted.

One afternoon we went over the story of my escape, and on another day we had a long session discussing the disposition of the Japanese defence-posts round the Argyle Street and Shamsuipo camps. We also talked of the prospects of again establishing regular contact with the camp. Cooper told me that one school of thought was very keen to carry out a raid to rescue all the prisoners in Kowloon, but the difficulty of the terrain made any such venture extremely hazardous until our ships could approach the coast, or until the land forces had been considerably strengthened. There was no doubt that the camps could be opened easily enough, but it would be a very different matter to get the inmates away without such a high casualty rate that the operation would fail in its main purpose of rescue. The first mail to arrive for a month came in one afternoon, among it a bundle of copies of *Life, Picture Post, Punch* and other illustrated papers, all very tempting. But my eyes were in no shape for reading, especially as the memory of my last attempt was so distressingly vivid.

I was ready to go on the 13th of August, but word came that the truck had not been able to leave Kweilin, so I had to contain myself in patience for another three days. Reports were coming in daily of fresh Japanese successes farther north, and chances of reaching Pingshek ahead of them were growing more remote. My health was not improving as it should have been, and my one wish was to reach Kweilin, no matter in what condition, for an American hospital had been established there. From the purely logical viewpoint there was no reason in the world to make so much effort to go on living, life certainly held few attractions, yet a burning hatred of the Japanese made me fiercely determined to cheat them of the satisfaction of having caused my death. If I could reach Kukong ahead of the enemy troops it would still be possible to rejoin a safe road by cutting across country for eighty miles, but if Kukong fell it might take me months to get out. Those thoughts were constantly at the back of my mind, and they kept my nerves on edge.

Saturday, the 12th of August, was calm and sunny, and on that day we visited the Chinese General in charge of the East River Area, to receive from him a pass that would carry me through to Kweilin. It was said that such a pass was not usually granted since the generals had no jurisdiction outside the areas under their immediate control, and though that was true my bona fides were never questioned at any future date.

We had to walk a mile to reach his headquarters, and I had my first really comprehensive view of my surroundings. The Mission Compound was situated on a long point lying between the East River and a tributary that flowed from Tamsui, on a stretch of easy rolling country that afforded vistas of charming rural loveliness. Venerable old trees cast their cool shadows on rich fields of grassland, there were cool green areas of rice, and along the river banks were large clumps and groves of giant bamboo, most handsomely decorative. Small lakes and waterways running in from the river mirrored perfectly the scene about them, while ducks and other water fowl fished or cruised lazily about, sending their tiny bow waves rippling across the still water.

Beyond the confluence of the streams the massed buildings of Waichow proclaimed a large city, and my companions said they would take me there that night to sample the fried chicken at a particular restaurant, which was famed, even in that land of fried chicken, for the excellence of its fare.

Sentries stopped us at the gate of Army Headquarters, and the delay while Major Cooper's papers were examined gave me a welcome rest. The General proved to be a mild inoffensive little man, by appearance much more addicted to the gentle art of philosophic reflection than to the massive planning and vigorous action of modern war. He received us with quiet ceremony, a boy placed tea silently on a small table, and after asking many questions about Hong Kong, the answers to which he probably knew much better than I did, the General handed my pass to Cooper and the interview was over.

My friends hurried off on business bent, while I sauntered slowly home in the sunshine, enjoying the peaceful beauty all about and resting frequently. Even so the journey tired me very much, and my hosts were disappointed when I turned down their offer of an evening in town, for in the full vigour of their youth they could not sense the dreadful feeling of weakness that held me in its grip. The day's walk had already been too much of an effort, and I passed another wakeful night with my heart and brain racing, until morning found me limp and lifeless. Caught in the uttermost depths of exhaustion I spent most of the day in bed.

Cooper told me that my next stop would be made at Hoyuen, twenty-four hours distant by river steamer, where another British officer was established. I was assured of finding good attention and comfort there, for most of the heavy stores belonging to the BAAG had been moved from Waichow to Hoyuen, which was a small place of little importance. The Japanese were expected to reoccupy Waichow at any time, but it was unlikely that they would drive any farther up the river. My kit had been increased by the addition of two sets of underwear, eating utensils, an electric torch, a light soft blanket and a pair of socks. In fact I was completely set up for the entire journey, and wished for nothing more. Shoes were the main trouble, and I was finally fitted with a pair of rope-soled sandals, made to measure in Waichow. They were very comfortable in dry weather, but they became hard and heavy when wet.

A pass written in Chinese was given to me by Major Cooper, and at the same time he informed me that I had been given a Chinese name, the characters of which formed a name which sounded similar to my own, Koo Te Wen. The written characters were shown to me, and I was informed that a "chop" was being made. Just for a joke my friends almost made me believe that I would have to write that name at military check points, and it caused me some worry as I could not see well enough, nor could I concentrate sufficiently, to be able to copy the intricate drawing.

One morning I took a leisurely stroll along the river bank, where the track passed mainly over firm sand, very comfortable on my bare feet. A fresh breeze tempered the heat, and there were patches of soft grass to rest upon in the shade of bamboos. Children passed driving water-buffaloes, huge powerful beasts in perfect condition, their dark-blue coats sleek and shining. Not anywhere else have I seen those fine animals showing evidence of better care or better feeding than they did in that country near Waichow, and I could not help thinking what a price one of them would bring in Hong

Kong, where even the racehorses had been sold over the butchers' counters.

Long narrow river sampans were under way, those going downstream passing swiftly in the middle of the current, those going up creeping along the banks, working into every little bay and eddy, "yolos" helping the sails. It was laborious going, but the crews worked away with a patience and a philosophic disregard for time that made me, who was so anxious to be on my way, feel envious of their calm acceptance of their lot. Their lives were spent on the water, the sampans were their homes and means of livelihood, their interests were those affairs that mean cargoes, food, toil and survival, and their world was compassed by the limits to which their sampans could attain. They were going up the river. The current was strong, but they could overcome it, and one day they would arrive; or perhaps a typhoon or a flood would overwhelm and drown them. What matter if the journey took seven days or fourteen; or if it ended suddenly? Inexorable Fate could not be hurried or delayed; what was to befall would happen at the appointed time, not one hour before, not one hour after. Therefore the wise man accepted what the gods decreed, wasting not his substance in futile yearnings over something which was not to be.

Realising the truth and wisdom of that outlook, yet such serenity was not for me. I was seething with impatience to be off.

That evening I went to the river bank to watch some buffaloes being washed by their youthful masters. How those great animals loved the attention. They lay on their sides in the shallow water while the lads scrubbed them all over with stiff brushes. Finally their necks and heads were carefully though vigorously scrubbed, during which operation the big black eyes of the animals expressed a mingled feeling of gratitude and supreme enjoyment that was laughable to behold.

One morning the Major invited me to go with him to his secret radio station about a mile distant, and very foolishly the invitation was accepted. The pace proved too much for me, and on arrival I could do nothing but lie down at full length to avoid fainting. To make matters worse my head was so clouded that I could not remember the way home, and when left to return at my own speed I wandered astray, and was finally guided back by a small child whose mother had understood my questions.

That was a very bad day, the one bright spot in it being the arrival of a signal announcing the departure of the truck from Kweilin. Arrangements were immediately put in hand for me to travel in a boat sailing the following night, and I was keen to be on my way. The journey up river usually took three days and nights, and that would be followed by a journey by truck over six hundred and fifty miles of atrocious roads. The time for that trip was highly problematical owing to landslides, bogged vehicles, bandits and breakdowns, and in spite of my enthusiasm to go I could not help wondering in what state I would reach Kweilin. Nevertheless it was with a light heart that I made my preparations, for although my hosts were doing their best for me, a feeling persisted that the food and medicines prescribed were making me worse instead of better.

Chapter 10

Waichow to Kukong

My last day, Wednesday, the 16th of August, was spent in lazing about and packing my kit in readiness for the road. A farewell dinner had been arranged for 7 p.m., and before it was over I was feeling somewhat embarrassed with the gifts that were presented. First in importance was my Chinese "chop", carved in characters of old script on the end of a light brown stone. That fitted perfectly into a case of polished buffalo horn, the sliding panel of which fitted so closely that only minute examination could disclose which side the panel was on, and from which end it opened. On one side of the stone there was an inscription in characters which read, "From the members of the British Military Mission, Waichow". The "chop" and case were beautifully made, and the little present which gave me so much pleasure at the time forms one of my most valued souvenirs of the war.

Then a linen handkerchief was given to me by the doctor, and that too had my name finely worked in characters in one corner. Lieutenant Thomas presented me with a half-pound slab of chocolate, while Corporal Tanner parted with a metal mirror in case my glass should be broken. Altogether we had a most enjoyable meal, and I scarcely knew how to thank my friends for all they had done for me in that dangerous and isolated outpost. Dangerous, for every Britisher in China had a high price on his head and there were innumerable traitors, Japanese agents, fifth columnists or just plain bandits who were only too keen to take a chance shot for the reward.

The Customs Station was only five minutes' walk from the Mission, and after dinner we strolled down there to meet the boat from Waichow. When she arrived there was a long delay while police and customs officials carried out an uproarious search, and after a time my friends departed, leaving me in charge of one of their agents, a Chinese who could speak a few words of English. Mr. Wu was given very explicit instructions regarding the attention he should give me, and he occupied an adjoining bunk so that he was always within reach.

The ship was just a shallow pontoon with a deckhouse running almost its entire length.   There was a narrow deck along each side, while inside the deckhouse a narrow passage ran fore and aft right down the middle. On either side of that passage there was a double-deck platform nearly six feet wide on which the passengers slept, heads to the wall, toes to the centre, packed in rows like sardines. I fancy that the upper berths were first-class and the lower ones second, but I am not certain of that and in any case there seemed to be nothing to choose between them. If you felt like luxury you could hire, for a small charge, a thin straw mat to cover the bare boards, but these had little to recommend them as they were no more than one sixteenth of an inch thick. Besides sleeping in your allotted space you also had your meals there, washed, shaved and generally made it your home, for there was nowhere else to go except to the lavatory aft which was reached by the narrow side-deck. In my tottering and generally unstable condition that journey became somewhat hazardous, and more than once I narrowly escaped falling overboard. The only safety device was a small hand-rail, missing in places, along the side of the deckhouse, for bulwarks and rails had been dispensed with so that men could move freely along the side-decks when poling the ship off mud banks.

My bunk was rather too close to the engine room, which was just an open space from which pungent fumes exuded, and as the passengers were shouting all night above the noise of the engines it was impossible to sleep. Also, I was against a narrow athwartship alley, and every other passer-by seemed to jab his elbow into my ribs or poke my legs. The bunk was just a few inches too short, so when my feet were hard against the footboard my head was inclined to protrude a little through the window. That proved to be too much of a temptation to one woman who was a frequent visitor to the stern, and every time she passed she persisted in poking her fan in my eye. The only way to minimise the knocks and bumps was to fold myself up like a jack-knife.

The engine was running on charcoal gas, but by the fiendish noise it was making in all its bearings it sounded as if it were running on road metal, and the mystery was that it ran at all.

One and a half hours after sailing, the ship was hard aground on a shoal, and I had visions of staying there all night, but in a little more than ten minutes stout men with stout poles screwed her off into deep water, and we had no further trouble. Ours was reputed to be the fastest ship on the river, and barring accidents we should reach Hoyuen by dark next evening. I sincerely hoped that all would go well, for twenty-four hours in that cramped space would be ample at one stretch.

A pleasantly cool breeze blew in my window all night, so that morning found me much refreshed. By 7.20 a.m. the river had narrowed to a quarter of a mile, and hills covered with grass rose steeply from its western shore to give welcome variety to a landscape which had been monotonously flat. The contour was the only thing that did change, for there was no colour in the view. Grey cloud spread its pall across the sky, and light rain was falling.

Breakfast consisted of soup followed by poached eggs on a little rice, and though my inside was still very disturbed I could not resist the meal. Possibly Mr. Wu had been told to see that plenty of food was sent to me, for instead of the usual small bowl of soup arriving, a full quart was sent in a bowl like a vegetable dish. First impressions were deceiving, for it looked like a flavourless watery mess with a few green leaves and minute pieces of pork floating about in it, but it was really delicious and I had no difficulty at all in emptying my bowl. The penalty came later when my journeys to the stern were made with monotonous regularity, though in fairness to the soup it could be assumed that most of my trouble was caused by the farewell dinner of the previous night. Although they meant well my hosts had acted with more hospitality than common sense, for they insisted on me eating a fat pork cutlet cooked in thick batter, and in the circumstances I could scarcely refuse.

Late in the morning another bout of shudders had me in its grip, and Mr. Wu was sent off for a pot of hot water. Having taken two aspirins and drunk the water as hot as I could bear it I wrapped myself in a blanket, though all the other passengers were fanning themselves to keep cool. When the shivering was over the usual horrible exhaustion followed in its wake, an exhaustion that gradually wore off as the day advanced.

By the time we reached Hoyuen at 8 p.m. that cycle was completed, so that, when Captain Powell suggested that he hire a chair for my conveyance, I was able to say that it was not necessary and we set off to walk the mile to his home. It was most enjoyable walking in the cool fresh atmosphere after the cramped conditions on board, though I realised that this was a deceptive access of energy that would not last.

Never could anyone have had more generous treatment than that which I received at Hoyuen. A hot bath was prepared at once, there were crisp clean towels, toilet soap and a new pair of pyjamas laid out for me. Then there were pineapples and bananas to eat, and afterwards I was shown to a room with a European-style bed, complete with wire wove and an embroidered pillow. The feeling recurred that this must all be part of some fantastic dream, such a gulf existed between my erstwhile lonely misery and this heavenly situation in which every possible comfort was provided by warm-hearted friends. Sleep was the one thing that they could not give me, but the soft bed was wonderfully restful to a wasted body whose bones had little covering and which had never become really accustomed to sleeping on bare wood.

Next morning it was just the same, every slightest suggestion was acted on at once, and I was quite overwhelmed with gratitude to Mrs. Lee, wife of the Chinese cook, who did everything humanly possible for my comfort. In the midst of all this happiness it was a pity that another attack of fever developed about midday, and in spite of every attention it left me too weak to move from my bed until evening. A barber had been summoned to cut Captain Powell's hair, and as mine badly needed cutting he agreed to cut mine too. Unfortunately for the barber's peace of mind, about half-way through the operation I fell out of the chair and was quite unable to sit up any longer. He waited at least half an hour in the hopes that I might arise and allow him to complete his masterpiece, but at last he took his complaining departure, no doubt feeling that my somewhat ragged coiffure was no great advertisement for his art.

That attack also robbed me of the pleasure of joining in at a special Chinese "Chow" arranged for my benefit, although I did sample a small piece of chicken, beautifully crisp and brown, cooked as only the Chinese can cook it.

Before she retired for the night Mrs. Lee brought in half a dozen slices of pineapple in case I should be thirsty, a little kindness that gave me pleasure beyond anything she could have dreamed.

Staying with Captain Powell at that time was a Russian named Illin, a young man who had had a very interesting and adventurous career as a rolling stone about the byways of China. When the Japanese occupied Hong Kong he was a member of the police force there, and by bluff and fast thinking he had secured a passage to Macao, from which place, by devious routes, he had made his way overland to Hoyuen and the employ of the British Army. Both he and a Chinese runner, Mr. Wu Hing, were to travel with me to Laolung.

Next morning my host gave me a fine khaki woollen pullover in case it should be cold on the journey, and it gave me a surprise to see the maker's tag clearly marked, "Made in Australia". One hardly expected to find British Army supplies in that isolated, far distant outpost, though possibly my own conception of its remoteness was somewhat distorted owing to the difficulties of my journey.

Hoyuen was as far as the large river boats could ply, and from there one had to travel in something much smaller than my ship from Waichow. A rather gloomy picture had been painted of the discomforts of these vessels, and after the trip in the larger craft I was rather dreading the next stage of the journey. However, owing to the forethought of my companions my fears were quite unfounded.

At 8 a.m. we went on board, and there I found that four berths had been booked for the three of us. That gave us ample room to lie fore and aft instead of across the beam, and instead of facing added hardships I found this part of the journey infinitely more comfortable than the last. Illin and Wu did all they could for me, and one big improvement was that we had three thicknesses of blanket to sleep on. The others had their own and Captain Powell had given me an extra one, so spread out on top of each other they took a great deal of hardness from the wood.

Continuous rain kept the temperature at a pleasant level, but the journey left little impression as my shivers returned and I felt too ill to notice much.

A twelve-hour journey brought us to the village of Lum How at 9.30 p.m., and we remained there all night, quite comfortable on a bed on which we could stretch out at full length. This was of particular advantage to Illin, who was at least six feet two inches tall, and who would have had a very uncomfortable time of it trying to sleep across the beam on benches only five feet six inches wide.

Sunday, the 20th August, saw us away soon after daylight, chugging along against the current of a narrow and very beautiful river. But my capacity for receiving impressions had gone altogether, my health had completely broken down, and long periods of semi-consciousness filled most of the journey. At 2 p.m. we pulled in alongside the steep river bank at Laolung, and my two companions almost carried me up to a cobbled pathway where a chair was waiting.

Accommodation had been arranged at a reasonably clean and comfortable hotel, and I was carried straight there to my room, to bed, and to a haze in which Illin and Wu Hing appeared fleetingly. They were making inquiries and arrangements on my behalf, but by that time I was beyond caring or taking any further interest.

Late in the afternoon Mr. Davis, of the Seventh Day Adventist Mission, called to see me, though I do not know how he learned of my arrival. He immediately began to be extremely helpful in a most practical way, realising my very low condition and making plans accordingly. He asked if I would like to see a doctor, and the answer was, "Yes, please, as soon as possible".

It was not long before he returned with Dr. Chun, a Chinese who had been trained in England, and who had worked in English hospitals. The doctor listened to my story and immediately diagnosed malaria, taking a blood-test to verify it. However, he was so certain that that was my trouble that he gave me an injection and some quinine pills to swallow and he said that two or three days' treatment would make me feel much better. My sincere hopes were that he was right, for the fever had been upon me for almost three weeks then, and I was feeling like death itself. My thoughts towards the doctor at Waichow were far from complimentary, for I had been very ill there for a week and he had never suggested that fever might be the trouble, nor had he made any tests to check my condition. Now a more generous view can be taken, for it must be admitted that none of the usual symptoms were present, and my belief is that my whole system was so starved and exhausted that there was little left in me for the fever germs to thrive on.

Mr. Davis proved to be a man of considerable energy, and towards evening he came back with a most marvellous mattress filled with rice straw, fully six inches thick. No bed of feather-down could have felt more soothing to my aching bones than did that simple mattress, and I was at a loss to know how to convey my gratitude for an act akin to ushering me through the portals of the promised land. But he had not finished yet, and when I was comfortably installed he produced a meal of malt syrup, whole-meal wheat bread, and some stewed pears.

It all seemed vividly reminiscent of some fairy tale of long ago, when Prince Charming escapes after untold hardships from the clutches of the Wicked King, and finds himself at last in the friendly and healing hands of the Good King, who heaps kindness and hospitality upon the miserable wanderer. Only in this case Prince Charming was translated into my own unprepossessing self, and there was no danger of a Beautiful Princess casting languorous eyes in my direction.

Such thoughts were drifting aimlessly about the hazy space that was my mind, and I made several efforts to pin them down to those realities which were actually occurring in a remote Chinese village; a village which, in the course of centuries, had witnessed the passing of only a handful of Europeans.

When everything possible had been done Mr. Davis took his departure, promising to send more food next day, and I settled down to a night of fevered imaginings. The quinine was making me feel rather sick in the stomach, but during the morning a deep sleep claimed me for three hours, the longest and most refreshing sleep I had had since leaving camp. Dr. Chun came again in the evening and found my temperature down to ninety-nine degrees, so he was quite pleased with that, and after giving me another injection and more quinine pills, he said that the fever would soon be better.

Then followed two days of fitful sleep, and a most amazing series of acts of thoughtful kindness. Always in the background was Mr. Davis, and his cook, preparing meals that arrived steaming hot in metal containers, and it seemed that each time I awoke there was something more appetising than the last on the little table by my bed.

The doctor pronounced my fever gone, and he said that good food and plenty of rest would soon put me back into circulation. That was good news, for when a bath had been prepared for me I could hardly recognise the shaking skeleton that stepped into it.

Major Urquhart and Captain Hutchinson arrived with the truck from Kweilin, Hutchinson on his way to Waichow, while the Major said he would return with me to Kukong as soon as the truck had been repaired. The old vehicle had almost breathed its last on the roads of China, and after several more or less serious breakdowns on the journey from Kweilin, repairs were going to take several days

Major Urquhart bought a rattan chair to add to my comfort, and that gave most welcome relief from the pain of sitting on the usual hard bamboo seats. Eggs, whole-meal bread, cabbage, chicken and bananas were in plentiful supply, and with the aid of those, all hands were doing their best to make me roadworthy again. Their combined efforts quickly achieved results, and on Friday, the 25th, five days after my arrival, I awoke after a restful night feeling immeasurably improved, and looking forward to a walk through the town.

As in all Chinese towns the streets of Laolung were narrow, tortuous and smelly, the cobbled ways having been built for pack-ponies and human bearers rather than for wheeled traffic. It was rather surprising to see how well stocked the shops were, though it was noticeable that most of the goods were of local origin.

The Major, Illin, Wu Hing and I walked slowly along to the Seventh Day Adventist Mission School, and after entering the garden through a fine avenue of trees we were greeted by one of the teachers, a Chinese girl with a strong American accent. In common with most of the Mission Schools seen in China this one was in a beautiful setting, and life there seemed to be very pleasant.

From there we strolled on to a tea-house overlooking a small lake, and settled down at a table near a window. The view took in fields of vividly green paddy stretching away to purple hills in the distance. Ducks were diving along the lake shore, feeding on the bottom, with their tails vertical and feet paddling the air in their efforts to grub deeper in the mud. Buffaloes were submerged to their noses to keep the flies away, and from somewhere out of sight along the river bank came the unmistakable thump, thump, thump of a boat builder's caulking mallet. It was a perfect scene of peaceful rural charm, and, since the noise and tumult had left my head, I was able to sit calmly and thoroughly enjoy the natural beauty all about.

Cakes and bowls of fresh boiled milk were brought, milk from buffalo cows, and to my unaccustomed palate it was the best milk I had tasted. A second bowl was brought before we left that delightful spot, and then I was very glad to climb into a chair to be carried back to the hotel, feeling tired but very much better for the outing.

News was brought that the truck was ready, and plans were made to leave at eight o'clock next morning. Major Urquhart was fixing a bed for me, and he was also lashing the rattan chair to the side of the truck so that I could sit up for a change. According to all reports a journey by truck over those roads was not one to be undertaken lightly, and though I was feeling much stronger we were going in easy stages, taking three days to reach Kukong instead of the usual two and a half.

Saturday, the 26th of August, saw me up betimes, packing my gear in readiness for an early start, but a telegram arrived to say that a mail-bag was on its way to our first stopping-place at Tangtap, and that we must wait for it there. That meant that there was no need to hurry, and I was only too glad to be able to lie down for most of the morning. Our party for Kweilin was growing, for Mr. Davis and one of his Chinese associates were also going with us.

We left about noon, and I must say that the Major had excelled himself in providing for my comfort. A bed of deep straw had been made athwartships just behind the cab, the straw being kept in place by a blanket drawn tightly over it and wedged down by the cargo. For this truck was a real cross-country tourer, and beneath its matting roof, stretched over semicircular iron hoops, there was a tremendous pile of oddments, among which two fifty gallon drums of petrol were major items. There were several cases, some boxes of ammunition, the luggage of the passengers, a Tommy gun, rifles and pistols for the men, and my rattan chair looking like a throne in its uncluttered seclusion.

In the Chinese Press there was a report that the Allies had landed in Norway and that Germany had sued for peace, but the Chinese news was notoriously unreliable and we took no notice of this latest headline.

In spite of the rough going I rode in astonishing comfort, and there was a convenient peephole low down in the cover through which I could admire the view. The road climbed and wound along the sides of low hills of no great altitude, and then it levelled out over a richly fertile plain. There were fields of sugar-cane, peanuts, soya beans, sweet potatoes, taro, green beans and other crops which I could not recognise; all of those in addition to the endless rice fields.

At 3 p.m. we reached Tangtap, and there Davis took charge of me. He had been in China for twenty years, many of them spent deep in the interior, and he knew all there was to know about Chinese food. First he ordered a bowl of boiling water, and then proceeded to wash all the utensils that we were to use, drying them with his own cloth brought for the purpose. It made me smile to think of the feelings of one of our fashionable restaurateurs if his customers came in and washed all the dishes on the table before they commenced to dine. No doubt our host thought these mad foreigners were over particular, but he made no comment, and I must say that the precaution appeared to be highly necessary. Quite apart from the sketchy wash they had originally received, the dishes had been left lying about where dozens of flies used them as a playground, and I made a vow to stick to Mr. Davis for the remainder of the journey.

We had rice, greens, bean curd and lightly scrambled eggs, and there was no holding us once fairly started on this sample of light fare. My friends ordered exactly the type of food to suit my needs, and on each day of the journey to Kweilin I was to enjoy a variety of fine dishes which did not look sufficiently appetising to temp one who was ignorant of their worth, and which I certainly would not have risked without someone to lead me.

While we were dining Captain Powell arrived with the mail from Hoyuen, and knowing that he had not been well I was surprised to see him looking so fresh after his long journey. When told that he was coming on foot I doubted very much whether we would see him at all that day, but we soon discovered that he had been carried in a chair. The endurance of the Chinese carriers is simply astounding, and no one seemed to think it at all unusual that Powell had been transported up hill and down for thirty miles in nine and a half hours.

A second runner also arrived with a bag of mail, and by that time we were a party which the Japanese would have been very pleased to capture, for we then had a package containing complete copies of the enemy records of prisoners of war in Hong Kong, besides other strictly secret information. Those records had been acquired by a brilliantly daring piece of patient espionage. It gave me a great deal of amused satisfaction to read the official Japanese report of my own escape, and to contemplate the loss of face with which the camp commandant must have conveyed that information to his superiors.

Leaving again at 4.30 p.m. we drove through a pleasant fertile valley to the outskirts of Chungshun, where there was a Catholic Mission Station. Father O'Brien was absent, but arrangements were made for me to stay the night there, while the others went on to find accommodation in the village.

The Mission occupied a large building of two storeys, with high airy rooms and large windows, delightfully clean and cool. There, as elsewhere, everything possible was done for my comfort, and after dinner I was shown to a soft bed made up complete with mosquito net. Someone there was a naturalist, for scattered about the rooms and corridors were cages of birds, animals and reptiles. In a large earthenware jar in my room several white rats were feeding on grain, and as there was no cover of any kind on the jar I had visions of being invaded by them in the night. There were also several baskets of snakes, but in spite of these unusual room-mates I soon sank into a deep and dreamless sleep. A new day was already starting with a gloriously fine and clear morning when I awakened, and although my legs were still badly swollen with beriberi I was feeling much better and looking forward to going on again.

From my window there was a delightful view over an extensive plain through which a river wound its way, while beyond that the horizon was ringed with mountains. Down below, on one side of the house, there was a garden where tall maize, taro, sweet potatoes and beans were growing, while in front of the house bright flowers made a pretty garden round a lawn. Handsome trees spread their sheltering branches, motionless in the still morning air. There were the roofs and buildings of a village about two miles away, and in my moments of relaxation it seemed that this would be an ideal place in which to rest, to recuperate, and to forget. Then the urge to be off would return in all its nervous intensity, and I knew that there could be no rest until risk of recapture was far behind, and I was deep in the security of our own forces.

Soon after breakfast the truck arrived from Chungshun, and after my hosts had been suitably thanked for their hospitality we started off. The road began to climb, and soon it began to twist and turn in a tortuous struggle upwards, clinging precariously to a steep mountain-side. Slips partially blocked the way at frequent intervals, and when passing those, or rounding hairpin bends, our wheels skirted close along the outside edge from which the ground fell precipitously for hundreds of feet to a rushing stream. It was no road for a driver with poor nerves, and though our man was not afflicted in that way, his driving was of such a poor standard that I was far from happy in his care.

We must have climbed at least three thousand feet to the summit of that range, and then we began a long descent into the village of Linping. After lunch our tortuous journey was resumed, the road climbing again through narrow mountain gorges, though not rising to nearly such a height as it had done in the morning.

It was refreshing at last to come out of those gloomy defiles into a fertile plain where water-lilies were blooming in ponds along the roadside, and where rice fields and villages lent a more friendly aspect to the scene. The lilies were cultivated, for the Chinese use the roots as a vegetable, although without special treatment they are completely flavourless. The Japanese frequently supplied them as rations to the camp, but even after hours of boiling we could do nothing with them, they were so tough and hard. Our captors had agreed to supply a certain weight of vegetables each day, and lily roots were very useful for that purpose, for they usually came in caked with wet mud which weighed very heavily. Even as firewood they were scarcely worth their weight, and as food their value was exactly nil.

Steep, fantastic limestone mountains rose menacing beside the road, and we skirted their shadowing flanks to rumble into the village of Lungshien. That sizeable place boasted a clean and fairly new hotel, and it was very comforting, after a warm wash, to relax over a leisurely pot of tea. The bed in the truck had been a great success, and the travelling was no great hardship as long as the stages were reasonably short. However, my left foot and leg were still badly swollen, and periods of exhaustion persisted.

Next morning the party was roused early, and we were on the road again at seven o'clock. A straight road with a good surface ran through a wide fertile valley for the first few hours, and we made good time, following the course of a swiftly flowing river.

We stopped for refreshments at a spot where shade, trees and level sward made a cool picnic ground. There an old water-wheel was turning, raising two long arms by a primitive arrangement of wooden cams. At the extremity of each arm was a heavy pestle armed with iron, and as each cam bore down on the butt end of the arm, so the pestle was swung upwards until the apex of the cam passed and let it drop with a thud into a tiny well from which rice husks continually surged upwards. The only metal in that primitive contraption was on the end of the pestle, yet it looked as if it had been turning there for years. This was a simple milling machine, with no one in attendance, and there were only husks in the well.

Soon the road began to twist through uninteresting mountain passes, and we began to overtake Nationalist troops on their way to the northern front. All along our route small detachments had been encountered, but here was a large force on the march.

Never have I seen a body of men, except prisoners of war, in such a pitiable state. Uniforms and equipment were in tattered shreds, while hardly any of the men had boots. Except for hand grenades, which were quite efficient, their arms were ancient and worthless. Eighty per cent, of the men bore obvious signs of malnutrition, beriberi and pellagra were present in many forms, while nearly all had large running ulcers and many kinds of skin disease. They had the utmost difficulty in keeping on the move, and it was common for men to drop out by the roadside, to lie there and die. Not that they lay a long time and died slowly, death had already come while they still struggled along. It was only when the spirit could sustain the flesh no longer that the worn-out husk collapsed, and one more mortal found his eternal peace. The dead were to be envied; it was the living for whom we felt sorry.

Many have been the words of derision heaped upon the Chinese soldier, but how could those poor devils fight against the Japanese, or anyone else? Even had they had the strength to fight, what incentive could they possibly have? Conscripted into the army against their will in the first place, then systematically starved and deprived of almost every human right by corrupt officers who looked sleek and well groomed, why should they throw their lives away in hopeless war against an efficiently equipped enemy, who at least had the promise of loot and unbridled licence to spur him on? No; the blame for the collapse in 1944, when, after the fall of Hengyang, the Japanese drove virtually unopposed through the provinces of Kwangtung and Kwangsi and overwhelmed the American airfields, cannot be laid at the door of the Chinese soldier. One must look higher to the ranks of the senior officers and the politicians.

With Kukong some twenty miles ahead we took time off to visit the largest and most ornate Buddhist temple in Kwangtung. There were many buildings and terraces, the temple itself being guarded, just inside the entrance, by three huge gilded Buddhas some fifteen feet in height. All round the interior, right to the roof, were hundreds of coloured porcelain figures three feet in height, all representing real or mythical figures in Chinese history. Devils were well represented with their savage hideous faces and bared fangs, while there were many venerable old gentlemen with flowing beards, obviously poets or scholars of renown. Even Marco Polo was there, albeit his features had taken on a distinctly Oriental character, and his mother would have found him hard to recognise.

This temple was founded by three brothers, and their preserved bodies were among the proudest exhibits of this monument to their energy. The faces of the founders had been so frequently lacquered with a brown varnish that they might just as well have been made of wood or anything else, for though the features remained, one would never suspect that they were genuine human remains.

After that little interlude we had a large lunch before going on to Kukong. The delay had been enforced, since no traffic was allowed to move in the city between 8 a.m. and 2 p.m. The Japanese had frequently raided the place, always between those hours, and the restriction had been introduced to keep down casualties. Actually Kukong had been virtually evacuated, nearly all the buildings being in charge of caretakers, while the residents had been dispersed around the outskirts of the town. For a long time there had been raids or alerts every day, and I hoped that the Japanese would not time one of their visits to coincide with our arrival.

With only four kilometres to go, with the city clearly in view at the end of a straight level road, the engine spluttered a few times and then died altogether. The cause was a blocked petrol-pipe which proved difficult to clear, and our entry to Kukong was accomplished with a Chinese sitting on our starboard mudguard feeding petrol into the carburettor from a tin. With continuous priming and coaxing the motor took us through narrow, winding, congested streets in the city, and then out to the British Army Aid Group Headquarters situated two miles beyond.

Major Urquhart was established in a wooden house nicely situated among some old trees, on a hillside from which one obtained an extensive view across Kukong and the rolling country beyond. The Japanese knew that British were in residence there, but they had made only one strafing attack on the house, when many bullets went through the building without causing any casualties.

With that knowledge in mind I was sitting on the veranda admiring the view when an air-raid warning sounded in the town, and I wasted no time in looking for a ditch to dive into in case anything should come our way. The Americans had a similar "Intelligence" organisation, housed four hundred yards away, and their building too had been subjected to strafing attacks, but the Major assured me that the Japanese much preferred the larger target of the town.

My route to safety having been decided upon I sat back in a marvellously comfortable cane chair, and while awaiting the advent of the planes was served with afternoon tea, tea with fresh milk, biscuits with best quality margarine, and strawberry jam. There was no wind, smoke drifted up from many kitchen fires about the town, and everything was so serene and peaceful that the war seemed to belong to another world. Yet even here Death stalked abroad in all his ugly guises, and in a recent round-up, one hundred and thirty pro-Japanese terrorists had been caught and executed in the environs of Kufkong. I was warned not to wander too far from the house without a gun, for sudden death was liable to spurt from behind the trunks of those pleasant shady trees. The warning was well heeded, for it was no part of my programme to leave my body on some hillside in remotest China, no matter how beautiful the setting.

The planes apparently had business elsewhere, and replete with rich food I drowsed off, feeling that life could hold nothing better than this calm, lazy, supremely comfortable residence, seemingly so remote from the intensity of effort which culminated on the blazing war fronts of the world.

Towards evening the commanding officer of the American station, Colonel Scott, came over for a few minutes, and he proved to be most friendly, very willing to do everything in his power to assist. When he learned of the (decrepit condition of our truck he offered to let me ride in a weapon-carrier that he was sending through, even saying that he would install a spring cot for me. Although the offer was very tempting I could not desert my friends at that stage, so the Colonel gave me a supply of ration biscuits, candy and vitamin tablets to help me on my way, gifts that were much appreciated.

Colonel Scott was the first American officer I met in China, but I met many more later, and the initial impressions gained in Kukong were strengthened as my journey progressed. So much so in fact, that on a number of occasions during my journey through India, when prejudiced persons were unfairly and ignorantly criticising Americans, my comments were usually more pointed than polite. My associations with Americans in China left me with nothing but the warmest feelings of regard for their spontaneous friendship and generous assistance.

While evening shadows settled down, my day ended with a big meal topped off with stewed pears and custard. This was the realisation of dreams of two and a half years of starvation, when thoughts of food occupied an inordinate number of our waking hours, and if I dwell too much on meals that normally are commonplace, you must remember that to me that food was sheer ecstasy.

Next morning was fine and calm, and it caused me no sorrow at all to learn that the truck needed repairs that would take at least two days to complete. Rest and still more rest was my great need, and days passed pleasantly enough just in eating colossal meals and in sleeping. The Chinese servants were most friendly and attentive, and while I slept they whisked all my clothes away to repair and launder them.

The Japanese southward drive from Hengyang was still my chief concern, for the only road from east to west ran through Pingshek, sixty miles north of Kukong, and if we failed to arrive there before the enemy we would have to leave the truck and trek seventy miles across country before we met the road again. It would have been quite impossible for me to accomplish the journey on foot at that time, and no matter how I was transported the trip would have been one of intense hardship. The Major assured me that Pingshek was still quite safe, while Colonel Scott said that he had trucks running every day to a post twenty-five miles north of Pingshek, and even that place was in no immediate danger.

My afternoon was somewhat spoiled by the arrival of a Catholic missionary of the worst type, a priest who was nothing but a beggar of the most detestable kind, playing his religion to the utmost in his efforts to enrich himself.

He poured his story out to the Major for more than an hour, and though I was in an adjoining room, feeling too weak to walk more than a hundred yards, that wretch's whining voice roused me to such a pitch of fury that it would have been a pleasure to kick him from there to the city. The priest had by some means, certainly without payment, acquired a powerful new motor cycle, and his immediate concern was to sell it by fair means or foul to the British Army. As there were no roads in the vicinity on which such a machine could possibly be used the Major was not interested, but the beggar whined and wheedled, and when he at last felt sure that a sale could not be effected, he started all over again on a new line, trying to beg free transport for himself and his cycle to Kweilin or Kunming. Nothing was beyond his powers of request. And be it known that he was not prepared to bargain about the price, he wanted half a million Chinese dollars, which at rates then prevailing might have been anywhere between the lowest rate of £600 and the official rate of £3,375. Even the lowest figure would represent a very good return for a useless article that had most assuredly been acquired for nothing.

The Major, although he remained adamant in his refusal to become a party to any of these schemes, retained a courtesy and tolerance which to me seemed little short of miraculous, and I was longing to hear his boot meet the visitor where it would do most good.

The day had been warm and sunny, so to calm my feelings I climbed slowly to an eminence which provided a splendid view across Kukong, and beyond to mountains which rose tier upon tier to the far distant skyline. At that point the North River was broad and shallow, and the city of Kukong occupied a large island in the middle, besides spreading along either bank. It was an empty city, peopled by soldiery, guards and the ghosts of its former inhabitants. A law forbade anyone to enter the town without a permit, and should a person be wounded there without possession of such a pass he would not only suffer from his injury, he would be fined as well.

That evening we paid a visit to the American station to listen to the BBC news, but reception was ruined by static, so we were yarning and enjoying the clear moonlit night when gongs of an air-raid warning sounded from the town. We stayed out to watch the fireworks, but the planes had other business and they roared past overhead without dropping their loads. There were dark glades to pass through on the way home, and it was not very comforting to remember that there was a high reward for the killing of an Allied officer, the scale rising with rank, and I was very glad to have a pistol on my hip.

The truck was in worse shape than we had thought, and we were delayed for four full days in Kukong. One of the worst faults occurred when the engine was running under test, for a new bearing ran so hot that it seized up. This could have occurred only through sheer carelessness, but there was nothing one could do about it. My nerves were racing and these delays appeared to be designed especially to hold me back, the feeling growing upon me daily that I would never succeed in escaping from this vast country, that held me with its distances and its inadequate roads as effectively as if I were held in by the enemy.

The days passed in eating, in lazing, reading a little and dozing. My eyes were still in bad shape, and sometimes half a day would pass before I could focus them clearly on any point. Also, the swelling would not leave my legs. Those were the visible symptoms of my debility, but the main trouble was a horrible weakness, as if every last vestige of strength had been burned from my body.

On the evening of Wednesday, the 30th August, six weeks and three days after my escape, the Major, Illin and I were invited to dine at the home of Colonel Scott. Arriving there we found him inundated with new arrivals, eight officers and about a dozen other ranks who had come in from Kweilin in four weapon-carriers. They had a great deal of radio equipment with them, and were part of the organisation that was rapidly being built up in China against the day when the war would be concentrated on Japan. It was good to see them there, and I am sure their presence must have been a great comfort to the many British agents who had been isolated in those areas for so long.

Some of the equipment was immediately put into use, and instead of struggling to hear the news through a maze of interference, we were treated to the BBC version as if it were coming from the next room. And the whole broadcast was full of disasters for the enemy and optimistic forecasts. Quite obviously Germany was rapidly cracking, and it gave us wonderful satisfaction to hear that clear voice recounting the deeds that spelt the ruin of the Nazi Colossus. We heard of the rapidly mounting weight and intensity of the air raids over Germany, of the battered towns and industries lying in their wake, and the significant news of the hardening attitudes of Rumania, Bulgaria and Finland.

A very good dinner, and the company of men who were really doing something in the war, made the evening most enjoyable after the weary months of utter negation in the prison camp.

The new arrivals gave a bad report of some parts of the road we were to travel, for the recent rains had caused many landslides and there were stretches where trucks were bogged down, resting on their chassis in the mud. The hazards of the road were such that Major Urquhart elected to accompany us to Kweilin, a very comforting decision as he carried a Government order which entitled him to receive assistance from any Chinese military or civil authority to which he might apply. This arrangement meant a delay of one more day, but that was nothing compared with the advantages which might be gained.

Just before nightfall a big "Liberator" began circling over the town, and it continued to fly round for three hours before the drone of its motors finally died away. We could only guess what its mission might be.

On the first of September news came that the truck had passed its tests, and that we would certainly leave on the morrow. It was a fine sunny day and there were several air-raid warnings of first and second degree, but no planes came over the town. The first alarm, two bells rung at regular intervals, was given when enemy planes were reported in the air. The second, groups of three bells, was given when the planes were headed towards the city, and the third, a continuous ringing of the bell, was given when they would pass directly overhead.

My day was spent in lazing with my feet up, for although I had walked only short distances on the previous day my legs were more swollen than they had ever been, and rest was of prime importance.

Chapter 11

Kukong to Kweilin

Next morning we left Kukong, our armament increased by a Tommy-gun loaned by the Americans, our passengers increased by the addition of five Chinese women. These people were the wives of Chinese employed as British agents, and they were being evacuated to safety before the Japanese could use them for the practice of their devilries. No torture or mutilation was too frightful to be meted out to such as these should they fall into the hands of the enemy.

An easy run brought us to Lokchong, at which place it was advisable to put the truck on a train for the short run to Pingshek. That section of line, about twenty miles of it, was the only part of the Canton-Hankow railway still in existence in Kwangtung Province. For three days we had been driving alongside the site of the track, but there was not one rail, one sleeper or one girder of a bridge to be seen; they had all been spirited away. But there was plenty of evidence that the enemy was well acquainted with the activity at Lokchong, for there were many blasted locomotives and wagons hurled down the river bank, or lying where they had been cast aside after bombs had done their worst with them.

With the truck lashed down on a flat-top car we started off, the other passengers riding in a carriage, while I preferred the horizontal ease of my couch. This railway followed the river deep down in a steep narrow gorge, frowning mountainsides preventing the penetration of low-flying planes, and no damage had been suffered by the track.

Our journey to Pingshek was uneventful, but having arrived there safely it was a miracle that the truck did not capsize in its descent from the flat car. There was no way of unloading except over the side, and a platform of heavy planks was placed diagonally from the road to the deck of the flat. Considering the number of trucks being transported it was amazing to think that such a highly dangerous arrangement could be tolerated for more than a day or two without being remedied, but the Chinese are a notoriously fatalistic race.

The reason for this train haul was that between Lokchong and Pingshek a very rough road climbed tortuously over a range estimated variously to be from three to five thousand feet in height, the driving time for the trip being at least five hours. By train we saved three and a half hours, a great deal of wear on truck and tyres, and over and above the freight charge some CNC $30,000 worth of petrol. It was no wonder that the railway was popular.

Pingshek was a mushroom town clinging precariously to a mountain-side, more than half the buildings showing the bright newness of their construction, and all accommodation was packed with refugees fleeing from the threatened areas to the north. We were lucky to secure rooms in a clean hotel built in modern style, its main disadvantage being that it had the usual Chinese wooden beds, and my bones were still much too close to the surface to enable me to lie on wood with any degree of comfort.

Sleep eluded me, and I was glad when grey daylight began to filter through an atmosphere that held a soft transparent mist of motionless suspension. Cries of the street vendors soon roused us into action, and after a satisfying breakfast we started off on the next stage of this fantastic journey, a seventy-six mile run to Linshien.

Most of that day's travel took us through wide open valleys bounded by low rolling hills, wooded with the largest pines I had yet seen in China. There was little cultivation anywhere and only a sparse population, for this was a lawless land where lack of security discouraged pioneering. A violent rain and thunderstorm swept over us, our matting-cover leaked like a sieve, and most of us received a thorough soaking. The experience made me hope that fine weather would favour us, for it was easy to imagine the state we and our luggage would be in after several days of jolting, and wetting, and trampling.

Late afternoon found us on top of a ridge from which we looked down on a broad valley in which an intensely dark grey township stretched along the bank of a river. This was Linshien, a typical Chinese town with its narrow streets, its teeming population, its buildings crowding and leaning against one another, with its pervading smell of cooking, of filth, of decay, and of dried foods of revolting odour.

The road down was much longer than we thought, but at last we came out on to level ground, skirted the town, crossed the river on an old pontoon ferry poled by stolid men who cared not if it took ten minutes or ten days to cross, and finally drove into the compound of an American Presbyterian mission run by Mr. and Mrs. Kunckle. This mission was in a most beautiful setting, with rambling buildings, huge old trees, lawns, and a school with a large attendance of happy-looking youngsters. Inside there was an atmosphere of friendly hospitality, and Mr. Kunckle said that they were always prepared to accommodate from eight to ten travellers who might arrive unannounced. Already several guests were staying at the house, and after our arrival three Americans came in. These men had come through from Kukong in a weapon-carrier, and they certainly looked as if they had had a wearing journey.

Everything that our hosts could do they did to make us comfortable, and then they presided in true colonial style at a dinner of delicious food served by well-trained Chinese boys. Here was the perfect existence of the foreigner in China, as pictured in the pages of romantic fiction. The evening passed rapidly in talk, for we were a varied band of wanderers in a strange land, and a great variety of adventures had befallen us. Most widely travelled "China Hand" was Bishop Hall, a name that carried an aura of fame that called for hushed voices when mentioned, but I am afraid that in my heathen ignorance it failed to make its due impression.

The Bishop was also on his way to Kweilin, and although we were already uncomfortably overcrowded the Major agreed to take him too. Fortunately for us there was plenty of room on the newly arrived weapon-carrier, so, with his numerous large boxes, our notable companion was given passage in that. Soon my head began to sag, and I excused myself from the party to settle down on the finest spring bed it had yet been my good fortune to find in all China. Not that my blissful rest was of long duration, for this was one of the traditional nights when devils were abroad in Linshien, and gongs and bells made a terrific racket all night long in their valiant efforts to keep the evil spirits off.

Maybe one more daring than the rest had secreted himself in our very compound, for when the portals were being opened for our exit next morning the whole massive gate crashed to the ground, several children who had come to see us off having a most fortunate escape from serious injury.

When the wreckage had been cleared away we waved goodbye as we swayed and skidded down the slippery approach road. All drivers of vehicles proceeding east had been unanimous in their condemnation of the roads they had traversed, and we knew that an unpleasant journey was in store. Landslides, washouts, damaged bridges, hairpin bends, slippery surfaces and precipices all lent their quota of hazards by the way, and we hoped sincerely that the weather would remain fine. The most cheerful part of the news was that the road was improving as there had been no rain for three or four days, and gangs were working at all the worst sections.

Well! we had been warned, and we were not disappointed. Hour after hour we struggled in low gear over an atrocious surface, and when trying to pass a truck that was down on its chassis in the mud, we stuck too. A horde of Chinese was milling round the other vehicle making ineffectual efforts to extricate it, and the unfortunate crew were fully occupied in trying to protect their load, instead of in giving constructive aid to the job.

When we asked him for assistance the leader of that gang of bandits demanded a fee that was almost half the value of the truck. We refused to agree to such an exorbitant charge, and going to work ourselves with shrubs and pieces of timber, we had the extreme satisfaction of running the truck out on to a firm surface after only fifteen minutes' work. In an hour that bad spot could easily have been made passable, for right alongside there was a high bank, heavily wooded with trees suitable for fascines. No doubt the Chinese found the bogged trucks highly lucrative, and they would make no move to repair the road as long as their source of income remained attractive.

The next block was complete, with two trucks embedded alongside each other, and there was nothing we could do but wait on firm ground until one of the wrecks was moved. Temporary repairs were made to the road, and then we sailed through the bad patch, going downhill at a good speed and slithering right through to safety. The truck was certainly taking punishment, but it was still going.

We had intended to stay the night at Patpo, but through various delays it was five o'clock before we rolled into the village of Tailing, some thirty miles short of our objective. An American who had just arrived from Patpo advised us strongly not to try to go through until next day, for he said that there was a two-mile climb over a very greasy hill which would almost certainly stop us for the night. He had just survived a number of very narrow escapes from skidding over a precipice, and he spoke with some knowledge and feeling. As there was no need to take undue risks we followed his advice, and a number of other trucks also remained until next morning. Our friend handed over some of his rations, about a dozen packets of biscuits, some tins of pork sausage, dried fruit bars and thick chocolate for making cocoa. He said he was being issued with more than he could eat as he preferred to live on the fresh Chinese food.

Tailing was not prepared for such a large influx of tourists, and the only rooms available were in a very poor hotel where there was a great noise of people shouting and tramping about all night. Sleep was quite out of the question with such a racket going on, and I was very glad when daylight brought the relief of action once more.

We were up and ready for the road bright and early, but more trouble with the petrol-pipe delayed us until half past eight. All the other trucks, about a dozen of them, had left at least two hours earlier, so we felt very much like laggards who had been too lazy to get up in time. Actually the delay was all to the good, for a hot sun came out during the morning, and by the time we reached the worst section of road the surface had been dried off until it presented not the slightest difficulty. For some reason or other I had been feeling very apprehensive of this stretch of road, the culmination of forebodings which weighed very heavily on me at Kukong. At that time all the dangers that had been successfully passed seemed as nothing compared with those gloomy fears that haunted my imagination and gripped my heart in sudden spasms of terror. No foundation in dream or premonition existed to sustain that feeling of impending disaster, yet it seemed that a great weight was lifted from my shoulders when we passed that hill of bad repute, and ran out on to a smooth level road.

Like so many other obstacles that tower menacing before us through the course of life, this one had crumbled into in-significance under the onslaught of direct attack; but who knows what danger may have been there? With different timing all the elements of tragedy might have fused in a tangled wreck among the rocks below, instead of which we actually experienced one of the best stretches of road on the trip. But it was plain to see why rain made it so dangerous, and I was very glad that the road was dry when we passed.

Our spirits rose as we ran along at good speed, until an unusually violent jolt set the motor racing. A pin had been sheared or dislodged from the clutch-plates, and we crawled along the last few miles to Patpo, unable to attain more than walking-pace. Had we known what was in store for us our impatience would have known no bounds, for our rendezvous was at a mission station where every comfort was provided and an excellent lunch was laid. My appetite was assuming disgusting proportions, and after more than doing justice to the good fare provided I felt like nothing so much as stretching out for an afternoon siesta. However, there was still a long way to go to Pinglo, our objective for the night, and when the truck had been repaired once more we started off in fine style, on a road sufficiently smooth to allow an average speed of thirty miles an hour. The scenery was now beginning to change, for we were well into Kwangsi Province and approaching the limestone mountains. All along the western skyline there rose a fantastic pattern of square blocks and pointed turrets, just like some artificial rampart of a colossal fortress.

Fifteen miles short of Pinglo the feed-pipe blocked again, and the motor spluttered to a stop. That looked like the end of our good fortune, for night was coming on and there was no town of any size nearby. The old trick of feeding petrol through the carburettor was tried again, and this took us on for two or three miles before the engine failed altogether, to leave us stranded. It was then 10.30 p.m., and it was agreed that the women should go to a small village which we had just passed, while the men would sleep at the truck to guard it. Nothing could be left anywhere on those roads without a heavily armed guard, and the seriousness of the bandit menace was brought home to us when the party with the women arrived at the village.

A great deal of shouting and argument arose, men gathered on all sides, and it was only after a prolonged and wordy battle of entreaty and convincing explanation that the women were at last allowed to enter. The reason given for this reception was that the villagers were afraid that we were bandits, and they were not taking any chances of having some members of the party in their midst. However, once they had been assured that all the men would retire to the truck they gave grudging consent for the women to remain, and we were able to settle down.

Illin, Wu Hing and I stretched out inside the truck, the Major was on a stretcher underneath, while Davis and his friend Mr. Hung slept on stretchers at the roadside. Fortunately it was a gloriously clear night with a moon just past the full, and no one suffered any great inconvenience from the enforced camping out, although it was not easy to sleep owing to the thousands of mosquitoes that gathered for the banquet.

With the first light of dawn our driver started to walk towards Pinglo in search of a mechanic, and Davis arranged for a large pail of hot water to be brought from the village. Along with the pail came dozens of curious children, and they gathered round, all eyes and amused interest, while we enjoyed a more than usually public shave and wash. They were all out to have some real fun, but at that hour of the morning I am afraid it was beyond my powers to participate.

Hardly had we finished our ablutions when the driver arrived back with a mechanic he had located a mile or two down the road, and while they went to work on the motor we repaired to the village for breakfast. Again we were a source of great interest to the children, and so numerous did they become around the restaurant that the proprietor had to clear them away to enable his customers to enter.

Fortunately the mechanic proved to be a mechanic and not one of that numerous band whose qualifications existed only in their imaginations, and when we returned to the truck the engine was running smoothly. A washer on the fuel pump had disintegrated, but the mechanic had been able to improvise with something which he felt certain would easily take us as far as Pinglo. His judgment was sound and we reached the town about 9.30 a.m., a town clinging and climbing about a steep river bank, its buildings saving themselves from precipitate descent into the river by means of a precarious system of crooked spindly struts and cross-beams.

When the truck had been despatched to have permanent repairs effected we went on board a houseboat owned by the YWCA. Half a dozen women were living there, besides a dozen children evacuated from Kweilin, and the two elderly Chinese ladies in charge carried an air of refined gentle grace that belonged to another age. They had brought their boat downstream from Kweilin to escape the imminent Japanese occupation of that city, and they were pathetic in their eagerness to know where they should go next; if they should continue going farther down, or remain where they were. Those were difficult questions to answer, for what could we say when charged with the knowledge that the Japanese were preparing for a drive up river from the south, as well as down from the north? All one could do was to advise them to take passage to Kunming if they could possibly arrange it, but it was evident from the look in their eyes that they had no intention of forsaking their home upon the river.

Looking at those gentle ladies my mind reeled with thoughts of what might happen to them in the hands of those brutes whose behaviour was so vividly imprinted on my memory, but one could see that whatever might befall them they would meet it with a calm heroic dignity that nothing could destroy. The final Japanese drive overran all that area, and I have often wondered how those charming people fared, my sincere hope being that they safely avoided any molestation by the invaders.

The boat was moored against the river bank, and high above it a spring of clear cold water issued from the rock, water which flowed on board through bamboo pipes. We all enjoyed a most refreshing bath in this convenient stream, the temperature of which was low enough to make our skirls tingle. Repairs to the truck took longer than expected, so when lunch time came the good ladies invited me to dine on board, and they favoured me with a most tasty fish. Fish was no great problem for them, and it was only an hour or two earlier that our lunch had been swimming gaily by, only to fall victim to a baited hook. Had he known the pleasure he could give when cooked he might have been the happier to die.

Climbing to the road again we went in search of our truck, and while waiting for one of the members of our party who had wandered off, I was tempted by the sight of some pastries that resembled small sausage rolls. They were coming out of an oven in front of me, and their smell was too appetising to resist. They proved to be filled with a mince of crushed sesame seed, and so pleasant were they to my palate that a dozen more followed the first one before my hunger was satisfied. After buying another two dozen to take on the way we started off, running down to the river ferry at 2.15 p.m. This was one of the usual punts, poled by three or four stalwarts, and they judged the swift current very nicely as they worked their heavy craft into position for the crossing.

For thirty miles a good road ran through a broad flat valley, intensively cultivated, a valley bounded on either side by steep limestone mountains, under whose buttresses nestled many large, compact villages. This was the most densely populated area we had yet seen, a fact which testified to the fertility of the rich river flat.

As we advanced the walls of the valley gradually closed in, until the floor was little more than a quarter of a mile wide. On either hand, rising vertically eight hundred feet and more from the level plain, were fantastic spires, rectangular blocks like giant chimneys, huge wedding cakes, minarets and carved towers. It was a strange impressive scene, filled with Nature's artistry in the grand manner, a scene steeped in mystery and menace.

Deep in a shady amphitheatre among those spires we stayed to rest and to let the tyres cool. All the available flat around us was vividly green with young rice and other crops. It was marvellously calm and peaceful after the long drive, a perfect spot in which to laze and dream, and let the imagination roam at random through those vast caves and crevices worn by wind and rain, caves that held how many stories of desperate adventure? For here was one of the natural highways of this ancient land, through which pursuers and pursued of many a princely house had passed in headlong flight, and it was easy to picture the last despairing effort of some exhausted wretch as he clambered up the cliff, to take his final chance of life in the dim security of those limestone vaults.

Again we climbed aboard and rolled along a level road with an almost flawless surface, putting the miles behind with an effortless ease which was very soothing after the thumping, jolting and crashing of the past few days. Then small shops began to line the highway as Kweilin came gradually into being, its size indicated by the fact that we must have traversed three miles of those small shops before the buildings of the main city were reached.

Just on dark we drove into the compound of the British Army Aid Group's headquarters, and there I was really at home. News of my escape had preceded me by quite a long time, and a number of people were very interested to meet me and learn the latest news of mutual friends who were still prisoners of war in Hong Kong. A doctor came to look me over, gave me more vitamin pills, and said that he would give me a thorough examination next morning. In spite of all that had been done for my comfort on the way I was giddy and tottering with fatigue, and after dinner it was grand to sink down on a most comfortable bed. This was in a cottage shared by two officers of another "intelligence" organisation, and they made me very much at home, lending me pyjamas and anything else that they possessed. Everything was perfect except that the place was literally swarming with mosquitoes, and they bit me with the greatest relish and persistence in spite of liberal applications of repellent.

Next day, Thursday, the 7th of September 1944, I began to learn a little about the situation at Kweilin and the prospects for the future. Japanese planes were coming over on every moonlight night, but I was told to take no notice of them, as so far they had been attacking only the airfields and other military targets. I felt in no mood for enduring any air-raids, and was very glad that we had had a quiet night.

An atmosphere seething with nervousness and unrest had the city in its grip, and all military headquarters were packing up in preparation for a hurried departure. All through the city troops were building sunken pillboxes in the streets, preparing for a stubborn defence which no one expected to materialise. For my part, when a "boy" brought freshly brewed tea with sugar and milk at 6 a.m., I felt that life could hold little more in the way of luxury, and sincerely hoped that the Japanese would remain away and allow me leisure to enjoy it. But there were unmistakable signs that this was a front-line city, and squadrons of planes were continually roaring overhead.

Prison-camp complex still had me in its grip, and it was only by an effort of will that I refrained from rushing out to see what was passing. In camp the roar of a group of planes was always the signal for craning necks, for we were ever on the lookout for the welcome markings on the American planes, or if, as usually happened, they were too high for us to see, we listened expectantly for the whistling bombs, or for the thump, thump, thump of the ack-ack guns. In spite of a certain amount of danger from falling bombs, the raids which the 14th Air Force made over Hong Kong were the greatest morale builders which the prisoners of war were granted during the whole term of their captivity, and asked whether they would rather have a raid or a Red Cross parcel, I believe at least fifty per cent, would have voted for the raid. And that is saying something in a hungry camp.

Colonel Ride, commanding officer of the BAAG, called me to his office, and after a prolonged questioning which left me feeling like a limp rag, he said he wished me to make a very full report. He wanted the story of the treatment we had received in camp, as much information as possible of the defences round the camp, and anything else that might assist in formulating a plan of attack. With my eyes still seriously affected and my brain incapable of any long concentration, that sounded like a formidable task; for I had with me four full diaries of very small writing, diaries that covered the whole period of my captivity. It would be necessary to go carefully through them to pick out the pertinent information, and it seemed obvious that long before that could be achieved Kweilin would be included in the Japanese version of a co-prosperity sphere. Having had an inside view of the working of that type of co-prosperity I had no intention of waiting for another look, so the problem of my next move came up for discussion.

One plan was that I should go to Liuchow by train and then by truck convoy to Kunming, but though it was enthusiastically pointed out that the trucks travelled through most marvellous scenic beauty, not the promise of a trip through Heaven itself could have tempted me to another seven days of such jolting. The next plan was that I should fly to Liuchow and then go by truck to Ishan, a matter of only three hours, where I could rest in comfort while writing the report. That sounded a little better, but it seemed fairly certain that if Kweilin fell Liuchow and Ishan would quickly follow, and I would find myself hurriedly bundled out on the road again. Such a prospect was appalling and I decided to make every effort to be flown out directly to Kunming, where security would be assured for some considerable time. Not that I expected the Chinese troops to be any obstacle to the Japanese if they wished to take Kunming, but the very distance and the difficulty of maintaining supplies over the intervening terrain would, I knew, prove insurmountable for the rapidly vanishing enemy transport system.

While those deliberations were proceeding a Chinese had been sent out to make some purchases on my behalf, and besides bringing a complete outfit of toilet articles he arrived with what he described as the largest pair of shoes in Kweilin. I imagined something that I could wade about in, but in fact they fitted perfectly and were a very real asset indeed. My instructions were to ask for anything required, and if it were humanly possible it would be procured. With prospects of an air passage in view my demands were very light; in fact I had to ask for exactly nothing, though I was strongly tempted to see what the reactions would be to a request for a packet of diamonds.

The doctor gave me a thorough examination and pronounced me in sound condition, though badly in need of a long period of rest and correct diet. He was very keen to send me to a convalescent hospital in Simla at the earliest opportunity, but Simla held no attraction for me at that time. If it were at all possible I wanted to spend my leave at home in Auckland. The immediate result of the medical examination was that I started on a ten-day course of quinine to kill the malaria germs, while a daily dose of vitamin tablets was administered. Possibly that mixture had something to do with my feelings, but certain it is that Friday, the 8th of September 1944, a fine sunny day, was a very depressing one.

On that day the general evacuation of Kweilin was ordered. Opinion as to when the Japanese would occupy the city varied between three days and two weeks, but everyone was bustling about packing up, with orders to get going as soon as transport could be arranged. The two officers whose

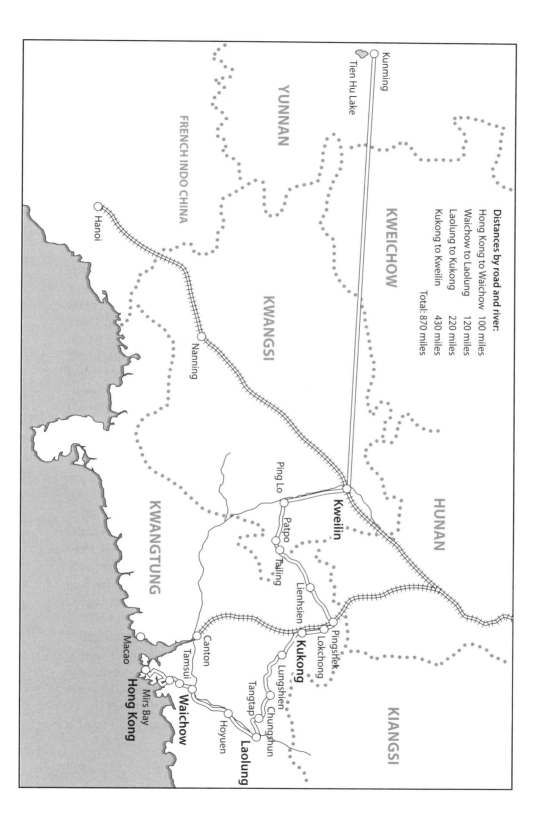

Distances by road and river:

Hong Kong to Waichow	100 miles
Waichow to Laolung	120 miles
Laolung to Kukong	220 miles
Kukong to Kweilin	430 miles
Total:	**870 miles**

Kunming

Tien Hu Lake

YUNNAN

FRENCH INDO CHINA

KWEICHOW

Hanoi

KWANGSI

Nanning

HUNAN

Ping Lo

Kweilin

Patpo

Tailing

Lienhsien

KIANGSI

Pingshek

Lokchong

Kukong

Lungshien

Tangtap

Chungshun

Laolung

Hoyuen

KWANGTUNG

Canton

Macao

Tamsui

Mirs Bay

Waichow

Hong Kong

quarters I was sharing were having great difficulty in finding transport for themselves and their baggage. There were trains standing at the station, but there was no coal to feed the fires of the engines, and it seemed doubtful if there ever would be any. All available trucks were already overtaxed in meeting the needs of the units to which they belonged, and it looked as if my friends would have to leave on foot. Then, in the midst of their depression, a miracle occurred. Two months earlier they had sent a man off to procure a truck for their organisation, and they had heard no word or sound of him since. At midnight they were sitting disconsolately among their cases and boxes, making plans for walking out over the hills if the worst came to the worst, when in marched their man to announce that he had an almost brand new truck with spare drums of petrol and oil for their whole journey. Talk about manna from Heaven; if that was not perfect relief from frustrated tension, I would like to see it improved upon.

In their excitement and pleasure they quickly made all plans for me to leave with them, but they overlooked the fact that I was then under Colonel Ride's orders and was a virtual prisoner until my report had been completed. They departed next morning, leaving the house a desolate place, for everything movable was being packed by the remaining Chinese servant. The owners had already flown to safer regions, and it was easy to imagine what the house would look like after it had been left vacant for a few days with the city under siege. I will back the Chinese looter against any looter in the world, including the white ant. When he has finished with a building there is nothing left but the walls, and if they are not built of mud or concrete they go too.

After the departure of my friends a feeling of great depression stole over me, for, as I watched party after party leaving in all their feverish haste, it seemed that no one had time to think about a stray PoW who had managed to get himself to Kweilin at the worst possible time. Well, not quite, for it would have been still worse for him had he arrived a little later, and found the Japanese actually in possession. The prospect of their imminent approach did not please me at all, and I was then beginning to make my own plans for walking out in case no other means of escape presented itself.

Indescribable scenes were witnessed along the railway, where thousands of Chinese had swarmed into and on the trains and engine in the hope that they would ultimately start. Some had been there for days, packed in a solid mass in carriages and wagons, while engines and roofs were covered with people. Every place on every train that offered a precarious hold was occupied by someone, and the story is well known of those who perished through being swept off the roofs when a train passed under a low bridge. Here was panic-stricken humanity making a last despairing bid to escape the terrors of the invaders.

After lunch-time Colonel Ride arrived from the airport with General Carton de Wiart, who had flown in from Kunming to make an inspection of the forward area. I was introduced to the General, and in spite of the many problems with which he was faced, he listened attentively to a short account of my escape. At the same time I voiced my own wishes to be allowed to go to Kunming to recuperate, and the request fell on sympathetic ears. Colonel Ride came along later with the most marvellous news that the General had given orders that a seat must be found for me in his plane, which was returning to Kunming that same afternoon. Arrangements had been made for Major Minshull Ford, of the Royal Welsh Fusiliers, to follow me to Kunming later, when he would put me through interrogations, and we would complete a report together.

Soon after noon an air alert sounded, and there was a great racket going on in the clear blue sky away above Kweilin, so high up that the participants could not be seen. Thirty fighters roared away into the upper atmosphere, climbing until they disappeared, and while they carried on their hate in noisy evolutions, groups of bombers came sliding in at tree-top level. It was all very exciting and one could only guess at what had happened, though it looked as if the bombers had been set upon by enemy fighters and the Americans had gone up to beat them off. It was very annoying to hear the engines screaming in dives and turns without being able to see anything, and then one broke away from the rest in a dive that had all the sounds, except the last one, of finality. The machine seemed to be headed from the ceiling to the earth, its motor screaming to a crescendo of pitch that was shattering in its intensity. I fully expected the end to come in a booming explosion as it hit the ground, but the screaming motor died out in silence, and added yet another blank sentence to the remainder of the indecipherable and unsatisfactory play being enacted overhead.

By the time lunch was over the sounds of fury had subsided, and those who had been inside were not even aware of what had taken place. For my part, it would not have surprised me in the least if a shower of bombs had descended from the blue.

Chapter 12

Kweilin to Kunming

My memory of the next hour or two is rather vague, but by some means I found myself in a large army truck on my way to one of the airstrips. The way was rough and rugged, and the vehicle bounced and thumped over deep pot-holes until my bones seemed to strike directly on the hard boards at every jolt. What flesh remained had entirely lost any properties of shock absorption that it might have once possessed, and I was glad when we pulled up alongside a C.47 transport plane bearing the roundels of the RAF. It was a long time since I had seen those markings, and it was good to know that they were again penetrating those Eastern skies, from which they had so ignominiously been shot during the black days of 1942.

There was a great deal of chatter and excitement from a British consular official who was certain that the plane was badly trimmed and overloaded. In his panic he made himself very hot and red in the face by moving luggage about the plane, and he then made himself further obnoxious by attempting to have some passengers left behind in order that he, and a ridiculous quantity of his luggage, should be assured of a safe passage. The captain of the plane must have been strongly tempted to throw the man and his luggage out, for those were my own feelings. To see an official making a public demonstration of sheer fright was not a pleasant experience.

With twenty passengers and a full load of luggage on board we were ready to go at 4 p.m., and the big plane lifted gracefully over the mountains surrounding the field. That was my first experience of flying in anything larger than a little two-seater, open cockpit "Avro", and I was greatly impressed with the steadiness and feeling of solid security in this big aircraft. We climbed steadily to twelve thousand feet and sailed over a vast area of steep barren ridges, over hundreds of miles of country almost entirely devoid of population. Rivers and streams ran in gorges too steep for any cultivation, and villages of any size were conspicuous by their absence. Occasional tracks twisting along the mountain-sides were the only evidence that men did live in this great inhospitable expanse of primitive terrain. Frequently the earth was obscured by layers of cloud, but as we went west, so we saw the streams change colour. Clear water gave place to rivers heavily charged with the deep red silt that characterises the rivers of Yunnan, and which is responsible for the name of the Red River which flows south to the Gulf of Tongking.

The sun went down to leave a landscape plunged in night below, while colour still tinged the topmost clouds. Pinpoints of light came into view, and after making several circuits over Kunming we landed on a sodden strip to find light rain still falling. Great pools of water were lying everywhere, and jeeps and trucks were dashing past, spraying water in all directions. Planes were roaring overhead, landing at frequent intervals, and there was a great confusion of noise and movement. My main impressions were of tremendous activity, of mud, of wet, and a feeling that it must have been raining for a long time. We emptied out of the plane, and there were wives and friends to meet some of the passengers. It occurred to me that these were the first white women I had been close to for two and a half years, and I looked again with renewed interest, but without being greatly impressed.

Someone put me in a jeep and drove for what seemed to be interminable miles around the airport, to the Royal Air Force Mess. To my disordered senses the coloured lights and the atmosphere of comfort within those walls seemed to be something from the pages of fiction. I was introduced to the commanding officer, Wing-Commander Lord Waleron, who told me that the Mess was unusually crowded because flying schedules had been disrupted by the weather. Normally there would be only three or four staying there, but that night there were more than a dozen. By the time dinner was over I was too exhausted to absorb any further impressions, and my conversation must have been rather wild, for next morning some of my friends were discussing the previous night with no little amusement. They said that my eyes on occasion had not encouraged argument.

Situated at an elevation of 6,000 feet Kunming has a very good climate, and I had thoroughly enjoyed the experience of needing a blanket to keep me warm during the night. The Mess was intended for the use of air crews staying overnight in Kunming, and as it was pressed for room arrangements were made for me to stay at the Mess of the British Military Mission in China.

Wing Commander John, RAF, Air Attaché in Kunming, gave me a warm rug and a pair of stockings, for he said I would need them for the flight over the "Hump" into India. My wardrobe was gradually increasing, though I was still not embarrassed with more luggage than could be lifted quite comfortably in one hand.

Lord Waleron arrived with a Jeep about 10.30 a.m., and we drove again round that enormous airfield, the first big one I had been able to inspect. There were literally hundreds of fighters, bombers and transports lined up in orderly ranks or strewn about in all stages of repair. That was the terminal of the freight route from India, the end of the most dangerous freight route ever flown, the seething, bustling outcome of one of the daring and imaginative projects of the war.

Right there before my eyes was the evidence of what had been achieved. Vast piles of supplies, great dumps of bombs, vehicles in amazing numbers from jeeps to huge six-wheeled trailers, all had been flown over the implacable mountains, brought by the one highway still uncontrolled by the enemy, the highway of the sky. All day and all night too the big transports were roaring round above the field, going out light to India, coming in loaded to capacity. Sometimes a plane was unable to reach the requisite eighteen thousand feet for safe flying, and then another transport would leave its scattered remains on some jagged mountain peak, there to be a constant reminder of the dangers of that bold adventure.

After a brief interrogation by an "intelligence" officer I was driven to my new home, a large house on the bank of a river about one hundred feet wide, which flowed into the Tien Hu Lake. A room on the first floor overlooking the river was assigned to me, and that really looked like luxury. It was a large room with bathroom attached, nicely furnished with furniture made in France, and it seemed wonderfully quiet. No one shared it with me, and for the first time in what seemed a lifetime I had somewhere to go on my own, somewhere to retreat to when I wanted peace and solitude. And how I wanted solitude. Always, when living in the crowded conditions of the prison camp, my vision of heaven had been a soundproof room with a door six inches thick, through which no unwanted guest, no grating voice could penetrate. The quiet seclusion of this room looked like the realisation of a dream, and I felt that it did not matter then if my whereabouts should be forgotten for a time. Besides a very comfortable bed with a tight wire wove, there was a large writing-table in my room, another of the things that I had missed very much while in camp, and although I was not feeling in the mood to write anything, it gave me great pleasure just to know that it was there and at my disposal when required.

Greta Eardley, sister of one of the men I had known in camp, came to see me one evening to learn the latest tidings of her brother. We decided to send cards back to the camp, including hidden information of my safe arrival in Kunming, and although they were addressed to various people in camp in the hope that one might go through, none was received there. Whether the Japanese picked up the reference, or whether they stopped all mail from China I do not know, but the attempt was made because not long before my escape Henry Eardley had received a letter from Kunming only six weeks after it had been posted. Compared with the usual twelve to eighteen months which our letters took, that had seemed like a telegram.

The Kunming office of the British Military Mission was headed by Lieutenant-Colonel Clark, an old "China Hand" who spoke the language fluently, and he invited me to dine with him one evening. Possibly I had premonitions of trouble to follow, for it was not an enjoyable meal, and I excused myself early. Within an hour a severe attack of diarrhoea developed, an attack which lasted for two days, with intermittent spells of vomiting to increase my discomfort. My only recourse was to stop eating altogether until this condition cleared up, and it was particularly annoying to have to look at a beautiful dish of peaches and pears that the cook had bought for me, without being able to sample them. Fruit had been one of the things we had missed more than anything else, and it was most tantalising to have the room filled with the scent of it without being able to satisfy my craving.

First impressions of Kunming were decidedly unfavourable, for there had been a lot of rain, streets were inches deep in black filthy mud, streets of houses were dilapidated and decaying, the majority of the people were dirty and poverty stricken, while many were diseased and stamped with vice. Those were first impressions, generally true for parts of the old city, but they were considerably modified on better acquaintance.

Thieving flourished on a grand scale, shops were stacked with goods of US Army origin, and it was said that complete jeeps could be bought by visiting two or three vendors of spare parts. Just before my arrival at the Mission, thieves had climbed into the compound from the river, jacked up a new Jeep, and had gone off with the four wheels. Chinese currency was in the throes of almost total collapse, and it was difficult to arrive at the true value of anything. Various exchange rates were operating, the lowest official rate being CNC$12 to the rupee, the highest black-market rate being CNC$120 to the rupee. Those were the days when Chinese on fixed salaries in official positions were almost starving, while coolies and other casual workers could be seen walking the streets with great blocks of notes under their arms, packs of notes six inches thick. Even at that no great amount of money might be represented, for there was a bewildering variety of notes issued in China, and when it came to CNC$10 bills, the notes themselves were worth much more than their face value. For instance, one sheet of writing-paper or one envelope cost $10, while a tin of shoe polish was $600. No wonder it was a common sight to see men strolling along with armfuls of banknotes.

The weather was delightfully cool, but it was not pleasant for walking as rain still continued intermittently and thunder was rumbling about the surrounding hills. Major West, in charge of the British Military Mission Store, took me in hand and fitted me out with two sets of underwear, another khaki shirt, a pair of shorts and a woollen jersey. This last I thought might be useful later when flying, and I did not realise at the time that in a few days I would be very glad to be wearing not only one jersey, but two.

Heavy rain continued for several days, and the river ran swiftly, thick with brown mud. The water overlapped the bank in places, and some of the old-timers said that they had never before seen it so high. During that time I was feeling too ill to want to go out, and since there was always plenty of interest in the life on the river, and on the roadway opposite, the weather did not worry me.

Transient officers were continually dropping in for meals, and I was rapidly feeling the pulse of their cumulative opinions of this enterprise in China. International policies decreed that Chiang Kai Shek must be supported in his alleged resistance to the Japanese, but there was not one honest foreigner in China who did not subscribe to the view that the Allies were backing a foredoomed failure. Never were indictments more bitter than those which came from the lips of those officers who had been toiling in danger and discomfort in the forward zones of China, where all their efforts ended in complete and utter frustration. And it was not only from the forward areas that complaints were heard. Right there in Kunming many men were wondering why so many gallant lives were being sacrificed in flying supplies and sinews of war over the "Hump", supplies which never by any chance were ever used against the Japanese.

Where did they go? Nobody could say for certain, but many were the views expressed. "They were delivered to the Chinese Army. They disappeared into the country; into the mountains; into Chiang's network of private stores. They were stacked in reserve dumps for use in the civil war to follow World War II." Undoubtedly much material was sold to the Japanese.

The Chinese Army was run on lines that could not be tolerated in any Western country. Corruption was rife throughout its higher ranks, with the result that, in spite of their miserable pay, its officers waxed fat and wealthy while its soldiers starved to death in rags.

Where did all those supplies go to? Why were the fine airfields, constructed so laboriously in Kwangtung and Kwangsi provinces, abandoned to the enemy without a fight? The final Japanese offensive through South China in 1944 was so weak, had so pitifully little behind it, that one determined defensive action would have killed it dead in its tracks. But there was no defensive action. The streets of Kweilin were a scene of feverish activity, with troops building sunken pill-boxes at every intersection and at every commanding position. A man who had been twenty years in China looked at the scene, and said with quiet introspection: "I wonder! I have seen exactly the same preparations made in a dozen cities in China, and not one of those cities was ever defended." He had no need to wonder, for Kweilin followed the normal pattern, and Japanese troops marched through the town. Every officer and man in China knew that his work, his best efforts, were utterly useless and futile, and it was no wonder that a bitterness of spirit was general among the forces there.

The American and British aid could have had a tremendous effect had it been co-ordinated and driven into a front-line striking force, but long before it ever reached the forward areas it had been dissipated into the private pockets of officialdom. That may sound exaggerated and untrue to those who heard only the clamourings of the official Press, but I was writing those lines at a later date in Shanghai, and here is my feeling at that time.

> Just now, it is July 1946, the newspapers are full of nonsense about the war raging with the Communists. Hair-raising accounts appear daily of the imminence of attacks on Nanking and Shanghai. "The 'Battle' for Shanghai is now On", "Reds Closing in on Yangtze Triangle", are typical of the headings in the newspapers. Foreign correspondents are confined to Nanking as "it is much too dangerous near the forward areas". Can one imagine it? Too dangerous for men who stormed ashore on the shell-torn beaches of Iwo Jima and Okinawa? Too dangerous to go into an area where only occasional shots are fired? No; the reason why journalists are not wanted is that the actual scenes are not for publication. There is no doubt about the Communist successes, but they are not

achieved through the pictured scenes of battle. It is my firm belief that in most of the battles which end in Nationalist defeat, the contending generals spill more ink than human blood in their intricate conniving.

Here, right now in Shanghai, is an exact replica of the sense of utter frustration that depressed the armed forces in 1944. Now it is the staff of UNRRA confronted with exactly similar conditions. They see huge quantities of relief goods piling into the ports of China, and immediately the rot sets in. Delays, difficulties, deliberate misappropriations, inefficiency, lack of control, private greed, official greed, all take their toll of supplies that were sent to save the starving, to rehabilitate the broken industries. Here the starving have starved through centuries, and they can continue to starve. Here the broken industries have no money to *buy* equipment, so it will go to those who can pay. Why? The cry is that China is bankrupt, yet in a speech made by Mayor Wu last week he apologised for the fact that there were so many millionaires in Shanghai – a strange state of affairs in a bankrupt nation. Just as the war supplies dissipated in China, so are the UNRRA supplies going, but I digress too far; this story concerns my escape from China, not my third return.

My immediate impressions of the people moving through Kunming were accented by comparison with those among whom I had lived in the provinces of Kwangtung and Kwangsi. There the climate was warm and friendly, the soil rich and productive, the people plump, round-faced, smiling, and pleasant to be among. Here many of the trains of ponies were tended by mountain folk, people with Tibetan features, dirty, faces pinched and mean with hard living in bitter climates and with struggling to extract a meagre subsistence from the barren mountain soil. Their minds and morals were formulated by the lives they led, and in their eyes were the seeds of murder, of thieving, of distrust, and of hate. Yunnan is a bad province for opium, and it could be bought at many street stalls packaged in cigarettes. These were bought by many depraved types, and when one saw the men who tended the passing caravans it was not surprising to hear that the mountain trails were dangerous for lonely travellers at night.

There were hundreds of tiny China ponies in the streets, really miniature steeds that barely reached to my elbow. They were harnessed into carts, or they had saddles and equipment to hold every variety of goods that could be done up in packages small enough for them to carry. One special saddle had a platform slung on either side on which piles of bricks were stacked, while another had harness for holding a large tub on either side, tubs in which bean curd was carried. Long convoys of these animals were continually passing, they being the only available transport that was able to cope with the steep and narrow mountain tracks. Most were fat and well cared for, but occasionally one saw some in pitiful condition – thin, badly chafed and obviously neglected by an ignorant or vicious owner. Continued use of such animals should not have been tolerated, but neither should human wreckage have been allowed to litter the streets as it did in every Chinese city.

One did not need to be sensitive to live in any degree of comfort in China, for the diseased beggars were nauseating. On every street those wretches grovelled, their bodies covered with hideous running ulcers, or with horrible deformities. The worst features of every ailment were invariably bared to public view and accentuated as much as possible by accumulations of filth, all done with an eye to attracting the maximum sympathy from the passer-by.

A favourite trick of the beggar with deformed legs, either real or assumed, was to drag himself about the streets through all the wettest and worst filth he could find, until he became just an utterly revolting sight, too disgusting even to attract sympathy.

Traffic in Kunming at that time was completely chaotic, with little or no control being exercised. Only at the worst intersections were American Military Police in charge. This hidden city of China had been designed for rickshaws and other wheeled vehicles that could be drawn by hand, and the advent of motor-buses, trucks, jeeps, petrol wagons and cars was playing havoc with the narrow ways. The mere pedestrian got along as best he could, threading through the maze of vehicles which had no respect at all for the sidewalks. Any stroll in town was bound to yield its quota of surprises, for the streets were blocked in a great variety of ways. At one point the crowd of walkers would be dodging out round some obstruction, and on reaching the spot you would find a small child, intent and unconcerned, doing its business with utter disregard of the passing traffic. At another place a pony munched a contemplative meal, while the crowd milled out among the vehicles to get by. No one questioned the right of the pony, or of the driver who sat alongside – they must have their food, it was time to eat, so what better place could be found than the one in which they happened to be? No! people might be killed in trying to pass, but no one would think of placing any blame on the pony.

Parked buses and trucks caused great confusion, for even when hard against a building they frequently blocked more than half the traffic way, and the drivers would disappear with no regard at all for the trouble they were causing.

Those were problems which came into being with the arrival of the sky train from India. Kunming was in the throes of a revolution that rocked it to its foundations, and in spite of, or because of, the fantastic prices prevailing, millionaires in China dollars were springing up like mushrooms. These people were putting their unstable cash into solid property as fast as they could, and whole new suburbs of houses were springing up, houses built of blue-grey bricks that looked quite attractive from the outside, but which by our standards were hopelessly deficient in plumbing. Then there was almost a whole street of substantial modern business premises and banks, all constructed during the past year, while more building was in progress.

One of those new structures gave me an interesting insight into Chinese improvisation. Excavations eight or ten feet deep had been flooded by recent heavy rains, and work was held up owing to lack of any pumping gear. So the contractors had gone to work and built a wooden contraption which shifted the water at surprising speed. An endless belt, fitted at frequent intervals with a board attached at right angles, ran up a sloping wooden trough, and as this belt was turned by teams of several workmen, each board pushed its quota of water up the trough. These water troughs were in general use throughout the land for irrigating rice fields. Of course the boards could fit only loosely and much efficiency was lost through leakage, so that four feet was the maximum lift possible at one time. This trouble was overcome by building a reservoir at that height, from which a second belt carried the water up to road level, and with both belts turning at their best speed a considerable stream poured out into the gutter. Next day the foundations were clear, and builders were at work.

Yunnan has a splendid climate for fruit growing, and all along the streets were vendors with their little stalls. Peaches were just going out of season, but pears and persimmons were excellent, and very plentiful. The weather was growing colder, and on several days I was wearing two pullovers. Chestnuts appeared at wayside stalls, and, cooked in burnt sugar in big iron kongs, they were very good. Every day I bought a bag to take home, but usually, if my walk had taken me some distance, there would be very few left by the time I arrived.

My health was improving and walks were taking me farther afield, so that I explored streets of coppersmiths, of vendors of porcelain, and of other goods of Chinese craftsmanship. There were some very beautiful vases and teapots that attracted me until their price was disclosed, when my interest waned suddenly. A pair of small vases was offered for five thousand Chinese dollars, while other articles bore similar crazy prices, ranging up to eighty thousand dollars. There was no Navy Office from which I could draw any pay, so the only money I had was that advanced by the British Army Aid Group, which was just enough to cover ordinary expenses incidental to living. My mind could not readily adjust itself to those prices which all seemed to have at least three noughts too many attached to them, especially as conversion to sterling required so much juggling with various exchange rates. The best typically Chinese work was represented by bronze figures of most hideous and ferocious mien – knights of old, and warriors of undoubted strength and savagery. There were really splendid examples of that kind of work, but they were much too heavy to tempt me to buy.

An interesting walk was that along the top of the old city wall from which one looked across wide fields of rice, stretching as far as the eye could see, to far distant hills. Those fields appeared to be as smooth and level as close mown lawns, but closer inspection showed the rice to be a full three feet in height, and carrying a very heavy head of grain. That was by far the best crop I had seen anywhere, and it was easy to see why this wide valley was famous for its fertility.

One of the ancient city gates presented a fine example of Chinese architecture, its ridges and curved eaves ornamented with a great variety of porcelain animals and fish. Then there was a long street of most noisome hovels, its old buildings falling to ruin, its yards and alleys cluttered with filth, its occupants dirty and slovenly in the extreme. The broad top of the wall would have made a lovely scenic walk had it been laid out with paths and gardens, lawns and seats to attract those with leisure to enjoy the undoubted beauty of the surrounding view, but here much of the pleasure was lost through the visitor having to pick his way through dumps of refuse and of human filth.

The British Military Mission Mess was situated close to the northern boundary of the city, so that in a few minutes one could walk out over a bridge and be right in the country. There were miles of paddy fields, with closely packed villages dotted here and there, the dark red walls of the houses in pleasing contrast with vivid green fields. Tall handsome trees lined river banks and often ornamented the villages, big dark clumps standing up like islands in the green level sea. I strolled through the villages, and on looking into one of the houses was greatly surprised to see a blindfolded pony trudging round and round grinding corn. In some of the larger rooms two ponies were at work, and on seeing them in what appeared to be purely residential houses, I wondered what other work might be going on inside those red walls, so closely packed for mutual protection.

At the approaches to most villages pillboxes had been constructed, and troops were in evidence everywhere. No one took any notice of me, except innumerable small boys who constantly shouted their greeting of "Ding-How" as they gave the "thumbs up" sign.

One day, when I was out walking with Mr. Pouncey, of the China Maritime Customs, we watched a little crude rescue work in progress. A crowd lined the banks of a river and there, in a sampan, the body of a man hung like a wet sack over a pole resting across the gunwales. Pouncey spoke Chinese fluently, and when he asked an onlooker what had happened we were informed that the man had just been dragged from the river. To all appearances he was quite dead, but later, when we were returning from our walk, the "body" was sitting up. Close by the track its clothes were drying by a fire of rice straw, while friends prepared a meal. As the river was little more than twenty feet wide at the place where he was fished out, it is more than likely that he was an attempted suicide, and no doubt he would be greatly annoyed at returning to his erstwhile unhappy state, after suffering all the major discomforts of dying. Some people have no luck at all.

One road in Kunming was lined with an avenue of magnificent blue gum trees, massive patriarchs from sixty to seventy feet in height, a gift from some early visitor who brought a reminder of his native land to keep him company in this, at that time, remote corner of the earth. Those gum trees were in full bloom, their soft yellow flowers making a most attractive display. It was a pity that their beauty was marred by hundreds of big black crows which delighted to roost in the spreading branches, where they made a deafening noise with their raucous caws in the mornings and evenings, the while they spattered the roadway with their droppings.

At one time a plague of hairy caterpillars invaded the house, unpleasant little brutes that persisted in crawling to some place where they would be squashed with the maximum of mess, and which had a nasty habit of stinging if one tried to pick them up. But caterpillars were not the only pests to worry us, for enormous rats made a happy hunting-ground of my room. Those unwelcome visitors became so acquisitive that at one stage it seemed that they might even walk off with me. My first loss was two cakes of soap, a commodity extremely difficult to come by, and then large quantities of fruit began to go. Secure places were gradually found for edibles, and then other belongings began to disappear. A towel was only just retrieved as the last few inches were disappearing through a hole in the wall, while a pair of stockings, apparently regarded as palatable, was left to me as a small pile of frayed wool on the floor. It was no easy matter to remember to lock everything away, but having exercised exceptional care one night I was greatly annoyed to wake in the early hours and hear a great racket going on in the drawer of my writing-table. Unable to find anything better to do, a large rat had managed to squeeze in over the back of the drawer, and it was having a great time tearing up all my letters and papers. Mr. Rat got a mighty whack from a stick as he leapt from the drawer, and although he was still agile enough to escape, the blow should have convinced him that paper tearing was not a profitable pastime.

Human thieves also went to work on the house, but this time I was not the victim. One wall was against the street, and on that side all windows were heavily barred. That precaution was merely a challenge and, by means of a long pole with a hook on the end of it, they had dragged through a broken window all the bedding and everything else that could be squeezed between the bars.

A week in Kunming passed rather slowly, for I was much too unsettled to relax and enjoy a life of lazy ease, and I seemed to be forgotten. Major Ford had gone to Ishan, and with the Japanese rapidly advancing on that area, both from Wuchow and from Kweilin, anything could be happening there. A black depression settled over me at times, but the constant flow of visitors from all parts of India and China kept me interested with their varied and dramatic adventures.

Nature had been lavish in her treatment of Kunming, for besides the rice and fruit, vegetables grew in great abundance. There were ordinary potatoes, sweet potatoes, cabbages, carrots and many varieties of beans and marrows, so that the food was an endless source of delight. The cook was an artist at his work and he turned out most attractive cakes and pastries. I made prodigious inroads on those delicacies, and my uncontrollable appetite was shameful. Still, the cook had no cause to growl, for the more he bought the more he made in "squeeze". It was said that although his official salary was CN$ 7,500 a month, he was really collecting between CN$ 45,000 and CN$ 50,000. That was how China functioned.

On the 19th of September Colonel Hooper, of the British Army Aid Group, arrived from India, and he said that arrangements had been made for my reception there. If hospital treatment were needed I would remain in Calcutta, but if only convalescence were required I would fly to Simla. He painted a most attractive picture of that health resort in the foothills of the Himalayas, where he said there would be beautiful girls to attend my every want. Such convalescence certainly sounded alluring, but I was growing hopeful of spending my leave in Auckland, and compared with that prospect any other appeared as a dying ember beside the sun.

Possibly as an indication of my improving health fleas began to invade my bed in large numbers, and while they bit me to their hearts' content, I could never catch one. There were no sheets to be had, and I fancy the fleas just poked their heads through the blankets while they were biting, so that they could make a precipitate retreat at the first movement.

Little highlights stand out in those days at Kunming, one of them being a dinner to which Colonel Hooper and I were invited by Miss Greta Eardley. On a lavishly stocked table pride of place was taken by a dish of perfectly browned roast pigeons, and I could not help thinking what her poor brother could have done to those. Henry Eardley was a young and very strong man with an enormous appetite, and while looking at all that luscious food it made me laugh to think of him lining up in the prison camp for his miserable portion of rice, probably with broken glass in it, and his small mug of green slime. This latter concoction was alleged, by the Messing Committee of which I was once a member, to be vegetable stew; but none of the names by which it was known in camp sounded anything like "stew".

Frequently people with whom I dined remarked that they could not eat big meals when they thought of the thousands of our people starving in the camps, but I am afraid no such qualms ever blunted my own appetite. Had it been humanly possible to deliver food to the camps it would have been delivered, but as it could not be done there was no point in feeling miserable over one's own good fortune, and thoughts of friends in camp brought mainly amusing comparisons to mind. I knew that they would have reacted similarly had our positions been reversed, and many of us have laughed about it since.

Friday, the 22nd of September, was a sunny day with a beautifully clear blue sky, and the "Air raid expected" signal was hoisted during the morning. A squadron of American fighters roared up into the realms of space, and thereafter all was quiet, no enemy planes appearing. Kunming had been heavily bombed a year previously, but no attack had been made for a long time and I sincerely hoped that my stay would be completed in peace. It was delightfully restful walking through the fresh green countryside on those bright days, and I felt that the crashing, rending madness of bombing would be too much to bear.

My interrogator was still missing, so I decided to settle down and write as comprehensive a report as possible. Any points which needed elaboration could be dealt with after his arrival, and as there was still a long wait to be endured, that idea was a good one. Neither my eyes nor my brain seemed capable of sustained concentration for more than two or three hours each day, and study of the diaries proved to be a very exhausting business.

Besides the basic plan of flying me to India once my services were no longer required in China, there were a number of local proposals advanced. Always hovering in the background was the danger that someone would decide to send me back to Ishan by one of the truck convoys, an idea which various visiting officers had put forward, but it was one which I had always strenuously opposed. If information was wanted it could be had in Kunming just as well as in Ishan, and there were limits to my endurance. Death would have been infinitely preferable at that time to two or three weeks of bumping and crashing over those shocking Chinese roads, and having already crossed China once, it was not in my scheme of the future to go thumping back over two-thirds of it again. Such little adventures might possibly be regarded with interest by those in the prime of life, but it was not hard for me to believe that my prime had occurred at some time prior to 1942. I was determined that any further hardships would be undertaken from dire necessity, and not from love of them.

A more attractive proposition was that my remaining time in Kunming should be spent at a quiet rest-camp at Shi Shan, some twelve miles distant on the shore of Lake Tien Hu, and that plan broke down only because the place was temporarily closed. So I remained at the Military Mission Headquarters, enjoyed strolling about in the country or in the town, and let others do the worrying.

On a Saturday evening a party of us went to see a film, *Casablanca*, my first for almost three years. Could that be a modern picture? Was that the film that was acclaimed a great success? As the story unfolded, my senses became more and more numbed, and I left the theatre feeling bewildered and insulted. What had happened? I used to enjoy seeing a film occasionally, but here was something so blatantly artificial, so childish in its pantomime, so seemingly antiquated in its technique that I could not believe that the silver screen could be offering such entertainment to normal, presumably intelligent adults. There were long sequences of close-ups that one associated with films of twenty years ago, and there was such a spate of ridiculously unreal adventure that it could be conceived only in the mind of a Hollywood producer, so immersed in his own realms of fancy that he had lost all contact with the world. My strongest feeling was one of anger that that was the plane on which my intelligence was judged to be, and it was a long time before my film mentality degenerated sufficiently to enable me to enjoy a programme without an occasional surge of anger at the fare provided.

In Kunming there was always something unusual happening to hold the attention of a Westerner, and I was greatly amused by the building of a two-storey house across the street from our Mess. On Sunday workmen arrived to erect uprights and rafters. Monday morning saw a wooden roof slapped on, temporary flooring laid upstairs, and a few weather-boards nailed on the upper walls. In the afternoon the furniture was hauled up: beds, a side-board, chairs and cupboards. I have no idea how long it took to complete the house, but the family moved in and slept there that night. It struck me rather forcefully that our own housing problems would soon vanish if we could move in the day after a house was started.

On the 30th of September my luxurious comfort came to an end, for the British Military Mission moved its quarters to a smaller house. There I shared a room with another officer, while a third bed was available for any chance visitor. The kitchen was not yet in operation, so on that first day we had lunch at the "Hotel de Commerce". The bill came to CNC$600 each, a sum which at the official rate of exchange represented £7, 10s. at the semi-official rate 15s., and at the best black-market rate 11s. 3d. In claiming expenses for an official visit a nice point would arise as to what rate of exchange one would be entitled to use.

Two days later Ford arrived, and life took on a more definite aspect once more. When the reports were completed he was to escort me to India, and his presence lent point and direction to my writing. With Ford was Captain Henry Chan, a Chinese member of the British Army Aid Group who had been working behind the Japanese lines. We had a most interesting stroll together one evening, and in discussing this most recent inrush of foreigners to China, he expressed annoyance at the attitude of the majority of Americans. His chief complaint was that they treated Chinese of every strata of society on the same level as the coolies, and there was no doubt that his censure had much to justify it. Not only

Americans came in for criticism, for he painted a vivid picture of the faults of many of the British in China; but he was generous enough to agree that his complaint was directed more against individuals than against the race. It was true that one frequently saw "officers and gentlemen" drinking themselves into a state of alcoholic stupor, and the Chinese, who are an abstemious people, looked on with anything but favour at the behaviour attendant upon such gross over indulgence. Henry was an educated thinker, and it was stimulating to hear the frank opinions of one of those people with whom we were attempting to be allies. Had there been more of his type among the ruling clique a different history would have been written for China, but it was a sad fact that he represented an infinitesimal minority. Personal interest and intrigue among its officials held the entire nation to ransom.

At that time no one in China had any illusions about the real state of affairs; it was the outside world, relying on Official news releases, that was given an entirely false conception of the situation. The tragedy for China, and for us, was that the Communist faction was the only one which had sufficient organisation to be a threat to Chiang's regime, and it was inevitable that America should support the established Government, in spite of all its deficiencies. Nothing as corrupt as that Government could survive, no matter how much external aid was applied. All that the big aid programmes achieved in China was a slowing down of the rate at which the country sank into the morass of internal dissension, and inevitably into the hands of the Communists.

But I digress too far again. A bottle of mulberry wine in a shop window attracted me one day, and feeling somewhat affluent at the time I bought it for CNC$600. That was the nicest drink I had had since my escape, for most of the locally made liquor available was concocted from alcohol distilled for motor fuel. There were many different labels on the bottles, such as gin, orange brandy, cherry brandy, whisky and various wines, while the contents were of varying hues. The colours and the names were snares and delusions, for underlying them all was the harsh flavour of raw alcohol. It was terrible stuff, and people who had over indulged staggered forth next day as if they had been through the Valley of the Damned.

News came on the 9th of October that arrangements had been made for me to go to Calcutta, Colombo and thence to New Zealand, so I was anxious to be off. My reports were almost completed, and a passage to Calcutta was booked on a plane leaving on the 17th of October. In the meantime, one Captain Jones and I explored the city and its environs, and frequently we would discover a street devoted entirely to one particular trade. In spite of the numbers of ponies everywhere we had not seen any harness shops, until one morning we came to a street where harness of every kind could be bought. Everything was made there, from the thread with which the leather was sewn, to the metal buckles and the wooden frames of the saddles.

The old city was most interesting, but it was only by peeping through open gates or doorways that much of its beauty could be seen. In courtyards behind high walls there were handsome examples of Chinese architecture, houses with wide curving roofs highly ornamented under the eaves, while along the ridges there were porcelain figures of dragons, fish animals, birds and people. There is no more beautiful roof in the world than the Chinese roof of green glazed tiles with its curved caves, and my "Ideal Home" would have such a roof.

Chapter 13

Kunming to New Delhi

Several conflicting signals arrived, for Army Headquarters in both Chungking and Kunming had been making plans for my future. Out of the resultant confusion one important change occurred, and that was the inclusion of a visit to Delhi.

At 8.30 a.m., on the 17th of October 1944, we rose from the Kunming field in a Dakota transport of the RAF. That plane had gone in with a full load of supplies, but as usual it was returning almost empty. The only other passengers were Ford, and three American fighter pilots who were going to India to fly three new planes back to China. They were a cheery group, very keen on souvenirs, so I gave each one a Hong Kong banknote that had been kept all through my captivity. Those autographed notes were eagerly received, and at least they had the distinction of rarity, for it can be safely assumed that they were the only souvenirs of their kind that changed hands in a plane over the "Hump" in the year of 1944. In return they confirmed me as a "Burma Roadster", a title conferred upon those who travelled the road, or flew over its course, in the years of war.

Yunnanyi lay bathed in hot sunshine in a level plain of paddy, and soon after passing its densely crowded, grey buildings, we flew over a lake of emerald green. The weather was beautifully clear and soon our wing-tip seemed to almost touch the rocks as we skirted rugged pinnacles of a mountain range. Away to the north the snow-clad peak of Mount Tali rose in pale ethereal splendour, twenty-five thousand feet into the blue sky. At least that was the height credited to the mountain by the pilots, who based their statement on the fact that a plane had crashed into it when flying several thousands of feet higher than the altitude recorded on their maps. For mile after mile our plane skimmed past rugged and savage looking mountain peaks, and it was no time to dwell on what would happen if an engine failed. Occasionally a village with terraced paddy fields appeared away down in some deep valley, and once we saw a village on the end of a mountain spur. On three sides the land fell precipitously for a thousand feet or more, and the only approach lay along a narrow ridge which in turn climbed to a higher mountain beyond. It was hard to guess how or why people lived in such a place, where no cultivation was possible, and where the climate, at an altitude of ten to twelve thousand feet, must frequently have been severe.

About ten a.m. one of the pilots said that American fighter patrols, flying from Yunnanyi, almost daily met Japanese planes not far south of our position, so there was still a chance of being attacked. No parachutes were in evidence in the plane, but the pilots appeared to be quite unconcerned about that. They suggested that as the old transport revelled in the not very flattering name of "The Snake", it had probably had plenty of experience in crawling along streams, or through the trees, when avoiding Japanese fighters. At wide intervals thin lines showed where tracks climbed tortuously over the mountains, though we could see no reason for their existence.

Soon a higher range came into view, its peaks buried in swirling cloud. We had been flying at 13,000 feet and now we lifted to 16,000 and plunged into the cold vapour. Ice formed on the wires and wings, and it was intensely cold, for the plane had numerous wide cracks around the door, through which the wind whistled in a chilly blast. The altitude was giving me a curious empty feeling in the chest, and I was quite content to sit perfectly still as instructed, and not waste strength in movement.

Seventy miles north of Miyitkina we broke out of the cloud and looked down upon a tropical jungle, so far below that we seemed to be looking into the black depths of an ocean. Then the mountains between Burma and Assam rose to meet us, and after the barren ranges of China these looked rich and vivid by comparison. Nature was on the rampage in this untouched wilderness of tropical profusion, where dense jungle covered the highest ridges, and where silver streams and rivers went tumbling down the valleys.

I enjoyed the scenery from the pilot's cabin, gazed on the range of snowy peaks along the northern horizon, and talked with the young Australian radio operator. He looked no more than twenty, yet he said he had been flying with the RAF for four years, and that that was his last trip before going home on leave. He said he might not have to go overseas again, and looking at his youth, and thinking what those four years must have held for him, I sincerely hoped that he would not. He had done his share.

At noon we came down at Dinjan in North Assam, and it was like landing in an oven.

Down on the flat plain of the Brahmaputra the heat was intense, and I quickly stripped off my two woollen pullovers. There were planes everywhere, among them one of the latest American night fighters, the "Black Widow". She certainly was a sinister and diabolically powerful-looking lady in her black garb, no fit companion for any growing lad on a dark night.

While the plane was refuelled we had lunch, and then we rose over tea plantations on the eastern side of the Brahmaputra, to fly south along the foothills, some four miles from the broad shallow river.

A fairly high range gave us a patch of very bumpy air, and then we were out over the broad plain again. We wound along through a beautiful cloud formation, where mile after mile of tall woolly pillars stood vertically in the still air. Down below a lace-work of rivers made a confusing pattern on the plain, and soon there were mile after mile of flooded fields.

Villages and houses appeared to be afloat on a lake that stretched as far as the eye could see, a lake that covered the rice-fields and was the forerunner of the tragedy of famine. At 4 p.m. the wheels touched down on the air-strip at Dum Dum, and Ford and I drove to the "E Group" Mess at 1 Ballygunge Park Road. After the primitive squalor of China's cities I could scarcely believe the sight of the wide, clean, tree-lined, perfectly surfaced roads of Calcutta, and it seemed that in a few hours I had been transported to a different world. No magic carpet of fiction could possibly have done more for me than had that battered, weather-worn old transport that revelled in the name of "The Snake".

That evening I enjoyed a luxury that had been dreamed about in camp, and I lay back and soaked in a proper bath with taps that really worked, and an efficient geyser from which unlimited hot water flowed. While the warm comfort eased the aches in my joints and muscles, my mind went back to the dank showers at Argyle Street in Hong Kong, where the bitter north-east monsoon whistled round our gaunt frames as we shivered in the cold slimy cubicles, and where huge loathsome spiders watched us with malevolent eyes. Many times when suffering the icy spray of those showers I had sworn that once back in the normal world I never again would submit myself to the discomfort of a cold shower.

A most appetising and satisfying dinner at Spence's ended a day of such events as could happen only in this modern age of science. We took it all as a matter of course, but we who have had the opportunity to do such things as travel from Kunming to Calcutta in a few hours should be grateful for the privilege, for we have taken a living part in an historical event of the most profound and far-reaching magnitude. Until a few short years ago Kunming was one of the most isolated spots on earth, for entry could be made only by weeks of travel over primitive roads. Now, through the demands of a world war, it was flung wide open to the most advanced achievements of science, and people who were exactly the same as their forebears had been for a thousand years and more, were suddenly thrown into violent contact with the distant, modern world. It was no wonder that the peasants looked in blank astonishment at the great planes that roared down upon them out of the sky, too utterly dumb-founded to try to grapple with the meaning of it all, unaware of the impending changes that were presaged by those winged visitors. China was at the threshold of a new era that would shake her to her profoundest depths, an era of change that would not end until she stood level with the remainder of the world, in science, in medicine and in learning.

Next morning I began the rounds of the shops, for Ford had orders to hand me over to the Navy in Calcutta, and although my official transfer was delayed, I had to look like a naval officer again. Some things were very scarce, and it was not until noon that I found an outfitter who could supply a cap and shoulder straps. The cap was my most valued possession for more than a year, for inside it was the name and address of the vendor. Every time I looked at it the experience gave a fillip to jaded thoughts, for the street in which that cap came into being was known as "Chandney Chawk". Something about that name had an immediate appeal, for it seemed to conjure up a host of transient thoughts, of themes for stories to be woven round it. Perhaps it was inevitable that a cap with such a brand should not grow prosaically old, but true it is that a year later it parted from me at Manus Island, in the Pacific, on a night when a warm trade wind gently stirred the coconut palms beneath a brilliant moon.

Commander Carrick RNVR, Senior Naval Officer Calcutta, entertained me to lunch, and it was soon apparent that my resistance to "gimlets", as supplied by the "Saturday

211

Club", was at a very low ebb. I can remember walking with extreme care and concentration in finding my way between the dining-tables.

Later in the day, after another shopping session, Ford and I witnessed one of those little scenes that could be enacted only in the East, or in the imagination of a cartoonist. Coming along a road at right angles to the one in which we found ourselves was a small grandstand, with five or six tiers of seats. The base of that contraption was level with the top of a fence, so that while it travelled steadily along the road we could not see what impelled it, or on what it was resting. We certainly were not prepared for the sight that confronted us when the structure came clear of the corner of the road, and we burst into fits of laughter. Looking for all the world like some grotesque centipede, it went across the intersection with each of its fifty or sixty legs resting on the head of a bearer. The actual raising and lowering of the burden must have called for some very delicate timing, but whatever difficulties were entailed there is no doubt that the total effort was one of perfect co-ordination.

On Thursday, the 19th of October, after a number of con-flicting signals had been received, a telephone message from New Delhi confirmed arrangements for me to proceed there on the following day. In accordance with the usual sadistic policy of Airways personnel, we were roused from bed at 3 a.m. Our luggage allowance was a generous one of 65lbs., but Ford sailed gaily out with a load of gear weighing 110lbs. When they saw that heap the officials were adamant, and we waited while he made a quick readjustment of packs, and sent some back to the Mess. It struck me then that if many people did the same thing that might be one of the reasons why intending passengers were forced to relinquish their beds several hours before the actual time to take off.

From Dum Dum field we rose into the still morning air at 6.30 o'clock, with a complement of eleven passengers and a full load of luggage and cargo. Through a thin transparent mist the plane climbed to 5,000 feet, where the air was perfectly smooth, and cool enough to make a blanket welcome. Down below were vast tracts of flooded lands, where villages and trees stood like islands in a placid silver sea. But that calm expanse of water was viewed with fear by the people living in those tiny houses, for they knew that when the flood had drained away their crops would be drowned and ruined; and that misery, starvation and death would surely follow.

Allahabad appeared as a city bathed in sunlight and pearly mists, and at 9.30 a.m. we landed for breakfast. There were dozens of planes on the big airfield – Hurricanes, Mosquitoes, Mustangs and the usual fleet of C-47 transports. Before our departure there arrived the most graceful and beautiful aeroplane I had yet seen, a four-engine "Ensign". If appearance meant anything that was a most perfect machine, but among airmen there were murmurings and shaking of heads, for that lovely bird had some mysterious faults in its design.

North of Allahabad the landscape was a checker-board of green and dun-coloured squares. Most of the rice had been harvested, and the bare ground looked hot and baked hard by the sun. Farther on the river twisted and turned through a plain dotted with round, dark-green trees, trees that threw welcome shade on a floor of burning heat haze.

Looking down between the starboard engine and the fuselage I could see our shadow racing across the fields, where herds of cattle grazed, and where oxen were ploughing. Then, spreading over miles and miles of plain, the great city of Delhi came into view.

My treatment in that capital which controlled the seething destiny of millions will for ever be a bright oasis in my memory, for it was a source of endless wonder to me that important, busy people should be so hospitable. Even my appearance must have been unpleasant, for several of my front teeth were missing altogether, one was just a broken sharp-pointed fang, while my face was bloated with beriberi.

Accommodation was granted in a large airy tent in the Viceroy's Leave Camp, where a section of the grounds of the palace had been set aside for junior officers on leave from the forward zones. It was a delightful place, the cool lawns shaded by large spreading trees where birds and squirrels played. I said the lawns were cool, but that was only by comparison with the sunshine in the scorching streets, for the shade temperature was 90 degrees. Business during my week in Delhi consisted of answering innumerable questions on a wide variety of subjects, and I realised then that the training given to anyone who is likely to become a prisoner of war is hopelessly inadequate. For instance, I was expected to remember what type of fuel was being used in certain industrial plants by the colour of the smoke from the chimneys; I should know the fuel available for transport by the type and number of vehicles on the roads; I should know the effect of Allied bombings on enemy transport by the supplies available in the territory through which I had been. Hour after hour I had to try to answer questions, until my brain went numb and became a total blank, when my torturers would desist, unsatisfied.

The long period of malnutrition in camp, the rigours of escape, and the weeks of burning fever, had reduced me to a state of severe nervous exhaustion. Although during my stay in Kunming my weight had risen by forty pounds, it was not healthy weight, and after a morning or afternoon of questioning I would feel horribly exhausted. However, to offset that was the hospitality and kindness shown to me by everyone with whom I came in contact. That first night in New Delhi was one to be remembered, for there, in that peaceful garden, it seemed that I found my first haven of complete rest, security, and utter relaxation. It was quiet; wonderfully quiet. Daylight faded from the sky, and the cool, dark infinite canopy above drew the burning heat swiftly from the hard ground, to concentrate it in a myriad stars that shone down upon the grateful earth below. Sitting there, alone under the stars, my tortured nerves relaxed until it seemed that I had reached that ultimate and everlasting peace to which all men aspire. At last I dragged myself inside and slept soundly under a sheet and blanket, until awakened in the cool of early morning with a soft "Salaam, sahib", uttered by a servant attired in spotless white. Beside my bed he left a tray with tea and a large ripe banana, and then departed as silently as he had arrived. No, it was not a dream, everything was real, the tea just right.

On Saturday, the 21st of October, I was at last officially handed over to the Navy, though it seemed a rather incongruous place for such a ceremony, so far away from the sea. Commander Hughes, RN, the Senior Naval Officer, was kindness itself, and he offered to let me share his house if my quarters should prove to be uncomfortable. A stay at Simla was still available should I wish to go there, but my mind was on New Zealand and home, and nothing but orders would delay my journey there. Lieutenant-Commander Hunt, RNVR, also was very kind, and he placed his room and office at my disposal; little kindnesses that helped to restore my faith in human nature.

The days passed quickly, in answering questions, strolling in the town, or just lazing at the camp. One afternoon I went to see General Telfer-Smollett, in charge of the Red Cross for the Eastern Theatre, and after listening for some time to my ideas of requirements in Hong Kong, he asked me to wait while he attended to other business. The result of that "other business" was that I suddenly found myself ushered in to see Lord Louis Mountbatten, who gave me twenty minutes of his valuable time, and who gave instructions that I was to proceed to Kandy to see the Naval Intelligence Section there.

Next day I had lunch with General Telfer-Smollett and Lady Raisman, and if the lady noticed that my eyes were too much upon her, it may be told now that with her greying hair and her peaches and cream complexion, she looked as if she had just stepped from the frame of a Romney portrait.

On another day a unique experience befell me, one that has given me many a laugh. Called to the telephone, I was informed by General Sir Charles Auchinleck's aide that the Commander-in-Chief, India, requested my company at lunch with him that day. The invitation caught me completely off balance, for I had to reply that I was extremely sorry to have to refuse, as arrangements had already been made for me to have lunch with the Viceroy. Surely the occasions must be rare indeed when such a situation would arise, when a junior officer would be in a position to turn down an invitation issued by the C.-in-C., India, because of an engagement which took social precedence.

Lunch at the Viceregal table was much less formal and terrifying than I had imagined, and my change of fortune could not help obtruding upon my thoughts. Three months before I was half starving, living little better than an animal, being ordered and threatened by guards who were certainly on the level of animals, while now I was being entertained in the highest strata of society. My hosts, Lord and Lady Wavell and family, were friendly and considerate in the extreme, and if my own shortcomings were rather obvious, they gave no sign nor hint that anything was noticed.

Later that afternoon Lieutenant-Commander Hunt took me to the Red Fort, where we enjoyed the lovely lawns, and where we admired the beautiful architecture and fine workmanship in the Pearl Mosque and the Emperor's Palace. The brightly coloured birds and flowers inlaid in stone in the marble walls were a source of endless wonder, for the delicate grading of the colours was so beautifully achieved that it seemed impossible that such a result could have been arrived at without the aid of an artist's brush. Yet those brilliantly plumaged birds were all made from coloured stones that had been selected and fitted together with an infinite patience. All through those buildings were decorations carved in white marble in the most exquisite workmanship. Strolling in the midst of so much beauty one wondered what the future would produce to equal those lovely monuments of a past era, for the popular philosophy abroad to-day appears to have its roots in utter mediocrity.

There was only one discordant note in my visit to Delhi, and that was struck one evening when a few officers were enjoying a cold beer at the Mess. One of them was stationed at a nearby camp where Japanese prisoners of war were held, and he was describing how he had had one of his sergeants removed from the guard because he had spoken harshly to the prisoners. When I asked him somewhat frigidly how that could possibly be a cause for having his sergeant removed, he said that if such behaviour had continued there would have been a mutiny in the camp. My God! there was an officer talking seriously about a mutiny among Japanese prisoners of war because they were being spoken to harshly, and my imagination tried to conjure up what would have happened to us if we had talked of mutiny as prisoners of the Japanese. There would have been machine-guns and bayonets, and tortures, and broken bodies beaten insensible with clubs. Listening to that person talking one wondered how it was that he had become an officer, and it was a disquieting thought that men might be asked to trust their lives to the commands of such as he. My feelings crystallised in a few biting phrases, and I left abruptly, unable to listen longer to such inane twaddle.

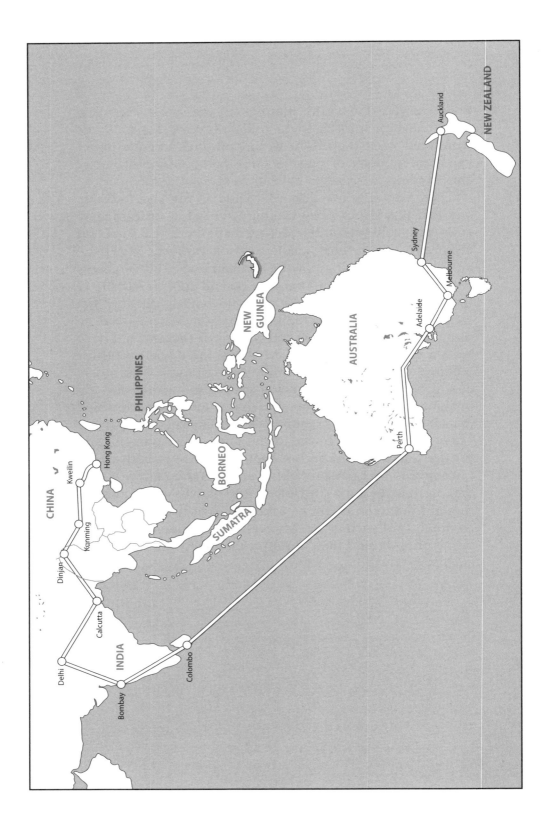

Chapter 14

Kandy, Australia, and Home

Airborne once more after a pleasant week in Delhi, we had a smooth flight to Bombay where a halt was made to refuel. It was 9.15 a.m. when we resumed the journey, and by that time the weather had deteriorated; there was a thick drizzle, and a very low ceiling of cloud. For a few moments we saw a pretty residential suburb, and then thick cloud engulfed us as we climbed higher and higher, until at last our plane broke out into a lonely, strange white world, 14,000 feet above the earth. It was very cold at that altitude, and we shivered, even though wrapped in rugs.

The weather grew worse, with huge clouds towering thousands of feet above, and we were ordered to return to Bombay. There was no break in that ocean of cloud below, and after retracing our previous course the pilot kept on flying until at last a hole appeared, and we could see water down below. Round and round we circled down through that welcome gap, until the surface of the sea was scarcely one hundred feet below, when a course was set for the coast. It was anxious going, for at times the mist was right down on the sea, and when the city came into view the tops of the buildings were buried in fog. Rising to a safe height the plane circled, seeking an approach to the airstrip, but visibility was nil. Finally we headed out to sea again, and then made a perfect landing at the small airport at Juhu, a few miles along the coast. We were all very thankful to be safely down, and when they stepped out of their plane the crew showed obvious signs of the strain through which they had been.

Of course there had to be the inevitable fool on board, a Brigadier who was so thankful to be safe, after shaking in his shoes for the past two hours, that he began to shout insults at the Air Force in general, and at our crew in particular. They had no right to discontinue their trip; it was imperative that he should reach his destination that day; the Air Force was manned by a gang of incompetents and cowards; blah; blah; blah. It was one of the most disgusting exhibitions of bad manners that it has ever been my misfortune to witness, and it was painful to see the emotions working in our pilot's face. He listened to as much as he could stand, and then, without uttering a word, he turned his back and walked away while the Brigadier continued his tirade. Anyone would have thought that the whole progress of the war depended on that nitwit, but I am quite certain that had he been lost in transit no one but the office boy would have noticed that he was missing.

Next day the weather improved rapidly, and we flew south over a great plain, where innumerable rivers, streams, lakes and swamps alternated on the landscape. At 11 a.m. we saw Bangalore, a sea of red roofs spread out among dark-green trees. It was a perfect day, the sky almost cloudless, yet it was pleasantly cool on the ground, and officers who had been stationed there said that the climate was very good. It seemed to be a most attractive place, and the dry air was crystal clear.

At 1.30 p.m., flying very high again, we crossed the coast and sailed along above a beautifully blue sea. Conditions could not have been better, but the altitude was affecting me, and I did not feel at all well. It must have been the rarity of the air that made me want to breathe quickly through my mouth, and caused a feeling of faintness that had no particular origin. Islands were seen to seaward, and then the flat jungles of Ceylon were below. Many tidal streams interlaced the jungle, and there were flat islands, large expanses of shallows, swamps, and huge coconut plantations. Villages with roofs of red tiles made bright splashes of colour in the sombre green.

Lieutenant-Commander Brotchie, RNVR, met me at the airport at Colombo, and then I had one of the greatest surprises of my life, when Lieutenant Tommy Parsons, RNVR, came along to take charge of me. Parsons had been in the 2nd MTB Flotilla at Hong Kong, in command of No.27, and in company with the other four surviving boats he had made a successful escape from the Colony on the night of the surrender. The sound of those motors warming up on Christmas night, 1942, is still with me whenever my thoughts drift back, just as I heard it at that time, from my hospital bed. My feelings were confused and violent. Pleasure that some of the boats were still afloat and would yet cheat the enemy; anger at my own helpless impotence; despair when the low roar faded into distance, and the feeling that the last link with freedom had gone.

At a later date, during our captivity at Argyle Street Camp, Mr. Parsons, senior, received a letter which informed him that Tommy was in hospital in England, after being wounded in an action in the English Channel. That was the last news received of him prior to my escape from Shamsuipo, and it gave me a great surprise to learn, when at Kukong in northern Kwang-tung, that Tommy was then in Foochow as a naval intelligence officer. From that place I sent a note by a runner and forgot all about him, so I could scarcely believe my eyes when he walked out to greet me at Colombo. It transpired that he had followed me closely out of East China, had flown past while I was at Kunming, and was then stationed temporarily in Colombo. We had three years' news to catch up with, and we talked late into the night.

My day or two in Colombo stretched to a week, lazy days which drifted one into another, with little to highlight their passing. One fright was administered when Commander Holmes, RN, asked me to talk about my escape to half a dozen naval officers, and when I agreed he suddenly confronted me with an audience of some eighty officers, including a batch of WRNS. On another day I had my first swim since the night when I tried to steal a sampan at Taipo, and this one was almost equally unsuccessful, for I spent much labour in the next two hours trying to clean black fuel oil from various parts of my anatomy.

Lieutenant-Colonel Jackman, of "E Group", Major Ford and I left Colombo for Kandy in a staff car on Monday, the 6th of November. It was a very pretty drive through most luxuriant tropical scenes filled with coconut palms, bananas, rubber trees, tea plantations, pineapples, paddy fields, and a great variety of palms. The banana season was at its height, and there were great stacks of bunches in every village. The wayside shops were loaded with a variety of fruit. Native women moving about looked very graceful and colourful in their bright saris, though very few had pleasing features.

That night the mosquitoes of Kandy heard that new blood had arrived, and they descended upon me in a musical horde, to keep me awake the night through with their vicious, stinging attacks. But before they could satisfy their lust I had enjoyed an excellent dinner with General Lamplough and Colonel Chapman, so I was fortified to some extent for the later ordeal.

Kandy was cool after the humidity of Colombo, and I enjoyed the views over mountain and valley. There were giant bamboos, eight inches in diameter, and another variety with bright yellow stems on which were painted longitudinal green stripes. There were papaias and bananas, jack fruit and areca nuts, coconuts and mangosteens. A big crowd of wild brown monkeys went swinging and racing through the trees, hurrying noisily to some fresh feeding-ground. One day I visited the "Temple of the Tooth", a famous Buddhist shrine which was once reputed to have held an original tooth of the great teacher, but this temple is a most miserable and uninspiring shrine, and for those devoid of the requisite religious fervour it has not one attraction. Its glory is in the same tradition as that of the fabled capital of the "Kandyan Kings", a glory that existed only in the imaginative minds of early voyagers.

Lunch with Lord Louis Mountbatten proved to be highly entertaining, for "Supremo" was in very good form with his stories of the difficulties encountered in persuading the Admiralty to accept the Oerlikon gun, and his account of certain tests of the prefabricated harbour for the Normandy landing, tests that were carried out in the Prime Minister's bath. Negotiations with regard to the Oerlikon became rather Gilbertian. The inventor was a foreigner, who was hurried to England for discussions at the Admiralty, where there was strong opposition to the gun. Difficulties were encountered in arranging a meeting with the officials concerned, and when a time had finally been set, the inventor could not be found. An intense and urgent search located him in gaol, where police had lodged him on suspicion, pending enquiries.

I went to a meeting in the War Room at South-East Asia Command Headquarters, where members of each branch of the Service gave a detailed account of front-line events of the previous twenty-four hours. The huge maps slid into position under electric control. When the routine work was over I was introduced as the guest speaker, and there was such a gathering of weighty rank, from "Supremo" downwards, that it killed my nervousness and I just talked of Hong Kong and of incidents of my escape for twenty minutes or more. The meeting then broke up, and I was very glad to escape into the peaceful garden.

Next day I returned to Colombo, and on Friday, the 10th of November, in company with Commander Milne, RNVR, I drove to Galle, seventy miles south of Colombo, at the south-west corner of Ceylon. There we found a delightful, sleepy, peaceful little town, huddled tightly within its fortress walls, a legacy of the Dutch occupation in the seventeenth century. The Portuguese had been there a century before the Dutch, but even they found a city with a history that reached into the deepest realms of antiquity. Placed in a lovely setting of natural beauty, the Galle of today carries an air of calm assurance which is the heritage of one of the most ancient and famed of all the seaports of the world. Moors, Arabs, Romans, Greeks and Chinese have all used this port as a trading centre, and it is more than likely that beneath the present town lie the foundations of Tarshish, of the Bible. We could have enjoyed a longer stay in that Old World spot, but the modern age was moving at a faster tempo, and next morning we were off.

At 6.30 a.m. we drove to the seaplane base, situated on a lake separated from the sea by a narrow strip of sand on which coconut palms were growing. It was a calm, clear morning, too calm; for our heavily laden machine needed help to climb off the water. There were only two passengers and a crew of six, but there was a full load of mail and petrol. The plane was one of those astonishing products of the war, a "Catalina" flying boat, or as the Americans named them, a PBY2. Once in the air on a reconnaissance job they seemed loath to come down, and they made some extraordinary endurance flights. I believe the record was in the vicinity of thirty-eight hours.

With two thousand gallons of petrol in the tanks we roared away down that glassy lake, until it seemed that we would never leave the surface. The palms came rushing towards us and still the tell-tale spray flew from our keel, but suddenly, just in time, we were airborne, and skimming over the palm tops. In a moment surf made a ribbon of white on the edge of the ocean, and then we were bound for Perth, more than three thousand miles away.

All armament had been stripped from the ship, and the space below the gun blisters had been converted to a cabin. With its plexi-glass blister covers that was an ideal place from which to view the scenery, while also in that cabin was a small electric cooker. Forward of the blisters was the main cabin, with three very comfortable seats for passengers on the starboard side, and two bunks for the crew to port.

After clearing the land a fresh following breeze arose, but by 1 p.m. that had practically died away, and down below there were glassy patches showing on the sea. We flew smoothly through a sky in which soft woolly clouds floated, and after lunch I tipped my seat back to its limit, and snoozed in great content. This was becoming quite a nice comfortable war after all. During the afternoon we flew round big tropical rainstorms from which cumulus clouds rose to a great height above us, clouds which our pilots treated with the utmost respect. Soon they were left behind, and we continued eastwards over a layer of soft trade-wind clouds, with nothing but the limitless blue above. Tiny white breakers on the sea showed that a steady south-east wind was blowing there.

The motors had been purring with a steady throb which instilled complete confidence, and the hours slipped by the while I dozed in easy relaxation. The small electric cooker was a great comfort, for we were able to enjoy hot cups of tea and coffee, but it was also responsible for giving us all a great fright. Just before dusk the port motor developed an oil leak that looked serious, and a big black patch swiftly spread across the wing. Underneath, it flowed on to the exhaust-pipe and carbonised there, forming a lumpy coating that would suddenly glow red hot. When it seemed on the point of bursting into flame, the whole glowing mass would break away and float off down to the sea.

Members of the crew spent varying periods standing in the blister watching developments with that motor, and in their anxiety they forgot that several cans of food were heating in a large container on the stove. All the water boiled away, and, with a violent explosion, a tin of meat burst. The commander of the aircraft, J.L. Grey, took half the contents in the middle of his back, while the remainder spattered over the cabin. At that time we were passing Sumatra at the point of nearest approach, and it would have been quite possible to meet Japanese patrols. I do not know whether that was at the back of my mind, but certain it is that I had a confused idea that the motor had exploded or that we had been hit by an explosive bullet. It was simply astonishing that a small tin could make such a noise in bursting.

Grey had to decide whether to take his ship down at Cocos Island or to continue to Australia with the defective motor. Arguments against stopping were that the plane would have to remain airborne until daylight since a flare-path was forbidden, and on another occasion, when a plane had landed, it had been subjected to enemy bombing. We continued on our way, and after the first two or three hours the oil loss was much reduced, though that disconcerting glow persisted round the exhaust pipe all through the night.

Dawn found us flying at 12,000 feet through a vast empty space, with the air as clear as crystal, and so smooth that no movement was perceptible. Down below was a solid layer of cloud, looking perfectly level until the sun raised its fiery rim. Then, all over the soft plain below, little pinnacles and hummocks of cloud glowed dull red as the sun's rays struck them, while some were edged with bright gold. It was a most enchanting dawn, and we flew along, a tiny speck in the limitless space, gliding above a world of fantasy wherein dwelt elves and fairies.

Soon the clouds scattered, and we could see a friendly blue ocean far below. It was a lovely day, and after we had been in the air for twenty hours the captain said we could make the coast on one engine if necessary, though the leak by that time had almost stopped, and the faulty motor was purring steadily. A small island came into view, and then we passed over a number of low coral islands, reefs and lagoons. The whole scene made a marvellous picture with its vivid colour contrasts; deep-blue ocean, sparkling white surf, brilliant viridian-green over coral sand, brown shallows over live coral, white beaches and dark-brown coral reefs. We sighted the coast of Australia, and flew south along a flat shore, barren and uninteresting.

Shortly after noon the city of Perth lay below, very pretty with its red roofs set among a wealth of trees, and at 12.30 p.m. spray was again flying from our keel as we taxied to a mooring. The time of flight, from water to water, was twenty-seven hours and two minutes. That was a long time to be airborne, and it is unlikely that any regular flights in future will last so long.

After lunch with the commodore I thoroughly enjoyed a drive through Perth, for its clean residential suburbs over-looking the Swan River seemed most attractive after the dirt, and smells and squalor of the Orient. Here was a country where the air was clean, and where one could enjoy sitting on the grass without feeling that it was polluted with filth. Anyone who has spent any time in China will understand that feeling, a yearning one gets to be able to stretch out in clean fresh grass, and to be able to fill one's lungs with clean sweet air.

The long flight had made me very tired, but next morning I was roused at 4.45 a.m., to proceed to the airport. We were in the air at seven o'clock on the way to Melbourne, flying over a flat plain which soon gave place to low wooded hills, through which the Swan River drew a winding, silver ribbon. My chief recollection of that flight was of passing over hundreds of miles of utter desert, with the whole brown landscape buried in a sea of heat haze.

At Kalgoorlie we saw the workings of the Golden Mile, and learned that there was an assured gold supply to keep the mines operating for twenty-five years, while further surveys were expected to reveal much more extensive deposits. The next stop for fuel was made at Forrest, and it was as well that the name contained two Rs, for the fuelling-station was planted in a wide expanse of sand in which no tree grew, and nothing could have looked less like a forest. Short stops were made at Ceduna and Adelaide, and soon after leaving Adelaide we watched the sun set. Above Melbourne the night air was clear and still, and the great city made a beautiful sight, appearing as a huge magic carpet, patterned with a myriad twinkling lights. That was the first city I had seen illuminated since the war began, and it was a wonderfully cheering sight.

The Royal Navy had been doing everything possible for me, and in Melbourne the Royal Australian Navy took charge. Everything was done that could be done for my entertainment and comfort, and my especial thanks went out to Lieutenant-Commander W.J. Seymour, RAN, who was sympathetic kindness itself. I am sure that none of those who helped realised just how much their hospitality meant to me, for the pleasure of mixing with families in quiet, secure homes was deeply moving.

The flight from Melbourne to Sydney took only a little over two hours, for a strong tail wind drove us along. Sydney was buried in a pall of smoke from bush fires in the Blue Mountains, and the city was sweltering in a heat wave. My memory of the one day spent there was one of answering interminable questions, and of talking into telephones by the hour. Many wives and families of internees in Hong Kong had been evacuated to Sydney prior to the outbreak of war, and news of my arrival soon spread. At midnight I tumbled into bed feeling desperately tired, and reluctantly gave instructions for a call at 4 a.m.

In Sydney the morning of Friday the 17th of November 1944 broke fine and perfectly calm. A Navy car took me to the flying-boat base at Rose Bay, where I boarded a comfortable "Sunderland" which lifted from the sea at 6 a.m. We circled the harbour, going almost as far west as the Bridge, but the view was marred by smoke which still lay in a heavy pall over the landscape. Then the ship swung round and we headed away to the eastward, out over the Tasman Sea. Notorious for its storms, on this occasion the Tasman was perfectly calm, and we enjoyed an uneventful crossing.

Never had I thought that a sight of New Zealand could affect me so profoundly as it did then, for when I looked down on the pastures near Whenuapai intense emotion gripped me. For hundreds upon hundreds of miles over Australia the landscape was brown and scorched by drought. For hundreds upon hundreds of miles over India the landscape was dun coloured, sweltering under a burning heat. Below me, then, on the narrow peninsula that separates the Waitemata Harbour from the Tasman Sea, was a fine expanse of grazing-land, vividly green and lush after an unusually wet spring. The air was clear, and everything was washed to a sparkling freshness that stirred the deepest feelings in my heart.

At the Tasman Empire Airways Terminal at Mechanic's Bay, Auckland, family and friends were waiting to meet me, and a few minutes later I was home. There my mother was waiting for me, and she was exactly as I had always pictured her, with her snow-white hair and her lively brown eyes in which a vivid interest shone. Her joints were stiffer with the passing of more than eighty strenuous years, but her unquenchable spirit was as bright as ever.

I was home after an amazing adventure in which luck played hand after hand in my favour, until I came to believe that the enemy could not prevail; that my ultimate escape was something inevitable and pre-ordained; that I had, in fact, an alliance with Destiny. That belief still persists. At various times before the war faint thoughts or dreams would intrude upon my consciousness, fancies in which, in some mysterious way, I found myself walking abroad in China. Why? At that time nothing could have been more remote than thoughts that I would ever visit that distant land. Again, from the moment of Hong Kong's surrender a feeling of certainty persisted that sooner or later my escape would be effected, and so strong was that conviction that all through the worst periods of my captivity an emergency kit was kept in a state of readiness.

Two and a half years was a long time to wait, but I was certain that I would *know* when the right moment came. That belief was proved true by events, for when the dog-kennel was moved from the sea-wall at Shamsuipo, I *knew* that the time had come.

From that moment the drama ran through its varying scenes to final curtain fall, an individual drama in which it was my privilege to be granted a successful leading role. In the circumstances it was inevitable that there should be some resentment at my escape, and in closing this account I wish to tender my regrets to all those prisoners of war who suffered additional privations through my action, and to those particular friends who suffered arrest, interrogation and all that that implied. I tender my sincere thanks for the generous reception they accorded me when we met again at Hong Kong, on "Liberation Day".

Appendix I:
Escape Kit

FOOD

2 x 8oz. tins beef

2 x 16oz. tins meat and veg.

1 x 8oz. tin creamed rice

1 x 4oz. tin biscuits

1 x 4oz. tin pork and beans

1 x 11oz. tin condensed milk

1 x 16oz. tin "Bemax"

1 x 16oz. tin soya bean powder

1 x 6oz. bottle peanut oil

1 x 2oz. bottle black pepper

CLOTHING

1 khaki shirt

1 pair khaki shorts

1 pair rubber-soled shoes

1 hat

1 pair stockings

1 part of gas cape

} Lost at first fence

EQUIPMENT

1 canvas haversack

1 water-bottle

1 50ft. length thin rope

1 small ball hemp cord

1 reel thread

1 small box dubbin

1 small pocket-knife

2 "Mae West" life jackets

1 safety razor

1 tin opener

1 plastic shaving-stick container with:

    2 needles, 3 razor blades, paper for diary, pencil, matches, a watch with broken spring

1 pack of papers tied in waterproof cloth containing:

    (*a*) Lists of all inmates of Shamsuipo Officers' Camp

    (*b*) Details of all movements of personnel from Argyle Street Camp

    (*c*) Diaries from date of internment

    (*d*) Maps of the area as far as Waichow

    (*e*) Hong Kong dollars, $180

Appendix II:
Anglicised Chinese Words

Sampan   A small Chinese rowing or sailing-boat.
Junk   A large Chinese sailing-craft.
Kong   An iron cooking-pot shaped like a deep saucer.
Yolo   A single oar which is shipped over the stern to scull with.
Chow   Food.
Chop   A seal used throughout China with which to endorse a document, instead of using a signature.

Glossary

BAAG	British Army Aid Group
BBC	British Broadcasting Corporation
Cdr.	Commander
HKRNVR	Hong Kong Royal Naval Volunteer Reserve
HMS	His Majesty's Ship
HMT	His Majesty's Tug
Lt.	Lieutenant
Lt.-Cdr	Lieutenant-Commander
MTB	Motor Torpedo Boat
PoW	Prisoner of War
RAN	Royal Australian Navy
RAF	Royal Air Force
RAFVR	Royal Air Force Volunteer Reserve
RE	Royal Engineers
RNR	Royal Naval Reserve
RNVR	Royal Naval Volunteer Reserve
RNZNVR	Royal New Zealand Navy Volunteer Reserve
Sub. Lt.	Sub Lieutenant
Surg.-Cdr	Surgeon-Commander
UNRRA	United Nations Relief and Rehabilitation Administration
VAD	Volunteer Aid Detachment
YWCA	Young Women's Christian Association

Index